Accidental Millionaire

Accidental Millionaire

The Rise and Fall of Steve Jobs at Apple Computer

Lee Butcher

c.1

Paragon House Publishers
New York

First Edition

Published in the United States by

B

JOBS, S.

Paragon House Publishers
90 Fifth Avenue
New York, New York 10011

Copyright © 1988 by Lee Butcher

Library of Congress Cataloging-in-Publication Data

Butcher, Lee.
    Accidental millionaire.

    Includes index.
    1. Apple Computer, Inc.—History.   2. Jobs, Steven.
3. Computer industry—United States—History.
4. Businessman—United States—Biography.   I. Title.
HD9696.C64A863   1987   338.7′61004′0924 [B]   7-9414
ISBN 0-913729-79-5

To Peter Miller, a literary film agent who makes big things happen and who has been a source of inspiration to me.

Contents

CONTENTS

Introduction

It isn't possible to write a meaningful biography of Steven Jobs without including Stephen Wozniak. Wozniak was the young electronics genius who created the first Apple computer, but the two men were friends before Apple. They were separated in age by four years and, consequently, the various events that shaped their lives and eventually led to Apple Computer did not occur in tandem. The first portion of this book is an attempt to present cameos important for each, but not necessarily in chronological order. The difference in their ages and the discrepancy in their paths made such an approach impossible.

Jobs, for example, had more than a passing interest in electronics, but he never achieved notable expertise. He contributed nothing to the creation of the first Apple computer other than the shape of its case. He was a mercurial young man jumping from one interest to the next, becoming a self-appointed expert in anything he undertook. Jobs was also a true child of the sixties, a youngster who explored the world of mind-altering drugs, tried hippie communal life, and had an avid, if short-lived interest in alternative lifestyles and philosophies. He spent a good part of his youth in Hare Krishna communes and made a sojourn to India to study Eastern philosophy.

Wozniak, on the other hand, was immersed in electronics even before he reached high school. All other activities paled in the shadow of his all-consuming passion. He was considered an outsider by people who knew him, including members of his family, but he didn't realize that he was missing anything important in life. Unlike Jobs, Wozniak was a "straight arrow" who had a healthy distrust of drugs. He also escaped experiments with alternative lifestyles, largely because he was so involved with electronics.

I have shown Wozniak and Jobs at separate pivotal points in their early lives. These sometimes occurred simultaneously but more frequently were distinct. A high school freshman who jumps from one thing to another is quite different from an older friend who has plunged into electronics at the expense of all other pursuits.

The lives of the two young men were entwined at different points in the early years, but they did not start to run in tandem until Apple Computer was actually formed. Nevertheless, the early adventures and development of Wozniak and Jobs are important to their later association with Apple. These formative years are shown in order of importance rather than chronological order. I begin with a chapter on the metamorphosis of electronics from vacuum tubes to microprocessors because, without the microprocessor, it would not have been possible for Wozniak to create the first practical personal computer.

Corporations are notorious for trying to use the press to their best advantage. Few companies have been better at this than Apple. In the early days, enormous efforts were made to promote Apple and, in doing so, Apple created the legend of "the two Steves," giving the impression that both Jobs and Wozniak invented the personal computer. It is patently untrue. Now that Jobs has been fired as both operating head of the Macintosh division and chairman of the board, the same publicists who were so adept at promoting him in the early days have slammed down an iron curtain around Jobs's time at Apple. The Regis McKenna Agency, which handled Apple's publicity and helped develop marketing strategies, would say nothing about Apple for this book. John C. Sculley, who became Apple's third president and who ousted Jobs as chairman of the board, will not talk about any aspect of Jobs's tenure at Apple. Sculley's publicist at Regis McKenna would say nothing about Sculley except that "He is a very sweet man who hates the term [often applied to him] 'professional manager.'" Regis McKenna himself would not talk at all about Apple. Neither would Michael Scott, who was Apple's first president, and who had a lengthy war with Jobs. Jobs's reaction was typical of his attempt to exercise control. It came through one of his close associates who said, "Mr. Jobs will decide if a book should be written. He will also decide *when* it should be written, what it will contain, and he will choose the author."

Of the principals originally involved with Apple, only Stephen Wozniak was free with his time, explanations, and elucidations. This book is an attempt to tell the truth about Apple and the role that Steven Jobs played, not only in its beginnings but through stormy years when he almost tore the company apart. Jobs and Wozniak were once best friends, but their friendship was shattered because of corporate politics and Jobs's never-ending quest for power. Recently they have mended some of their fences and see each other once in a while, but their relationship is guarded because Wozniak does not trust Jobs.

The reader's indulgence is begged during the portion of the book describing Jobs and Wozniak growing up. Years have passed, and many of the people who knew them have been scattered far and wide. The early chapters are an attempt to put people and events in perspective and to show how the two men came together to start Apple Computer Company in a portion of a garage in California.

Because Jobs had so little to do with the creation of the first personal computer that led to Apple Computer, many people feel that he became important only by hanging onto Wozniak's shirt tails. Hence the title, *Accidental Millionaire.*

Judy Smith and Frances Nelson are fictitious names for real people who were important in Steve Jobs's life. Their names were changed because they are not public figures.

Dozens of people intimate with Apple Computer, Steve

Jobs and Steve Wozniak talked freely, many of them off the record. Dozens more refused to comment even after being guaranteed anonymity. I would particularly like to thank Stephen Wozniak, who took time out from his busy schedule to talk to me for several hours. I would also like to acknowledge the contributions made by Nick Arnett, former high-tech writer for the *San Jose Business Journal* and now a personal computer columnist for *American City Business Journals;* Cindy Privett, high-tech reporter for the *San Jose Business Journal;* Tim Bajarin, vice president of microcomputer research at Creative Strategies in San Jose; Ash Jain, vice president of the Apple enhancement products division for AST Research in Irvine, CA.; Trip Hawkins, former Apple employee, and now president of Electronic Arts; Jef Raskin, who created the concept for the Macintosh computer at Apple and is now president of Information Appliances in Menlo Park, CA.; Bana Witt, one of Apple's first employees who is now starting a singing career; and Stephen Jones, another high-tech reporter with the *San Jose Business Journal.* I also thank Don Keough, who made it possible for me to be in Silicon Valley during the time this dramatic story was unfolding. Without the help of these people, and dozens of others who cannot be mentioned, this book could not have been written. My heartfelt thanks to all of them for talking candidly about a very sensitive subject.

CHAPTER 1

From Monsters to Microchips

Steve Jobs and Steve Wozniak were not only children of the sixties; they were the inheritors of advances in the science of electricity that had begun when Thomas Edison invented the first commercial light bulb. Edison's achievement, a scientific breakthrough, also heralded a marriage between science and commercial interests that would change the world. When Edison invented the light bulb, electricity heated a filament inside a vacuum bulb to create light, but it performed no "intelligent" function.

It remained for Lee DeForest, an American mathematician and engineer, to create vacuum bulbs that could do something other than generate heat and light. The vacuum bulb he invented could amplify sound, a rudimentary sort of "intelligence." DeForest's invention shattered the science of electricity and created the field of electronics. His invention made radio, radio telephone, wireless telegraphy and long-distance telephone service commercially feasible.

DeForest's invention came in the early 1900s, and the vacuum tube remained the heart of the new science of electronics for years. Vacuum tubes, however, were cumbersome and took up a great deal of space. Today a radio can be smaller than the size of your hand, but with vacuum tubes, the first radios were encased in cabinets about the size of a trunk. No significant gains were made for years, and vacuum tubes remained the building blocks of electronics systems when the computer age was born during World War II. During that time, the military recruited an army of physicists, mathematicians, and electronics engineers for creating radar and computer systems to locate enemy aircraft and ships, and to compute the trajectories of rockets and artillery shells. The computer created by this mass effort was called ENIAC, an acronym for Electronic Numerical Integrator and Computer, which was heralded as America's first electronic brain.

ENIAC contained thousands of vacuum tubes and was incredibly complicated. Furthermore, vacuum tubes had a distressingly high rate of failure. In 1943, before ENIAC, Howard Aiken of Harvard tried to solve the problems created by vacuum tubes by using a series of electromagnetic relays in a computer called the Mark I, but it was quickly made obsolete by ENIAC. The hugh ENIAC was five hundred times faster than the Mark I. It could add five hundred numbers in one second and multiply two twenty-three-digit numbers in less than five seconds. ENIAC used an enormous amount of power, and industry legend claims that whenever it was switched on, the lights dimmed all over Philadelphia. The computer was so huge, expensive, and power-hungry that it seemed to have no future other than for government use. It was actually more of a room than a machine. The behemoth contained eighteen thousand vacuum tubes, seventy thousand resistors, ten thousand capacitors, six thousand assorted switches, and an almost inconceivably complicated maze of electrical wiring. Ten feet high, one hundred feet long, three feet deep, and weighing thirty tons, ENIAC was an engineering nightmare.

Not long after the war, an improved computer arrived in the form of UNIVAC I, but it was still expensive and cumbersome.

It separated from military operations when Remington Rand sold one of the computers to the U.S. Bureau of the Census. A UNIVAC I helped CBS predict Eisenhower's 1952 presidential victory over Stevenson on the basis of early returns at the ballot box. Universities and large electronics companies began to take a keen interest in computer development. New research led those involved in electronics to believe that computers could eventually be reduced in size, and that the cost would drop enough to make them commercially feasible.

One reason for optimism was the development of a revolutionary device called a transistor. Only a handful of electronic engineers and physicists, however, recognized its potential. *The New York Times* wrote about the transistor in 1948, but the development created so little interest that the story was buried deep in the inside pages. The *Times* wrote:

A device called a transistor, which has several applications in radio where a vacuum tube ordinarily is employed, was demonstrated for the first time yesterday at Bell Telephone Laboratories, 463 West Street, where it was invented.

The device was demonstrated in a radio receiver, which contained none of the conventional tubes. The transistor was employed as an amplifier, although it is claimed that it also can be used as an oscillator in that it will create and send radio waves.

In the shape of a small metal cylinder about a half-inch long, the transistor contains no vacuum, grid, plate or glass envelope to keep the air away. Its action is instantaneous, there being no warm-up delay since no heat is developed as in a vacuum tube.

The working parts of the device consist solely of two fine wires that run down to a pinhead of solid semiconductive material soldered to a metal base. The substance of the metal base amplifies the current carried to it by one wire and the other wire carries away the amplified current.

Although the *Times* clearly missed its importance, the transistor was heralded as a major breakthrough in electronics.

3

Visionaries saw smaller, simpler, cheaper computers that would use far less power than the monstrous ENIAC. Three physicists who worked on the transistor received Nobel Prizes for their efforts.

The transistor was the harbinger of the microchip, which was still several years away. The transistor was slow to catch on because few electronics engineers understood it, and even those who did had little faith in it. Trade journals did not recognize it as a major revolution until years later. Vacuum tubes continued to be the basic building blocks in the science of electronics.

Work on the transistor paved the way for rapid advancements in the use of solid-state material in electronics. Bell Laboratories was one of the most aggressive companies in pursuing research to develop a solid-state amplifier. Two people on Bell's research team were to play a role that far transcended their involvement at Bell Labs: Walter Brattain and William Shockley. Brattain, an engineer with a Ph.D. in physics from the University of Minnesota, joined Bells Labs in 1929 and, after devoting some research to vacuum tubes, he was assigned to work on developing solid-state materials. Shockley, who was eventually to play a major part in making Silicon Valley the nation's leading high technology center, joined Bell in 1936 after receiving a Ph.D. in physics from MIT. Like Brattain, he served a stint in vacuum tube research, working under the supervision of Clinton Davidson, a Nobel laureate. Shockley's interest in solid-state physics eventually led him to Brattain where he joined the team researching the new field of semiconductors.

Bell also created a group of chemists and metallurgists to investigate the properties of silicon, which had been studied intensely during World War II as a semiconductor. Except for oxygen, silicon is the most abundant element in nature and forms the basic ingredient for sand, quartz, glass, bricks, and concrete. It becomes an excellent semiconductor for electricity when it is in a relatively pure form. In 1945 Shockley's group concentrated its efforts on silicon, along with another substance called germanium, which also makes an excellent semiconductor, but the team had come to a standstill in its attempt to create a solid-state amplifier.

It was John Bardeen who finally made the breakthrough. In late 1947, Bardeen and Brattain placed the thinnest wires possible on a piece of germanium. The wires were so small that the contacts were only two-thousandths of an inch apart. On December 23, 1947, they conducted a demonstration at Bell and were successful in amplifying a voice. The semiconductor had no moving parts, relays, vacuum tubes, electronic grid, or any other elements used in mainstream electronics. Nevertheless it was a true solid-state amplifier. It was called a transfer resistance device which was shortened to "transistor," a name that stuck. The possibility of using solid-state electronics and a device a hundred times smaller to replace the vacuum tube had been successfully demonstrated.

Shockley, Bardeen, and Brattain won the Nobel Prize in physics in 1956 for discovering the transistor effect, and by that time, some twenty-six companies were manufacturing transistors under licensing from Bell. Semiconductors were well on their way to making radical changes in the world of electronics. Helping pave the way was the U.S. Department of Defense, which created a Subpanel on Semiconductor Devices to augment its Panel on Electron Tubes. The new organization promptly poured $5 million into transistor research. The Department of Defense was anxious to find a replacement for vacuum tubes which had an alarmingly high rate of failure. It bought almost all of the ninety thousand transistors that were manufactured in 1952, and emphasis shifted from the use of germanium to silicon, which had far more promise for even smaller, more powerful semiconductors. A major advantage of silicon is that its melting point is 1420 degrees centigrade, making it ideal for high stress environments such as those created in rockets and missiles.

Even with advances in semiconductor technology, the vacuum tube was a long time dying. Production of semiconductors was both costly and slow. The purchase of a large number of semiconductors by the Department of Defense during the Korean War helped lower their cost but, at the same time, the government encouraged research in vacuum tubes. When IBM decided to go into the computer business, it relied on vacuum tubes in its mass-produced 701 electronic computer, and the military was its major customer.

A computerized information system three decades ago was a very cumbersome affair. Whole rooms were filled with various devices to perform different functions. Information had to be punched into cards in a noisily clacking room; the cards had to be sorted on another machine, collated on yet another, and sense made out of them on still another. The system was not only hardware intensive, it needed dozens of trained people to make it operate. Through the mid-fifties, IBM dominated the market, relying on vacuum tubes for their machines. Neither IBM, or anyone else, foresaw the radical change that was to come about in computers because of semiconductor electronics.

Several things occurred in 1955 that brought new emphasis to solid-state electronics and which shifted the geographical emphasis from the East to the south San Francisco Bay Area, now known as Silicon Valley. IBM began to realize that transistors were important in building computers, and William Shockley returned to Palo Alto, California, where he had previously lived. Shockley said goodbye to Bell Labs in 1954 to form his own company. He chose Palo Alto as the home of his new enterprise largely because of Stanford University and a maverick professor there named Frederick Terman, who was dedicated to the task of integrating university research with high technology businesses. Terman encouraged graduating students not to seek their fortunes in the East and tried to sell them on the benefits of staying in the area and starting their own companies. Two graduates who took his advice were William Hewlett and David Packard, who stayed in the Valley, became garage tinkerers, and eventually formed Hewlett-Packard Company. Now one of the world's largest electronic manufacturers, it would have a major impact on the lives of Steve Jobs and Steve Wozniak. Terman's determination to marry the needs of university research with high-tech business bore fruit with the creation of Stanford Industrial Park, where graduates could start their own companies.

It was an ideal situation for Shockley Semiconductor Laboratories. Shockley began to hand-pick employees and they, and other bright young scientists like them, formed a tightly woven cadre of scientists centered around Stanford, all making strong efforts in semiconductor research. The Valley was largely agricultural in those days, with fruit trees and acre upon acre of prune orchards. But the air was charged with expectancy. Several companies, such as Hewlett-Packard, Varian Associates, Admiral, General Electric, and Sylvania, were already operating there. A group from IBM had been transferred to San Jose to open a research center.

Shockley Semiconductor Laboratories, established as a subsidary of Beckman Instruments, was the first semiconductor company in the Palo Alto-Santa Clara area. It was oriented toward research and was closely tied to Stanford. Its goal was to develop the technology necessary to manufacture semiconductors at a profit.

Because he was the father of the transistor, Shockley had great success in recruiting the very best young semiconductor talent. Before long, he had surrounded himself with brilliant engineers and physicists who plunged headlong into research to create semiconductors that could be economically feasible and reliable. Making semiconductors was an expensive and inexact science. By themselves semiconductors represented what was then the most advanced technology in the world, but their process of manufacture was archaic. The end product concluded with an assembly line procedure in rooms filled with women who painstakingly cut and sorted the finished semiconductors with tweezers and scissors.

In 1957, seven dissident employees broke off from Shockley and found financing with Haydon Stone, who was involved with Fairchild Camera and Instruments. The president of Fairchild, John Carter, was aware of breakthroughs in semiconductors made during the war and urged his company to help Fairchild buy into the solid-state transistor world. The group planned to use silicon as a semiconductor.

The group, dubbed "the traitorous eight" by Shockley, convinced Robert Noyce, a physicist, to join them. Noyce was the son of an Iowa minister and had spent long hours taking Model Ts apart and putting them back together during his boyhood. He earned an engineering degree in physics at Grinnell College and, while he was there, became entranced with solid-state electronics. His interest was piqued even more when he earned his Ph.D. at MIT and worked in the transistor division of Philco after graduation.

Noyce drew people to him like a magnet. His angular features gave him a rather fierce look that belied a gentle manner. When Noyce joined the "traitorous eight," he was twenty-nine, the financing deal was struck, and Fairchild Semiconductor started operations near Palo Alto and Mountain View. Fairchild Camera and Instrument had an option to buy the new company if it achieved success. Noyce believes that the creation of Fairchild Semiconductor marked a turning point in the Valley and the beginning of the entrepreneurial spirit. He says it suddenly dawned on him that people, such as himself, who had thought they would have to rely on salaries for the rest of their lives, now had an opportunity to get stock equity in a start-up. "It was a great revelation and a great motivation, too," he says.

World events also played a significant part in the development of the semiconductor. In 1957, the Russians launched Sputnik, the first man-made satellite to orbit the earth. The military was alarmed and its interest in miniaturization became even more intense. The smallest functional technology was necessary if the United States was to launch its own satellite and to catch up and overtake the Russians in the space race. The Department of Defense funded dozens of research projects to create solid-state electronics. This was not a new idea; how to do it was the question that bothered research engineers.

The end result of these programs was the invention of an integrated circuit, known as a microchip, created simultaneously at Texas Instruments and Fairchild Semiconductor. Noyce was made head of research and development at Fairchild in 1959 and began serious work on silicon transistors. Although silicon was ideal for high-stress environments, the manufacturing process was still cumbersome, requiring end-wiring by hand. Noyce and Gordon Moore, a physicist, searched for a way that transistors could be connected in a solid state without the use of wires. They believed that if a single transistor with no moving parts could be created with a few lines of wire on a small, doped piece of silicon, why couldn't dozens of smaller resistor and other electronic circuits be crammed onto a single piece of silicon? Not only was this successful but the *smaller* the semiconductor, the *better* it seemed to work. Noyce filed a patent for a semiconductor integrated circuit on July 30, 1959, about the same time that Jack Kilby at Texas Instruments filed a patent for "Miniaturized Electronic Circuits." A lawsuit followed with no conclusive results and Kilby and Noyce became known in the industry as co-inventors of the integrated circuit.

Soon other "copycat" companies began making minor changes and making their own semiconductors, a problem that still plagues the Valley today. Fairchild Semiconductor was bought by the parent company and grew quickly to a $150 million a year business. Millions of dollars flowed into the Valley as semiconductor manufacturers began to multiply. Electronics would never be the same again. In the 1950s, a cubic foot could hold a thousand vacuum tubes. By 1958 the same space would contain a million solid-state transistors with the capability of performing incredible functions.

Several new companies were born, including National Semiconductor and Intel, both now leaders in the semiconductor industry. Charles Sprock, who broke away from Fairchild Semiconductors, headed National Semiconductor while Noyce defected to form Intel. The semiconductor business was so hot that new founders didn't even have to present business plans to venture capitalists. They simply said they were going into semiconductors and the money came, almost as a matter of course.

Dozens of new silicon chips began to pour out of the Valley, each more sophisticated than the next. Intel made history in 1970 when it learned how to manufacture semiconductors cheaply and put more complicated functions into the chips. When Intel introduced the 1103 random access computer memory chip (RAM), the electronics industry buzzed with excitement. The Intel 1103 could store more than one thousand bits of binary computer data, and it broke ground for building smaller computers that were much more powerful than mainframe computers.

9

Old-timers in electronics shook their heads in amazement. The microchip contained a maze of electrons that moved through microscopic channels on a piece of silicon. It even had the capability of handling arithmetic and logic processing circuits on the same chip. All the remaining components for a complete system could be put on two other chips. Intel had created a computer's central processing unit (CPU), which is the very heart of a full-blown computer, and it had done it on one tiny chip that measured one-eighth by one-sixth of an inch. On this tiny chip were 2,250 individual circuits that could be seen only by looking through a microscope.

Although the CPU could perform no functions alone and had to be connected with other electronic circuitry which fed it information, it seemed to have unlimited applications that depended only on an engineer's imagination and expertise. Soon it appeared in digital watches, microwave ovens, and in electronic devices that could make any variety of sounds. But in the beginning, no one saw the radical way that the chip would change the computer world. Robert Noyce said:

> The whole computer business was an area we just didn't see in the beginning. It just seemed impossible that this phenomenal level of electronic sophistication represented by the microprocessor could ever be reduced enough in cost so that the consumer requirements could be met. Doorlocks, for example. There are many microprocessor-controlled doorlocks today, but then, it just didn't seem possible to ever get the cost of these sophisticated electronic devices down to the point where you could do the job, compared to the price of a simple mechanical doorlock. The home and hobby microcomputer market was an area we really didn't see in the beginning either, and so was the whole field of electronic games.
>
> At one point our people estimated there were at least 25,000 different applications for the microcomputer, so it was clear that we couldn't follow up on them.

In its September 1977 issue, *Scientific American* compared the microprocessor to ENIAC:

Today's microcomputer, at a cost of perhaps three hundred dollars, has more computing capacity than the first large electronic computer, ENIAC. It is twenty times faster, has a larger memory, is thousands of times more reliable, consumes the power of a light bulb rather than that of a locomotive, occupies 1/30,000 the volume and costs 1/10,000 as much. It is available by mail order at your local hobby shop.

The CPU was the invention that paved the way for personal computers, but hardly anyone saw its possibilities. There were two teenagers who did—Stephen Wozniak and Steven Jobs.

CHAPTER 2

The Golden Boy

Steven Jobs was born in 1956, the same year that William Shockley returned to Palo Alto. He was promptly adopted by Paul Jobs and his wife, Clara. Paul moved from one job to another and, when Steven was five months old, the family left San Francisco to live in South San Francisco. The senior Jobs worked at different times to collect bad debts, to reposses cars whose owners were behind in their payments, and to help check loans for automobile dealers.

Paul Jobs had sensitive features and wore his hair closely cropped. Embarrassed by his lack of a formal education, he compensated by being bluff and brusque. He grew up on a farm in Germantown, Wisconsin, but he moved with his parents to South Bend, Indiana when the farm was unable to support the family. He left high school when he was in his early teens and, after combing the Midwest for a job, finally joined the Coast Guard.

Jobs had a touch of whimsy in his soul and more than a bit of romantic daring. While his ship was being decommissioned in San Francisco following World War II, he made an unusual bet with a shipmate. He wagered that he would find a wife there. On his excursions to shore on liberty, he shopped around for a prospective mate, and found one when he met a woman on a blind date. Clara had spent most of her life in the San Francisco area, but she packed up and moved back to the Midwest with Jobs after he was honorably discharged.

Jobs spent a number of years in the Midwest. He worked as a machinist, then tried his hand at selling used cars. The family was making ends meet, but Paul believed they might do better back on the West Coast. In 1952 Paul and his wife moved back to San Francisco and in 1956 made the major decision to adopt a baby boy they named Steven. As he grew up, Steven Jobs was unusually inquisitive and daring and, because of that, managed to get into an inordinate amount of trouble. Once he burned his hand when he stuck a hairpin into an electrical outlet. A few months later he was poisoned when he and a friend set up a chemical laboratory and Steven drank some of the ant poison that they were using for experiments. He had to have his stomach pumped in the hospital. Steven was joined by an adopted sister a few years later and Paul Jobs, being a conscientious father concerned about the well-being of his family, bought insurance policies to cover his funeral expenses and to help the family out if he died prematurely.

When the finance company for whom Paul worked transferred him to Palo Alto, he bought a house in Mountain View, part of what was starting to be known as Silicon Valley. Steven was not a good sleeper. He woke up early and disrupted the household until his parents bought him some toys and a phonograph to keep him occupied. Steven was also the star of home movies made by neighborhood children and would often play a spy, dressed up in his father's raincoat and hat.

The area was rapidly growing into an electronics center and a large number of engineers and technicians lived in the Jobs' neighborhood. Many of them brought working pieces of equipment home that had been discarded because of cosmetic flaws, and they tinkered with various electronics devices in their garages, showing off their proudest accomplishments by displaying them in their driveways. Steven's attention was piqued when a Hewlett-Packard engineer brought a carbon microphone home, connected it to a battery and speaker, and was able to amplify sound. This fascinated Steven, who had learned a little about electronics, because it went against the traditional rules he had learned. Since Paul Jobs couldn't explain it, Steven acted in a way that was to become one of his trademarks in later life: he descended on the engineer and bombarded him with questions until he understood the electronics principles involved. Impressed with Steven's quick mind and inquisitiveness the engineer began spending time with him, explaining the vagaries of electronics.

Paul Jobs was far more interested in tinkering with cars than he was in explaining electronics. He had been rebuilding cars and swapping or selling them since he was a teenager, and he continued his money-making hobby into his adulthood. Paul would become enthralled with a particular model, throw himself into it wholeheartedly, and rebuild it until it was as good as new. He became an aficionado of collectors' cars that caught his experienced eye, and kept photographs of his favorites in a scrapbook. Jobs would comb the junkyards looking for parts, and it wasn't unusual for him to spend a whole weekend on his pet project. He tried to get Steven interested in mechanics but Steven resisted. "He didn't want to get his hands dirty," Paul explained. But Steven enjoyed the haggling between his father and the junkyard dealers, and it may have been those early experiences that later would make him one of the most ferocious negotiators in the business world.

Paul Jobs was still struggling to support his family and became convinced that he could provide a better life for them if he sold real estate. He earned his realtor's license and went to work. Although successful during his first year, he didn't like the business in the least, especially the fawning he had to do with prospective customers and the irregular paychecks. His distaste increased when he fell on hard times and had to mortgage his home to feed and clothe his family. Clara took a part-time job to help out. Paul Jobs became so disillusioned with real estate that he decided to give it up and return to his earlier profession as a machinist. He was finally hired by a company in San Carlos, but he had no seniority and had to work for rock-bottom wages.

The family was forced to cut back on some of the meager luxuries it had previously enjoyed. Vacations were out, the furniture was used, and a black and white television replaced the color TV. Steven Jobs didn't like the change in the family fortunes and, when he was in the fourth grade, his teacher asked the students in his class a macrocosmic question: "What is it in this universe that you don't understand?" The young Jobs gave a microcosmic answer. He said he didn't understand why the family was suddenly so broke.

Steven was troublesome in grade school. He was expelled from one class for misbehaving when he was nine years old. A friendly teacher came to his rescue. Jobs recalls that she bribed him into doing his school work, sometimes giving him money for outstanding performance. Money was something that Steven understood and wanted. He rose to the bait and became an outstanding student. Although he skipped the fifth grade, his sixth grade report noted: "Steven is an excellent reader. However, he wastes much time during reading period." It explained further that he saw no purpose in studying his reading assignments and that he was sometimes a disciplinary problem.

Steven did not get along with his fellow students and, when he began taking swimming lessons, he was the kind of kid that others taunted and snapped with wet towels. At the Mountain View Dolphins Swim Club, Steven met Mark Wozniak, Stephen Wozniak's younger brother. Mark remembers that, "He was pretty much of a crybaby. He'd lose a race and go off and cry. He didn't quite fit in with everybody else. He wasn't one of the guys." Clara Jobs took babysitting jobs to pay for Steven's swimming lessons, a sacrifice that was consistent with the way his parents constantly sought the best for him. Bana Witt, who years later was one of Apple's first employees, said, "They absolutely doted on him. He was a golden boy who could do no wrong. They instilled that in him, and I think that's where he gets all of his confidence."

The sacrifices they made for Steven went far beyond those made by most parents. When he changed schools and had to attend Crittenden Elementary School in Mountain View, Steven didn't like it. Most of the students came from lower class neighborhoods; they were rowdy and frequently caused enough trouble to bring the police scrambling. After Steven had attended the school for a year he became an outcast. He confronted his parents and told them he would not go to school if it meant he had to attend Crittenden. Paul Jobs, concerned for his son's welfare, and aware of his stubbornness, gave in. They moved closer to the Palo Alto and Cupertino school districts so Steven could be in a better school. No sacrifice, it seemed, was too great for their golden boy.

One of Steven's friends was Bill Fernandez, a student who shared an interest in electronics. Both young men were shy and withdrawn and not the least bit comfortable with their peers. Jobs especially was disliked by other students, who considered him an oddball. Fernandez met him at Cupertino Junior High School, and the two hit it off. "For some reason the kids in eighth grade didn't like him because they thought he was odd," Fernandez recalls.

Fernandez introduced Jobs to Stephen Wozniak, who was four years older. Wozniak was also a loner, although he was so engrossed in electronics that he didn't feel deprived. Jobs said he liked Wozniak immediately because, "He was the only person I met who knew more about electronics than me." Wozniak said that was a gross overstatement. "Steve didn't know very much about electronics," he said. "He never did get to be very good at it. He got to the point where he was on the borderline of becoming a fairly good young engineer, but it took him years to get there."

Nevertheless, they became best friends, and it was probably the most important friendship either of them would ever have. Although Jobs and Fernandez tinkered with electronics, neither came close to Wozniak's level of expertise. Jobs and Fernandez created elementary gadgets in a garage, although they hadn't the knowledge to do anything very complicated. Contrary to popular opinion, Jobs had nothing to do with building the first Apple computer, but encouraged that perception. Wozniak took Jobs's claim in stride and never did much to discredit it, although in the early days of Apple he was hard-pressed to give Steve credit.

"Reporters would come in to me and ask, 'Well, did he develop the hardware?' I said, 'No.' Then they would ask, 'Well, did he develop the software?' I had to answer 'No,' again. I created the whole computer. I had no help from anyone, no one I could turn to. I did it all by myself."

Stephen Wozniak had plunged head over heels into electronics at an early age. His father, Jerry, was an engineer who went to work for Lockheed when he was in his thirties. Lockheed in those years was deeply involved in military research, and it was a very secretive corporation. By the time Jerry Wozniak went to work in the missile division in Sunnyvale, the space race was well under way. The Russians had launched Sputnik, and the American Vanguard rocket had blown up on the ground. Lockheed was making space age components for Discoverer, Explorer, Mercury, and Gemini, names that have become household words. The company was researching a new rocket fuel, and engineers had constructed a mock-up of a space station that looked like a wagon wheel with spokes.

Jerry Wozniak had played football at the California Institute of Technology where he earned a degree in electrical engineering. After holding an engineering job for a short time after graduation, he and a partner spent a year designing a stacking machine. They lasted one year before going broke, but Wozniak still thinks it was a good idea that failed only because neither he nor his partner knew how to operate a business. The failure of the stacking machine, along with the birth of their first child, Stephen, convinced Jerry and Margaret Wozniak to consider a more secure future. Wozniak hit the job market and worked as a weapons designer in San Diego, then designed autopilots for Lear in Santa Monica before he joined Lockheed.

Lockheed's involvement in highly sensitive projects made it a tightly controlled company. The work prompted much wild speculation about Russian spies. Stephen Wozniak and other neighborhood children kept a close watch on people they imagined were working for the KGB. America could sleep well with

Wozniak's miniature counter-spies working hard to keep the nation safe.

The Wozniaks enjoyed a contented home life. Jerry Wozniak played ball with his children in the back yard, coached a Little League baseball team, and won a father-son golf tournament with Stephen. Margaret Wozniak was a feminist before the movement swept the nation. She served as president of the Republican women's club in Sunnyvale and often had the children help out with precinct work. She ran the family with a firm but gentle hand.

The senior Wozniaks tried to instill culture in their children by osmosis. They played classical music often, hoping that the children would gain an appreciation for it. The children had other ideas. Leslie preferred pop music and her brothers were addicted to television spy and science fiction shows.

Silicon Valley literally crackled with electricity in the mid-sixties. There were new and exciting advances being made every day, and dozens of new firms were springing up to manufacture electronics devices. Stephen Wozniak was caught up in the excitement. When he was in the fifth grade Stephen was given a kit and succeeded in making a voltmeter. Wozniak and other children did odd jobs for neighborhood engineers in exchange for electronics parts. The engineers were generous in passing their knowledge along, and one of them caught young Wozniak's attention with a ham radio. Stephen built his own 100-watt ham radio and obtained an operator's license when he was in the sixth grade. Before long, he created a house-to-house intercommunications network by wiring speakers in the homes of neighborhood friends.

About this same time, Stephen also created an electronics tic-tac-toe game using the kitchen table for a work bench, much to the dismay of his mother. He hammered nails in a board to connect the electrical components and installed lights on the other side, and figured out circuits that would simulate the moves a human being might make. Wozniak was starved for knowledge about electronics and read all of the trade magazines he could get his hands on. One time he spotted a diagram for a simple calculator called a One Bit Adder-Subtractor which could do basic arithmetic. The diagram marked a turning point in Wozniak's life. He understood part of the diagram, but there were other aspects of it that were completely foreign to him. He had discovered that electronics could perform logical functions by the use of various switches and components. He studied the diagram intently until he understood it, then decided to build a machine he called The Ten Bit Parallel Adder-Subtractor, which was far more powerful than the one he had seen in the magazine.

Wozniak designed the circuits by himself and placed all of the necessary electrical components on a small board that had two rows of switches on the bottom, one row for adding, the other for subtracting. The solution to the arithmetical problem was displayed on a configuration of lights. It was Wozniak's first attempt at building a computer and it won him first prize in the Cupertino School District Science Fair. Later, competing against students who were much older, he entered it in the Bay Area Science fair and won third place.

Electronics courses taught at Homestead High School became the focal point of Wozniak's interests. He learned about theory, design, function, and practical applications. Wozniak was the star pupil in the electronics class taught by John McCollum, who was a genius at finding spare parts his students could use. Wozniak used most of his spare time, including homeroom study periods, to delve even more deeply into electronics. He was no longer thinking in simple terms, but considering how to have computers perform logical functions. One of his student friends, Elmer Baum, chanced by Wozniak's desk in homeroom and noticed the complicated sketches Wozniak was drawing on a sheet of paper. They looked like Greek to him.

"I asked, 'What are you doing?' And he said, 'Designing a computer.' I was impressed as hell."

Wozniak had always been a jokester and his growing knowledge in electronics helped make them more sophisticated. On one occasion he used sticks from an old battery, attached an oscillator and some wires to it, and created what looked like a dynamite bomb. Wozniak placed it in a friend's locker where the ticking of the oscillator soon attracted attention. The police bomb squad was called but, before they arrived, the school principal, William Byrd, took matters into his own hands. He grabbed the "bomb" at risk of life and limb and made a mad dash to an empty football field, where he pulled the wires out.

When it was discovered that the bomb was a fake, it didn't take school officials long to link it with Wozniak. He was called to the principal's office and went cheerfully, thinking he was to receive congratulations for winning a math contest. Instead he found himself chewed out, then escorted by police to San Jose's Juvenile Hall where he spent the night incarcerated. Margaret Wozniak retrieved her son the next day and screamed at the authorities that they should have tattooed a number on her son's chest. Wozniak's sister, an editor on a school newspaper, threatened an exposé. Wozniak returned to class and received a standing ovation.

Wozniak also learned more about computer mainframes and software. He taught himself how to design programs in computer language, and he learned how to design machines that would perform complicated mathematical tasks, including figuring square roots. Wozniak was already an electrical wizard by the time he met Steven Jobs. Jobs, who had learned how to perform simple electronics tasks, wasn't even close to possessing the wealth of knowledge and creativity that Wozniak had accumulated, but Jobs was interested and pursued electronics, after a fashion.

Jobs and Fernandez listened to rock music and made dazzling laser displays in the garage as they worked on electronics devices. Jobs bored easily and it was hard for him to stay with any one thing for very long. On the other hand, he was especially interested in science fairs, where he could show off his creations. At Cupertino Junior High School he constructed a silicon-controlled rectifier which could be used to control alternating current. When he entered Homestead High School, he enrolled in an electronics course taught by McCollum, who had been Stephen Wozniak's teacher two years earlier. Wozniak had been a star pupil, but Jobs was not nearly up to that standard. He dropped out of McCollum's classes after a year, distinguishing himself from other students only by his strange way of looking at the world. McCollum described Jobs as a loner who had a "different" way of thinking. Once, when he couldn't get a part at school that he wanted, Jobs placed a collect call to the public relations department of Burroughs in Detroit. McCollum said that it wasn't kosher for Jobs to do that. "I said, 'You cannot call them collect,'" McCollum remembered. "Steve said, 'I don't have the money for the phone call. They've got plenty of money.'"

Although Jobs dropped out of the electronics class, there was enough excitement in the air to keep him interested. He continued to attend meetings of the school's electronics club and made several visits to the NASA flight simulator at Moffett Field in Sunnyvale. He was one of the many students who attended evening talks by Hewlett-Packard scientists. The talks were about the latest advances in electronics and Jobs, exercising a style that was a trademark of his personality, collared Hewlett-Packard engineers and drew additional information from them. Once he even called Bill Hewlett, one of the company founders, to request parts. Jobs not only received the parts he asked for, he managed to wrangle a summer job. Jobs worked on an assembly line to help build computers and was so fascinated that he tried to design his own, but did not have the expertise necessary to see the project to completion.

Although only average in his understanding of how to use electronics components, Jobs developed a superior understanding of what those products could do. He became an expert at finding them, usually at rock bottom prices, prowled electronics hobby shops, and ordered various components from mail order houses. A huge electronics store named Haltek, which was housed in a building a block long, became one of his favorite haunts. It was filled with thousands of electronics devices, including vacuum tubes, which had long been outdated. Some of the parts were brand new, but it took months for them to reach Haltek. There were no clerks to help locate parts so customers had to be certain of what they wanted, then have the patience to find them. No one was better at this than Jobs.

In high school, he had a job working nights and weekends at an electronics shop in Sunnyvale and became knowledgeable about the going rate for various parts, from semiconductor microchips to less exotic components. He was so good at finding deals on his own that he once spent a Saturday rummaging through parts at the San Jose Flea Market, bought some transistors, then sold them at a profit to the owner of the electronics shop where he worked. Stephen Wozniak was with him on the flea market excursion and was dumbfounded when Jobs told him what he was doing. "I thought it was a flaky idea," Wozniak said, "but he knew what he was doing."

Jobs had interests that ranged far beyond electronics when he was growing up. This was the decade of the sixties where established beliefs and institutions were being challenged. It was the "hippie" era where young people rebelled against almost everything and experimented with various drugs. Jobs became caught up in the movement. He was natually curious about everything and spent almost as much time studying literature, philosophy, and the arts as he did experimenting with laser beams. He gave up his hated swimming classes and, for a while, tried to play water polo but says he quit when the coach encouraged him to be unnecessarily rough. He wasn't very good at it anyway. "I wasn't a jock," he said later. "I was a loner for the most part." His different viewpoint estranged him even more from his classmates, who considered him weird.

He also had a light-hearted side that sometimes manifested itself. Encouraged by Wozniak, who loved pranks, Jobs, Wozniak, and Elmer Baum tie-dyed a sheet in the school colors that featured a large hand gesturing obscenely. They had persuaded Baum's mother to paint the signal, telling her that it was a Brazilian good luck sign. They combined their initials at the bottom to read SWABJOB PRODUCTIONS. Jobs was on the carpet in the principal's office while his Father did his best to convince the school official that it was nothing but a harmless prank.

While Jobs was unpopular at high school, he was able to make friends with older, off-beat types. His first car, which he received in high school, allowed him to visit friends at both Berkeley and Stanford. Being on the campuses broadened his interests and he began to experiment with various drugs and sleep deprivation. Once he stayed up for two consecutive nights and regularly smoked marijuana and hashish, and affected an intellectual appearance by puffing on a pipe. Paul Jobs found marijuana in Steve's car once, but didn't know what it was.

Steve didn't blink an eye. "It's marijuana, Father."

Nothing came of the incident.

Jobs started dating his first serious girl friend when he was a senior in high school. The girl, Judy Smith, was very pretty and was two years younger than he. Wozniak didn't understand what Jobs saw in her. "She was pretty but she was kind of a druggie person," he said. "She didn't have a whole lot to offer intellectually. But they stayed together for quite a few years and she even worked at Apple for a while."

Jobs met Smith when she was working on an animated film project, largely done on the sly because school officials didn't approve of it. Jobs dropped in occasionally to watch the progress, and Wozniak thought that Jobs might be engaged in helping produce a pornographic movie. At the time she met Jobs, Smith's parents were starting to break up and they argued frequently. Smith said it was driving her crazy and that she was vulnerable at the time. Jobs helped take her mind off of troubles on the home front. "He was kind of crazy," she said. "I think that's why I was attracted to him."

Jobs and Smith often skipped school, opting instead to talk and partake of the fruit of the grape. Jobs took LSD for the first time with Smith and it blew him away. He said that he had been listening to Bach, when suddenly the wheat field he and Smith were in seemed to explode with Bach's music. He described it as the most wonderful experience in his life. He felt like he was a conductor and the strains of Bach were coming from the whole wheat field.

When Jobs graduated from high school he was thin to the point of gauntness and his school photographs were so unflattering that his mother bought only one. He and Smith had decided they were going to live together for the summer. It posed no problem for Smith because her parents were splitting up, and Jobs had long since demonstrated his ability to bend his parents to his will.

They rented a small cabin in the hills, then Jobs told his parents, "I'm going to live with Judy."

"No, you're not," Paul Jobs said.

"Yes, I am."

"No, you're not."

"Bye," Jobs said, and left the house.

The first few weeks were a treat. They took long walks. Smith painted, and Jobs took to picking a guitar and writing poetry. Wozniak visited them occasionally and they sat around listening to Bob Dylan records. The idyllic summer came to an abrupt end when Jobs's ever unreliable car caught on fire and his father had to tow it home. To make ends meet, Jobs, Wozniak, and Smith took jobs in a San Jose shopping center dressed up in *Alice in Wonderland* costumes. Smith was Alice while Jobs and Wozniak alternated as the White Rabbit and the Mad Hatter. Wozniak had a sense of the absurd and loved it, but Jobs hated wearing the heavy costumes. He said that after three or four hours he felt like "wiping out some kids."

The stint at the shopping center must have seemed especially trying to Jobs, since he and Wozniak had been intermittently engaged, over the past few years, in a somewhat less innocent and more profitable pursuit.

CHAPTER 3

The Blue Box
Escapade

When Jobs was still in high school, he and Wozniak began to outwit the telephone company. It was a highly illegal venture involving the ability to make telephone calls without the nuisance of paying for them. Wozniak first stumbled across the existence of a large underground network of "phone phreaks" who got their kicks from making free calls around the world. The discovery of this network led to the first Jobs-Wozniak commercial venture.

Wozniak's mother was indirectly responsible for turning her son toward a light-hearted criminal pursuit. It began when she saw an article in *Esquire* magazine describing how the underground network operated. The outlaws had created "blue boxes," which duplicated the tones that the telephone company uses to simulate numbers that are dialed. The outlaws gave themselves code names to protect their identities. There was Cap'n Crunch, Dr. No, Peter Perpendicular Pimple and other peculiar pseudonyms. The phone phreaks regularly phoned each other, made calls around the world, hooked into computers and generally drove the telephone company crazy trying to figure out how to stop them.

Knowing her son's fascination with such things, Wozniak's mother innocently gave him a copy of the article to read. Wozniak had not been interested in telephones previously because they were too simplistic. Phone phreaking opened up a whole new world that appealed to both the engineer and rebel in Wozniak. He devoured the article with growing excitement. Here was a challenge he could sink his teeth into and, perhaps, meet people with kindred minds. Before he had even finished reading the article, he telephoned Jobs and the two pored over the *Esquire* article, giving whoops of glee and feeding one another's enthusiasm for such an outrageous and risky adventure. They decided to make their own blue box.

It was not as simple as it first seemed. The telephone companies had seen the article and had zealously helped purge the libraries of operating manuals in an attempt to stamp out the growing number of phreaks. Jobs and Wozniak diligently searched through libraries to find a manual that might give them a clue on how to proceed. Finally the pair found a book that had been overlooked, and they rummaged through the pages for technical data to help them build their very own blue box. They discovered that the details about circuitry in the manual coincided with those described in the *Esquire* article.

The problem was that all the references were fairly general. They had to figure out a way to design a blue box that would exactly match the tone signals used by the telphone company. They started by building an oscillator to create tones they recorded on tape. Unfortunately for them, the oscillator was too erratic to provide the exact tones that were necessary. They tuned the oscillator with the enthusiasm of fanatics, but still couldn't get it right. Once they believed they had achieved success, but the tones on their tape recorder still didn't work.

Wozniak decided to try something different. He believed he could create more precise tones by using digital design. It was much more difficult to create, but if it was successful, it would be far more precise than the oscillator. Wozniak's competitive spirit was aroused by the success of other phone phreaks, many of whom had become legendary in the underground. Cap'n Crunch had discovered, quite by accident, that a toy that came with a box of Cap'n Crunch cereal duplicated the necessary tones. Hence his code name. Another phreak had cracked the telephone company system just by whistling. Wozniak's digital blue box would create a precise tone whenever a particular button was pressed. Wozniak was so intent on succeeding that he even wrote a program to run on one of the computers at Berkeley to help with the configuration of circuits.

Wozniak worked for weeks before he completed his first blue box. It ran on a 9-volt battery, had a small speaker, and didn't need an on/off switch since the power was only activated when buttons were punched. When the time came for a test, Jobs and Wozniak decided to call the latter's grandmother in Los Angeles but reached a wrong number in Angeleno. Nevertheless, they were gleeful about their success in making a long distance call free of charge.

The pursuit for a reliable blue box continued, and both Wozniak and Jobs became obsessed with getting linked into the underground network of phone phreaks. They telephoned the author of the *Esquire* article, who claimed the journalistic prerogative not to reveal his sources. They were particularly interested in finding Cap'n Crunch, who was the universally acclaimed king of the phone phreaks. They were up against a brick wall until Jobs discovered that Cap'n Crunch had recently been interviewed on a radio station in Los Gatos. Wozniak and Jobs went to the radio station, hoping to get Cap'n Crunch's real identity, but they ran into another wall of journalistic protectivism. Fortunately for the two, the world of phone phreaking was relatively small and word leaked out that Jobs and Wozniak were desperate to meet Cap'n Crunch. The underground network went into operation and Cap'n Crunch turned out to be a man who worked at a radio station in Cupertino. Jobs called the station and left a message for the receptionist to have Cap'n Crunch give them a call. They were elated when the call came and the legendary Cap'n Crunch was on the other end of the line. An appointment was made for Cap'n Crunch to meet them a few nights later in Wozniak's dormitory room at Berkeley.

On the evening of the appointment, Jobs and Wozniak could scarcely contain their excitement. They waited, sitting on the edge of the bed, wondering if the legendary king of the phone phreaks would actually arrive. Then came the knock on the door, and Wozniak opened it and stared in shock. A thin, disreputable looking man with bad teeth, wearing blue jeans and dirty tennis shoes stood there with a lopsided grin on his face.

"Are you Cap'n Crunch?" Wozniak asked.

Cap'n Crunch answered in a manner befitting his position. "I am he," he said regally.

"He looked absolutely horrid," Wozniak said later. Although Cap'n Crunch's appearance and his quiet, ferret-like movements unsettled Jobs and Wozniak, they found the man a wealth of information. He demonstrated his prowess over the phone company by making several free long distance calls, including one that crossed international barriers. He telephoned far-away cities to get weather forecasts and tapped into long-distance lines to automated services that told jokes.

The unshaven, unkempt Cap'n Crunch was undoubtedly the king of phreaks in spite of his unsavory appearance, which bothered both Jobs and Wozniak. He was a whiz at phone phreaking. He amazed the two when he showed them how to "stack" calls going from one relay to another around the world, concluding with a ring at a telephone just across the hall. It was a marvelously exciting experience for Jobs and Wozniak.

Following the demonstration, they went to a pizza parlor where Cap'n Crunch looked at Wozniak's blue box. He was impressed with the clarity of its tones, but said they sounded a little thin. Cap'n Crunch gave Wozniak some advice, along with the telephone numbers of other phone phreaks and codes that would allow them to place a call anywhere in the world free of charge. He also ended with a somber warning: Always make telephone calls from a pay phone so they couldn't be traced to them. For Wozniak, it was the most astounding encounter he had ever experienced. It came close to ending in disaster.

On their way back to Los Altos, where Wozniak had left his car, Jobs's famous Fiat broke down yet again. Jobs and Wozniak found a pay phone and used their blue box and tried to call

Cap'n Crunch for help. They dialed an 800 toll-free number with the blue box, but turned to jelly when an operator came on the line to see if they were still there. They were afraid their call was being monitored. They were so unnerved by this that Jobs put the blue box in his pocket and was dialing a legal telephone number when the unexpected happened. A police cruiser screeched to a halt and the officers ordered them out of the booth, thinking they were concealing drugs. Wozniak and Jobs stood helplessly against a wall, their legs and arms spread out in a pose that is now familiar on television, while police searched the area for contraband. It is perhaps an illuminating insight into Jobs's personality that, just before they were ordered against the wall, he slipped the blue box to Wozniak. If anyone was to be caught with something illegal, it wouldn't be Jobs. The police found the blue box, but weren't interested, having been more intent on finding illegal drugs.

One policeman asked what the blue box was.

"A music synthesizer," Wozniak said.

Another cop wanted to know what an orange button was for. "That's for calibration," Jobs said. Wozniak quickly followed up by telling them that it was a computer-controlled synthesizer. The police officers were convinced that the pair were not carrying illegal drugs and gave them a ride. Then, to the utter astonishment of both Jobs and Wozniak, one of the police officers looked at the small box and said: "Too bad, a guy named Moog beat you to it."

Sure, Jobs replied. He was the one who had sent them the schematics.

Jobs and Wozniak were a suspicious pair with their long hair, scruffy appearance and strange attitudes, but the police had no reason to hold them. Even so, it had been a harrowing experience for both young men, and the night still had a frightful event in store for Wozniak. When he picked up his car and headed back toward Berkeley, he fell asleep at the wheel and crashed against some road barriers. Fortunately, he wasn't hurt.

After their meeting with Cap'n Crunch, Jobs and Wozniak became even more fanatical about phone phreaking. One of the first things they had to do was find code names. Wozniak chose

Berkeley Blue because of his school colors and Jobs selected Oaf Tobark. Wozniak was far more taken with phone phreaking than Jobs. He was almost totally involved in the pursuit during his first quarter at Berkeley. He voraciously read every article he could find on the subject and taped some of them to his walls for edification or mirth. He subscribed to various underground publications that were devoted to phone phreaking, but still maintained a consuming interest in computers. Both he and Jobs hung around computer nerds at Stanford and continued to learn more about phone phreaking that had somehow found its way into the computer memory banks.

Wozniak was proud of his blue box and showed it to numerous friends, including Allen Baum. Baum was astounded when Wozniak used the box to make a telephone call from one booth to another, but that was not nearly as impressive as the time Wozniak made a toll-free call to a kibbutz in Israel where his sister was. Jobs was the first of the two to see commercial possibilities in the venture. They had both discovered that college students were perpetually short of money and that they wanted to make more telephone calls than they could afford. To Jobs, this seemed to be a tailor-made market for their highly illegal venture. Wozniak was not so keen on the idea, but Jobs convinced him that they could turn a profit. "He wanted to make money," Wozniak recalled. They conspired like spies to devise a code to use when seeking out prospective customers. It was a hit and miss marketing plan, at best. They would visit dormitories, knock on doors and ask if a certain person who was interested in a blue box lived there. If the prospective customer showed an interest, they asked him to attend a demonstration to see the advantages and ease of making free telephone calls. Should the prospect seem confused or suspicious, they made a hasty retreat and moved on to the next room.

The blue box business became fairly lucrative as the word spread through the campuses. Wozniak relished showing the benefits and power of the blue boxes. He would hook a tape recorder to the telephone lines with alligator clips, then make telephone calls to friends of those in his audience. They were not above playing practical jokes, and Jobs once made a toll-free call to a hotel in England to organize a party. Wozniak once called the Vatican, pretending to be Henry Kissinger, and asked to confer with the Pope. It was nighttime at the Vatican and the Pope was asleep, but, incredibly, the official in Rome said he would wake him. Wozniak quickly hung up.

Jobs and Wozniak gradually honed their sales techniques. They made tape recordings of the telephone numbers their customers usually called and sold them. They reached an agreement on how their partnership should work. Jobs supplied the parts, which totaled about $40, while Wozniak spent four hours or so wiring the boxes, which sold for $150 each. Wiring the boxes by hand was a tedious, time-consuming task, but Wozniak solved the problem by having circuit boards printed, reducing his manufacturing time to about an hour. Always interested in innovation and improvement, Wozniak added an automatic dialing feature to the box, and, when it was ready to be sold, he or Jobs taped a hand-written guarantee on the bottom. The card read, "He's got the whole world in his hand." Wozniak was proud of his work and promised to repair any box free of charge if it was returned to him with the card. He lived up to his part of the bargain.

Even the blue box adventure was unable to captivate the mercurial Jobs for very long. He grew bored and became increasingly nervous about the possibility of getting caught. He dropped out of the partnership after about a year. It was an opportune time for him to quit because the telephone company was coming down hard on people who used their lines illegally. Telephone company officials even hired informants who pretended to be phone phreaks to infiltrate that underground world.

Jobs also fretted about the seeming instability of Cap'n Crunch, who was not careful enough about his phone phreaking activities to suit Jobs. Jobs thought Cap'n Crunch was a space cadet who, sooner or later, would get into trouble and possibly lead authorities to him and Wozniak. Jobs was right to be worried because officials at General Telephone had managed to trace some of the calls that Cap'n Crunch made. Jobs's home number was on the list that General Telephone gave to the FBI. Cap'n Crunch was tracked down, fined one thousand dollars and placed on five years of probation. He was to enter the lives of Jobs and Wozniak once more in later years to create unsettling events.

Since it was illegal, the blue box business had to be conducted on the sly, and Jobs and Wozniak ran into unsavory customers. A few, realizing the perilous position the two were in, simply refused to pay for the boxes by threatening to turn them in. Jobs and Wozniak had no recourse when they were cheated. There was also the very real threat of physical harm. Jobs once found himself staring into a pistol when he tried selling a blue box to a customer in the parking lot of a fast-food pizza outlet. Jobs considered several scenarios, all of which ended up with him getting shot, and turned the blue box over to the gun-wielding bandit. That was enough for Jobs to call it quits.

Wozniak, on the other hand, never worried much about being caught. He was a free spirit filled with fun and enthusiasm for his new money-making hobby. He continued the business without Jobs and made additional improvements to the blue boxes so they could be used in airports and hotels. Once he used a box to tap into a line in San Francisco where he listened to conversations taking place with the FBI. Jobs, however, was so fearful of being nabbed by the police that he put as much distance between himself and Wozniak and the blue boxes as possible.

Even though Jobs had dropped out of the business, Wozniak still considered him a partner because he had turned it into a money-making venture. He displayed scrupulous honesty, a trait he was to demonstrate time and again over the years, by splitting half of the six thousand dollars he made on the blue boxes with Jobs. Not once in their friendship was Jobs ever to show such generosity. In fact, he was to take advantage of Wozniak several times during an association that gradually deteriorated into bitterness and distrust.

Wozniak employed a loosely connected sales force and continued to sell the blue boxes around various campuses in California. He made several airplane trips to deliver the gadgets, putting them in a suitcase and checking them through baggage so they wouldn't be discovered by security X-ray machines. Eventually, he left the business when it got to be too troublesome for him although he still retained an almost fanatical zeal for the electronics aspects of cheating the telephone company.

Wozniak had managed to create a blue box from an original design that was as good, or better, than any that had been designed. Most importantly, he never got caught, as did a lot of other phone phreaks. He continued to be fascinated with blue boxes and worked on them to the detriment of his college career. It wasn't long before he received a letter from the dean complaining about his lackluster performance in school. Wozniak found himself on the carpet in the dean's office, which had become familiar territory.

CHAPTER 4

Woz the Wiz

By the time Stephen Wozniak entered high school, he was already well on the way to performing wizardry with electronics. He learned even more in John McCollum's classes at Homestead High School in Cupertino. Wozniak absorbed physics like a sponge and became familiar with tasks that various electrical components and their electrons could perform. He also recognized that design must conform to human requirement or it is almost useless. Wozniak experimented with capacitators and resistors in both series and parallel, and learned how to manipulate direct and alternating electrical currents. He was moving deeper into the heady realm of a world that remained a mystery to most people, and was accumulating knowledge that gave him power to manipulate electrical currents.

The various devices created in McCollum's classes could create a wide range of sounds, using solid-state electronics. Wozniak learned how to jam electrical frequencies, a subject that was not on the high school class agenda. For all the excellent instruction in McCollum's classes, he did not teach anything about computers, which had become Wozniak's most pressing intellectual pursuit. Without supervision or guidance, he started designing machines that could do simple arithmetic, then advanced to more sophisticated mathematics. Wozniak piled up awards in science fairs and shared an interest in computer design with his friend, Elmer Baum.

Although McCollum did not teach computer science, he bowed to a request from Wozniak, his star pupil, to find a place where the budding computer designer could learn. McCollum used his influence with a friend who made it possible for Wozniak and Baum to spend Wednesday afternoons in the computer room at GTE Sylvania. There Wozniak came into contact with his first mainframe computer, an IBM 1130. It was about the size of a refrigerator, shook the floor when it operated, and was so loud that shouting replaced normal conversation. A keyboard punched holes in cards to enter information onto the computer's large reels of magnetic tape. The engineers at GTE were helpful and did their best to explain to the two youngsters how the system worked.

Wozniak learned, much to his astonishment, that a compiler was used to translate letters into electrical commands that were turned into computer language in the form of binary codes. He didn't realize that the compiler was a program. Instead, he thought it was the computer itself, not an instrument that was part of the computer's infrastructure. The engineers helped Wozniak find answers to questions that stumped him when he was building a relatively sophisticated calculator.

Wozniak and Baum learned how to write programs in FORTRAN, a computer language, and used the keypunch machines to punch holes into stiff paper cards that were fed into the computer. As their expertise grew, they wrote increasingly more complex programs. One program calculated moves on a chess board while others dealt with complex mathematical problems. Wozniak learned so much at GTE that McCollum sometimes invited him to give lectures to the electronics classes at Homestead. The only thing wrong with the lectures, McCollum said, was that Wozniak was talking at such a high level that most of the students didn't understand him.

Wozniak and Baum augmented the knowledge they gained at GTE by visiting the Stanford Linear Accelerator Center as often as they could. Although the Center was involved in many aspects of electronics, Wozniak and Baum spent their time in the computer center. There they found an IBM 360, which was IBM's most popular mainframe computer in the sixties. The engineers and technicians were just as helpful as those at GTE and the two teenagers were allowed to use keypunch machines to write programs they ran on some of the center's smaller computers. Wozniak was learning rapidly, and soon he was receiving technical material from about a dozen electronics firms in Silicon Valley.

By this time, the semiconductor companies in the Valley had started manufacturing increasingly smaller chips. A large number of computer functions could be placed in a relatively small space so that computers shrank and became known as minicomputers. These computers, which were about the size of a chest of drawers, were almost as powerful as the larger mainframes then in use. Various technical publications talking about the power of semiconductors began to appear and these were of particular interest to Wozniak. He read them voraciously and also pored through a book published by Digital Electronics Corporation entitled *Small Computer Handbook*. At the time, the "computer on a chip" had not been invented and designing a computer meant that a person needed almost complete knowledge of the diagrams and schematics that showed how semiconductors worked.

The more he read, the more enthralled Wozniak became. He studied a minicomputer designed by Varian, trying to understand all of its complexity. Then he tried to design his first minicomputer using microchips but couldn't. He knew what a computer was, but he still couldn't master the circuitry needed to make it work. The walls of ignorance fell with each new discovery Wozniak made; he became zealous in his pursuit to create a computer that would use a minimal number of chips. He became ecstatic when he found new ways to use computer language. Wozniak discovered how to make components of a computer perform as many tasks as possible. Wozniak's work baffled his parents, who didn't comprehend what he was doing, and he soon left Elmer Baum in the dust. Wozniak was performing such advanced work that Baum was unable to keep up with the electronics wizard that Wozniak had become.

Wozniak's interest in computers didn't diminish when he went to college. Rejected by Cal Tech, Wozniak ended up at the University of Colorado in Boulder. Jerry Wozniak was torn about his son's departure because he didn't think he was mature enough to enroll in college and leave home at the same time. Wozniak's love of practical jokes didn't diminish, and he took great delight in using an oscillator to jam closed circuit television sets in his classrooms. He could hardly restrain his laughter as the teachers struggled in vain to regain a picture. Once Wozniak carried this kind of joke too far: When some students were watching the Kentucky Derby, he jammed the broadcast just as the horses were closing in on the finish line.

Although there was no doubt of Wozniak's brilliance, he was a terrible student. He spent far more time at the university's data center, learning more about computers and FORTRAN, than he did in class. He badgered programmers and engineers, making a general nuisance of himself. Wozniak did not seem particularly concerned with academics, and his knowledge of computers, coupled with his prankish personality, found a new outlet. He ran several programs in the data center that printed reams of paper reading FUCK NIXON. Once again, history repeated itself and he ran afoul of college officials and left the university after his first year. He had only F's to his credit and a batch of computer designs when he returned home to enroll at De Anza Community College.

In familiar territory again, Wozniak began prowling for electronics components rejected because of cosmetic flaws and started tinkering with computer design. His obsession with computers continued to the detriment of his school work, but he managed to squeak through the year. During the summer, he and Baum were hired as programmers at Tenet, a small company that made computers. Baum didn't remain long, but Wozniak worked long and hard, increasing his knowledge of computer programming. Wozniak stayed with Tenet until the company went belly up during the recession in 1972.

Undeterred, Wozniak continued his study of computer design, often reading photo copies of material that Baum sent to him from MIT. He haunted science fairs. One item at a science fair caught his attention: it was a machine that performed different functions in sequence, giving out predetermined signals at each step. Wozniak was so captivated by it that he took a schematic of the machine home and translated the mechanical functions into electronics. He had learned something important: that electrical circuits could complete a number of functions in sequence before responding to a command. He realized then and there that he could design computers.

Shortly after this realization struck home, Wozniak began looking at the inner working of a Nova minicomputer designed by Data General. It had the capability of processing sixteen binary digits simultaneously, using more than one hundred semiconductor chips that were linked by solder lines on a laminated board. Although much more advanced, it used the same principles that Wozniak had incorporated into his adder-subtractor when he was only thirteen. Because of progress in the semiconductor technology, the same electronic tasks that had forced Wozniak to use a large board could now be performed on a single chip of silicon.

Wozniak and Baum devoured information that was sent to them by various semiconductor companies. They drew diagrams of circuitry as they designed different computers. Wozniak fully intended to build every computer he designed and was prevented from doing so only because he couldn't afford the parts. Jerry Wozniak, impressed with his son's progress, arranged for him to meet with a friend who had designed a semiconductor chip for Fairchild. From him, Wozniak got practical advice concerning semiconductors and circuitry.

Wozniak concentrated on miniaturization and was determined to translate some of the schematics he had drawn into a working computer, using as few parts as possible. Bill Fernandez, his neighborhood friend, happily joined in the effort and volunteered space in his family's garage. Wozniak began scrounging for various memory chips and other components and went to work. He designed the computer and its function while Fernandez concentrated on timing circuits that would make lights blink on at the proper command.

Fernandez was two years younger and did not have the wealth of knowledge that Wozniak possessed. Nevertheless, he made important contributions, especially in the demanding work of connecting components. Wozniak remembered in later years that Fernandez did not have an engineering background, but that he was exceptionally neat and methodical. The two youngsters drank quarts of cream soda and listened to rock music as they worked on the computer. Because of the quantities of the soft drink they consumed, they dubbed their machine The Cream Soda Computer. The machine was almost finished when Fernandez invited his friend, Steven Jobs, to meet Wozniak and see the computer. It was the start of an important friendship and, although Wozniak didn't realize it at the time, he had laid the basic groundwork for a machine that would revolutionize the world of computing and create a whole new industry.

Margaret Wozniak, ever anxious to get recognition for her offspring, convinced a reporter and photographer from the *San Jose Mercury* to witness a demonstration of the computer. Unfortunately, the computer shorted out in a shower of sparks because of a faulty chip. There was no picture or story in the newspaper.

CHAPTER 5

The Rebel

Unlike Wozniak, who had zeroed in on computers and programming during his adolescence and early adulthood, Steve Jobs entered that same period of life rather aimlessly. He had toyed with electronics, poetry, and music but he never achieved any degree of excellence. The consistent part of his personality was that he was strong-willed and mercurial, becoming even more so as he grew older. As a young adult preparing to enter college, he had no particular goal in life other than to broaden his living experiences. He was on a spiritual and intellectual fishing expedition.

Jobs had always been stubborn and, when it came time to choose a college to attend, he was just as obstinate. He read through college brochures, sneering at many of them, considering them too staid or undemanding in academics. He rejected both Berkeley and Stanford where he had prowled around for a few years while in high school. Jobs decided that he wanted to attend Reed College in Portland, Oregon after he visited a friend who was enrolled there. This was not at all to the liking of Paul and Clara Jobs, who wanted their son to have a more traditional education. They tried to talk him out of it, but Jobs was unshakable.

During elementary school, he had made his parents move to another school district by stubbornly asserting that he wouldn't attend school if he had to return to the same one. He used the same ploy in convincing them that he should attend Reed. Jobs told them that if he couldn't attend Reed, he simply wouldn't go to college. Although Paul Jobs could ill afford the high tuition at a private college such as Reed, he and his wife agreed to their son's demand. They drove him to Portland and, when they said their goodbyes, the parting was far less than cordial. Jobs didn't want his parents seen on campus. He had a rather romantic idea of how he wanted to appear to the other students. He said he wanted to look and feel like an orphan who had spent a few years bumming around the country, hopping on freight trains or riding in eighteen-wheelers.

Reed College, with its ultra-liberal, anti-establishment attitudes, was guaranteed to appeal to Jobs' quest for new horizons. In the seventies, it was a stop-over for wayward poets, rebels, and other anti-establishment types. It was a group of Reed students who started The Rainbow Farm, a haven for hippies and other far left people, and who pioneered experiments with mind-bending drugs. It was a place where students welcomed with open arms and minds such people as poet Allen Ginsberg and Timothy Leary, the high priest of hallucinogenic drugs. The rebelliousness of the students was tolerated by professors only if the students made up in academic excellence what they lacked in self discipline. The drop-out rate was high among juniors and seniors, with only about a third of each class returning at the beginning of each school year.

Jobs enjoyed the ultra liberal atmosphere at Reed and came into contact with a wide variety of people, many of whom were looking for lifestyles that were other than traditional. In the words of one student, Reed was a campus peopled by loners and freaks. Even in this anti-establishment environment, Jobs stood out as an oddball who was considered weird by people who knew him. He found one friend in Daniel Kottke, who had been raised in a New York suburb with affluent parents. Kottke had won a National Merit Scholarship and was at Reed only because he had been rejected by Harvard.

Jobs also became acquainted with an unusual student named Robert Friedland. He was a few years older than Jobs and won great notoriety by wearing Indian robes and campaigning to become president of the student body. Friedland had been arrested for using LSD and eventually was sentenced to two years in prison. At his trial, he had told the judge that he shouldn't pass judgment until he had tried LSD himself. The judge was not amenable to the suggestion and passed sentence. Friedland, who had manufactured and delivered some thirty thousand tablets of LSD, was paroled before serving his full term and became a Reed student.

Jobs, as McCollum had noted in his high school electronics classes, had a different way of looking at things. If anything, that difference had grown into full blossom, so that he could calmly face situations that might cause others to flee in shock or embarrassment. He met Friedland when he was trying to raise money by selling his typewriter. When he arrived at Friedland's room with the typewriter, Jobs found Friedland making love to his girl friend. The intrusion didn't bother either Jobs or Friedland, who invited Jobs to wait until he was finished; then they would take care of business. Friedland's calm in the face of intrusion during this intimate act impressed Jobs.

Friedland became Jobs's friend and teacher. Jobs was in hot pursuit of spiritual enlightenment and he believed that Friedland held the keys to the kingdom. Jobs had come to believe that enlightenment was the highest level of intellectual achievement and was determined to achieve it. Friedland recalls that Jobs was "one of the freaks" on campus. He rarely wore shoes and he had a straggly beard and longish hair. He gained a reputation for being exceptionally intense and threw himself obsessively into things that interested him. Jobs seemed to enjoy being different or exercising power over people. One of the things he enjoyed doing was sitting and staring at people for long periods of time, saying nothing, never blinking, and watching them squirm under his mesmeric scrutiny.

Even though his behavior was more often than not considered bizarre, Jobs had moments when he was interested in the traditional. He joined a dance class, hoping that he would meet the girl of his dreams and fall in love, his continuing relationship with Judy Smith notwithstanding. But, like most things, dancing didn't hold his attention for long, and his interest in classes faded as well. He attended for a semester, then stopped, opting instead for a Bohemian lifestyle while living in the dormitory. Paul and Clara Jobs were upset at the money they were spending to support their son's self-indulgence but could do nothing to change the situation. Jobs began to be a "floater," moving from one dormitory room to the next as they were vacated.

For all his peculiarities and disinterest in classes, Jobs had a keen mind. He was interested in macrocosmic questions: What are we doing here? Where are we going? What is the purpose of life? He became interested in karma and experimented with various drugs and diets that seem outrageous today. Whatever he did, he did with intensity. There was never a half-way point with Jobs; he either discarded ideas if he wasn't interested or plunged body and soul into things that grabbed his attention. Jobs spent several hours talking with Jack Dudman, Reed's dean of students. Dudman recalls that Jobs had an inquiring mind and challenged every new thought. It was impossible to gloss over a new idea because Jobs would respond with a bombardment of questions, usually playing the devil's advocate, until he was either convinced or dissuaded of the idea's validity.

Both Jobs and Kottke, who had a disdain for material things in spite of his privileged upbringing, began a serious reading program of various religions and philosophies, a pursuit not unusual for inquisitive youths of their age. They read about Yoga, Zen, and Buddhism. Jobs was particularly entranced with Zen Buddhism because it emphasized experience rather than intellect. He became even more convinced that intuition and enlightenment were more important than intellectual understanding.

Jobs's interest in Buddhism took him to the Hare Krishna temple in Portland. He and Kottke would hitchhike to the temple on Sundays and receive a free vegetarian meal, spend the night in a communal house, then go out and pick flowers to place at the Krishna shrine. The flowers were generally plucked from private gardeners, the owners of which had little use for Hare Krishnas.

After floating around the dormitory, Jobs left Reed after a year and rented a room for twenty-five dollars a month. There followed a period where he was intensively secretive about his life. Wozniak sometimes brought Judy Smith to visit Jobs on weekends, and even they didn't know what Jobs was up to. So far as they could tell, he was doing little except reading, engaging in occasional fasts, and meditating.

The money that had flowed from his parents became a trickle now that Jobs had left Reed College, and even a monk has to eat. Jobs borrowed money from the college, then found a job as maintenance man for electrical equipment used in the animal experiment laboratory. He knew more than enough about electricity to do the job. In fact, he was rarely satisfied with simply repairing something that was broken; he usually made improvements.

Even with the maintenance work, Jobs was still financially strapped. Portland winters can be brutal, and Jobs didn't have heat in his room. He would sit in a down jacket, throw coins, and try to master the mysteries of the highly ambiguous *I Ching*, the Chinese Book of Knowledge. He was so poor that he sustained himself for three weeks by eating a gruel made of Roman Meal cereal and milk that he "borrowed" from the college cafeteria.

Physically, Jobs was wasting away. Kottke and his girl friend worried about it and often invited him over for meals. The three of them were against eating meat and consumed various vegetarian dishes. All of them were interested in expanding their minds and spirits and tried to rejuvenate both mind and body by trying various diets and drugs. Jobs had used drugs before for recreation, but now they became tools in the search for mental enlightenment.

During this period, Jobs discovered *The Mucusless Diet Healing System* and *Rational Fasting,* written in the nineteenth century by Arnold Ehret. He became fascinated with the unusual dietary conclusions Ehret had reached. Ehret believed that every aspect of the body and spirit was affected by diets creating too much mucus in the body. Mental illness, Ehret maintained was the result of an unhealthy diet that caused gas pressure on the brain. Ehret eschewed meat, potatoes, rice, and milk as unhealthy culprits and taught that mucus could be eliminated by eating figs, horseradish mixed with honey, and other vegetables, nuts, or seeds.

As usual, Jobs became obsessed, this time with a mucusless diet. He even studied the diets of other primates and became convinced that man is a natural fruitarian. He began lecturing his friends and warned them that they were harming themselves by eating the "unhealthy" foods that Ehret had listed. Ehret wrote that he had once lived for two years, eating nothing but fruit, and Jobs tried to follow his example. He carried it even further. He began to fast, at first for a day or two, then increasing the fasting period for weeks.

Jobs noted the changes that occurred in his body during fasts like an outsider studying a laboratory specimen. One of the more interesting aspects of fasting was that Jobs's skin turned different colors. He found that fasting made him feel better than eating. After the first week, he said he felt great, then, as more time passed, he started to feel fantastic. He was convinced that his body was building strength and vigor because it wasn't diverting energy to digest food. Jobs learned to break his fasts by drinking vast amounts of liquid and eating roughage and, in his typical manner, began to lecture acquaintances about fasting benefits. The small group of friends Jobs had made learned to accept the fact that Jobs would become overbearing when he was obsessed about something, and tolerated his sermons as a matter of course.

Robert Friedland had embarked on his own regimen of diet, philosophy and drugs. He believed that everything was composed of electricity, a conjecture that some scientists believe today, and thought he could reach the electricity of love through the teachings of Neem Karolie Baba, an Indian guru. Friedland managed to spend the summer of 1973 in India and returned with tales of an "electric atmosphere of love" that he had discovered during various meditations. Friedland described it in such detail and enthusiasm that Jobs burned with a desire to go to India and have the same experiences.

Jobs considered the possibility that certain components of electricity might be the means to achieve love. He was very much taken with the idea of a world that lived in peace, where love was paramount to everything else. If electricity was the answer, he thought he might find it in an electrified atmosphere. He left the periphery of Reed College, went back home to his parents in Los Altos, and began looking for a job in electronics. The job he sought would not be permanent, but only a means to save enough to visit India and come into personal contact with a philosophy of life he believed to be the salvation of his soul and means of reaching the long-desired dream of enlightenment.

One morning he spotted a classified ad in the *San Jose Mercury* and saw that Atari was looking for someone to help design video games. Jobs was not familiar with the company beyond knowing that it had created a video game named *Pong* and others, that had become popular in households and in video arcades around the country which had previously been dominated by pinball machines.

Jobs was in a high state of excitement when he appeared at Atari's lobby in Sunnyvale. He hadn't bothered to clean up, was on one of his fruitarian diets, and presented a picture of a totally unkempt young man. But he was talking a mile a minute, an art he had perfected because it often overwhelmed people. The people at Atari listened to Jobs explain how he had been working for Hewlett-Packard, which he hadn't. He told them he could make vast improvements, and his mile-a-minute monologue bowled over a supervisor at Atari, who signed him on without bothering to check with Hewlett-Packard. Had he done so, he would have discovered that Jobs had never been associated with the company except on a part-time basis when he worked there on an assembly line when he was in high school. His friends were surprised when he got the position because they didn't think he was qualified.

He might not have been hired by a more conventional corporation, but Atari was an unusual operation. Nolan Bushnell, a young Silicon Valley engineer, founded the company in 1972. It was originally called Syzygy, but was renamed Atari when Bushnell discovered there was already a company with the former name. While he was in college, Bushnell was one of thousands of students who programmed college computers to play a game called *Space War*. Computer enthusiasts around the nation's colleges learned how to program computers to create rockets and space craft on video screens. They could control a rocket's firing system and movement with a joy stick. Some of the programs were so sophisticated that there were often messages running across the screen: YOU ARE HITTING THE MOON AT A SPEED OF EXACTLY 0276.20 MILES PER HOUR. BLOOD, GUTS, TWISTED METAL.

College administrators considered the game a waste of time and didn't appreciate the unauthorized use of their computers. Bushnell played *Space War* as enthusiastically as anyone else, but he was looking at it in a different way than other hobbyists. He had worked at amusements parks during summer breaks and concluded that people liked simple games with only a few basic rules. He also noticed that parents would sometimes use games such as pitching balls at wooden bottles to keep their children occupied while they ventured off, childless, to other pleasurable pursuits.

Bushnell was struck with the idea of creating a game, such as *Space War*, putting a slot on the computer to start it working, and having people lined up five deep to play. *Space War*, he decided, was too complicated for a large audience, so he created a simple game called *Pong*. He needed a computer that was small and inexpensive enough to produce to make it feasible. Fortunately for him, the microprocessor, "the computer on a chip," came along just in time and, in 1972, he found the financial backing to start his company.

Bushnell was an unorthodox man who considered business a type of war. He was interested in inventing other games and he did not discourage the use of marijuana during brainstorming sessions because he believed it enhanced creative thought. Bushnell stood six feet four inches tall, dressed in flashy clothes, and was not above stretching the truth to get his employees fired up about a project. He put a burr under the saddle of Al Alcorn, the chief engineer for *Pong*, by telling him that the machine had been ordered by General Electric. Bushnell admitted that he had no contact with GE, but used the ploy to "test Al's abilities." So when Jobs came to Atari looking for work, his appearance and mannerisms were not all that unusual for a company that was accustomed to strange employees.

The success of *Pong* surprised even Bushnell, who admitted that he didn't think there was much of a market. But the first machine placed in a Sunnyvale pool hall proved him wrong. Before long, people were lining up outside to play the game. When additional games started to appear, a few people thought the company was being controlled by organized crime. Financiers kept a close watch on operations, fearful that it could make a serious mistake and go under. Bushnell, who had the Regis McKenna Agency representing him, countered these fears by starting Kee Games to produce additional games to compete with other companies that had gone into the business. McKenna bombarded the media with press releases about Atari's stiff competition from Kee, then invented a "crisis" that, he told the media, had been settled amiably. The press release read in part, "We are happy that the people at Kee and Atari have been able to resolve the problems that led to the original split." Bushnell believed in manipulating the media and chortled about how easy it was to use the press to gain a business advantage.

Management at Atari was lax, with Bushnell's brother-in-law taking care of day-to-day operations. At times, the company discovered that it was selling video games for less than it cost to build them. During one period, it looked as if Atari might go bankrupt and Bushnell, under a tremendous strain, broke down and wept in public. In spite of the problems, Atari managed to sell $13 million worth of video games in its first year and, a few years after that, Bushnell's net worth was estimated at $30 million.

Employee 54, Steve Jobs, noted all of this and, characteristic of his nature, filed it all away for future use. He found aspects of the company's operation that might benefit him later on and remembered the chaotic operations. But, in later years, Jobs was

48

to make most of the same mistakes that he had seen made at Atari.

Because he had no electronics expertise, Jobs failed to make any significant contribution at Atari. He also made an unfavorable impression. The other employees thought he was weird and that he exaggerated his own importance. Bushnell recalls that Jobs would often look at the work of other technicians and engineers, sneer, and tell them they were "dumb shits." Jobs claims that he was better than all of the other engineers at Atari, not because he was brilliant, but because they were so inept. While at Atari, Jobs was following Ehret's mucusless diet, eating yogurt and fruit. He believed that the diet eliminated the need for bathing. Others disagreed. They said he smelled funny, and he created so much turmoil with his derogatory comments that Alcorn made him work at night.

Despite his lack of an electronics background, Jobs was a fast learner and Wozniak recalls, "He was smarter than anybody." He managed to pick up enough skills to refine a video game called *Touch Me* so that even Wozniak was impressed. Jobs had enhanced his electronics ability, but he was still a technician, not an engineer.

The lure of India continued to draw Jobs like a beacon. He longed to visit the country with Dan Kottke. In typical brash fashion, he asked Alcorn to pay for his plane ticket to the promised land. Alcorn couldn't believe it, and said there was no way he would pay for Jobs to visit a guru. Then, typically, Jobs lucked out. Atari had shipped games to Germany that were causing interference with television reception and German engineers needed help to correct the problem. Jobs boned up on the skills he needed, and Alcorn dispatched him to Europe to make the necessary adjustments to the games. From there, Jobs would go to India and, he thought, come closer to the enlightenment he sought by treading on sacred ground.

When Jobs arrived in Europe, the German engineers were stunned. What kind of a man was this? They cabled Alcorn to make certain the right man had been dispatched. However strange he might have seemed, Jobs managed to correct the television interference problem, and was off to India to visit the land of the gurus.

Jobs and Kottke arrived for their prolonged stay in India in high spirits, but the reality of India was somewhat less than Jobs had expected. This was the land of enlightenment and yet he found abject poverty intermingling with a faith that there was something better just around the corner. Kottke thought of the trip as a pilgrimage with no definite goal in mind. Jobs watched with interest the religious rites there and observed dead bodies floating in the Ganges, India's sacred river. A guru befriended him and shaved his head; then Jobs spent an all-night vigil sitting around a fire in an abandoned temple with a Shivite who had covered his body with ashes.

New Delhi was his base, and he walked with Kottke through the town only to discover that India was not at all what he thought it would be. He saw the most abject poverty he had ever witnessed. People ate out of garbage cans and, homeless, they slept on the streets. The luckier ones lived in huts made out of corrugated tin. Jobs and Kottke made a trip to Tibet where they were rewarded by getting scabies.

The guru Neem Kardie Baba had died and his body had been consumed by a funeral pyre, but Jobs and Kottke made a trip to Kainchi anyhow to honor his memory. They stayed there for a month, living in a one-room hut, which was fortuitously located near a field of marijuana, which they carefully dried and smoked. The hut was owned by a family of potato farmers. The wife provided primitive room service by serving them warm buffalo milk and sugar. Jobs, frequently combative and never afraid to speak his mind, accused the woman of diluting the milk with water. In a shouting match accompanied by numerous gestures to help bridge the language gap, the woman berated Jobs for being a criminal. In marketplaces where they bought food, Jobs haggled fiercely with peasants who sold their food from donkey carts. The bargaining experiences he had learned from listening to his father dicker for automobile parts was further augmented by this experience. The hard bargains he learned to negotiate would later be seen as both a blessing and a curse when he became associated with Apple Computer.

Jobs's summer in India caused him to question many of the beliefs that he had previously held. He was struck by the poverty that existed side by side with spiritual expectations. The harsh living conditions that he saw and experienced caused him to rethink his perception of India, and he left the country thinking that Thomas Edison had done more to improve the human condition that all the gurus that had ever lived. The change he had undergone when he returned to California was noticeable. He was gaunt because of dysentery, his shaven head sported a stubble of hair, and he wore Indian clothing. He was disillusioned with India, but still held fast to the phenomenon of enlightenment. There was also something strange in his behavior that struck his girl friend, Judy Smith. She remembers that he seemed detached, and had started staring intently at people with unblinking eyes. She says that he started to act like a guru but with a twist. He would ask a question, then stare as people tried to answer. His detachment, she says, took other forms. He would give her something one day, then look at it the next, and ask wonderingly, "Where did you get this?" She was unable to explain his behavior.

When Jobs returned from India near the end of 1974, he had no idea of what he wanted to do with his life. He was still trying to determine who he was and why he was here. He bounced around for a year and a half, rather aimlessly, trying to discover his destiny. Jobs had read *Primal Scream* by Arthur Janov, a California psychiatrist, and paid one thousand dollars for a twelve-week course at the Oregon Feeling Center. Primal Scream therapy was popular in the seventies and was based on the assumption that you could rid yourself of many anxieties and angers simply by screaming. The primal scream itself was named after the squawling that babies make upon the trauma of birth. Screaming, according to the Feeling Center, amounted to a spiritual and mental purge of unhealthy and negative feelings.

As Jobs struggled to get in touch with himself, he started to become curious about his natural parents. Judy Smith says that as Jobs thought of this, he often wept. Robert Friedland, who was managing the Feeling Center, says Jobs wanted to know who his natural parents were so that he could know more about himself.

He began to search for them, but never revealed much of what he discovered. He said only that they were both teaching at a university and that his father was a professor of mathematics. As usual, Jobs grew bored and disdainful of Primal Scream therapy and the Feeling Center, claiming that it offered too pat of an answer to things that were enormously more complex.

Jobs, having done his share of primal screaming, left the Oregon Feeling Center and returned to California, where he rented a room in Los Gatos. He worked off and on at Atari, where he continued to aggravate other employees to the point that he was finally demoted to consultant so as to preserve the peace. It was an ironic situation. No one involved in creating Atari products wanted him there, but Bushnell did. Bushnell liked the sense of urgency that Jobs brought to projects, predicting time of conception to completion in terms of weeks rather than months.

Wozniak, who liked video games, had started to wander in and out of Atari, playing games that were still on the assembly line. His interest piqued, Wozniak designed his own games and created his own version of *Pong*. Bushnell offered to pay Jobs a bonus if he could create a game that would smash a brick wall with a bouncing ball. Jobs's payment was to be based on cost of manufacturing it, which meant using the least number of chips possible. No one was better at using fewer chips in electronics than Wozniak.

Jobs tried to do the work himself, but it was over his head. He turned to Wozniak for help. The ever-trusting Wozniak agreed to design the game and split the $700 payment Jobs told him Atari had offered. "Steve wasn't capable of designing anything that complex," Wozniak says. "I designed the game thinking that he was going to sell it to Atari for $700 and that I would receive $350. Steven sold the game and gave me $350. It wasn't until years later that I learned that he had actually sold the game for $7,000."

Jobs did not bother to tell anyone that Wozniak had been involved in creating the game. Alcorn found out about Wozniak's contribution later on and offered him a job at Atari, which Wozniak refused. Jobs, in the meantime, had moved on to an

Oregon commune called the All One Farm. A number of spiritual wanderers dropped by the farm where the inhabitants tended gardens without benefit of insecticides or herbicides and also joined forces to pick apples and prune the trees. Jobs became one of the toilers in the apple orchards. He also became even more obsessed with his dietary experiments and frequently ate, only to force himself to throw up. Once more, Jobs became disillusioned and departed after a few months. He was still a seeker who had no idea what to do with his life. He knew what he didn't want: "I didn't want to grow up to be an engineer."

Jobs was twenty when he left the All One Farm. He had no particular expertise in anything and his college training, such as it was, had not prepared him for a job. Luckily for him, he was still friendly with Wozniak, who was making remarkable progress in computer design.

CHAPTER 6

Breakthrough!

As Jobs experimented with primal screaming, worked loosely at Atari, and tried to get in touch with his feelings, more down-to-earth events were happening in Stephen Wozniak's life. He had gone to Berkeley to pursue his education, dropped out during his junior year, gone to work for Hewlett-Packard, helped start a computer company, and married a girl he met during one of his telephone pranks.

He had also discovered the Homebrew Computer Club, composed of people who were avid computer hobbyists. Through it all, he continued his work on computer design, made both easier and more difficult because the semiconductor industry had invented the microprocessor, the computer on a chip.

The Homebrew Computer Club drew computer hobbyists, programmers, suppliers, and engineers from throughout California and, eventually, had members from around the world. At first it was like the permanent floating craps game in *Guys and Dolls,* moving from one place to another as membership grew at a surprising rate.

Homebrew was started by Fred Moore and Gordon French, computer devotees who had worked for the defunct People's Computer Company. There were no dues or fees and the meetings were loosely organized. People of like interests would gather to discuss computing and to share information. Among the members was the notorious Cap'n Crunch of phone-phreaking fame. The meetings were meant to bring engineers together to share information, but many of those who attended played their cards close to the chest. They were willing to show off the various devices they built but were not eager to give operational details. Wozniak was not one of them; he passed out schematics and diagrams to anyone who was interested.

"I wasn't too interested in making money," he says. "I just liked Homebrew. It became the most important part of my life."

One of the first members of the Homebrew Computer Club was Lee Felenstein, a Berkeley dropout who had tried to create a computer network using a computer that had been discarded by the Stanford Research Institute. His idea was to form a grassroots network to link people with similar interests. Unfortunately, the sentiment was far greater than the reality. Only a couple of places linked with the computer, and these used teletype machines to send and receive information. The process was so slow and cumbersome that it was much simpler to make a telephone call than to use the computer network.

There had been remarkable advances in electronics during the past few years, which fueled Felenstein's dream of making a small computer he intended to call The Tom Swift Terminal. Making practical use of microprocessors and other new electronics components were the central themes at Homebrew. Just how far electronics had come was brought home when a member of the club demonstrated the Altair 8800, which had received coverage in trade magazines as a breakthrough in computing. Kits for an Altair sold for less than $400. When put together, it was about the size of a liquor box. There were rows of switches and lights that blinked on and off at various commands.

What lay at the heart of the machine was the topic of interest. The Altair used the Intel 8080 central processing unit, a remarkable new device that was packed with power. Although it was wafer-thin, about one-eighth of an inch wide and a quarter of an inch long, this mighty mite was more powerful than the room-size ENIAC with its thousands of vacuum tubes and miles of electrical wiring.

The 8080 had almost infinite possibilities. Robert Noyce, co-founder of Intel and co-inventor of the microprocessor, had tried to calculate its applications and found no upper limit. Intel had introduced two other microprocessors before creating the 8080. Electronics functions that once needed a large number of electrical components could now be performed on a silicon chip so small you could hold it on the tip of your finger. The microprocessor itself challenged the intellectual limits of those who tried to make it perform. Without the necessary memory chips to give it orders in the form of electrical charges, the 8080 could do nothing. For Wozniak, who had long dreamed of making a computer with the fewest parts possible, the microprocessor seemed a godsend, but he had difficulty adjusting to this latest breakthrough in electronics.

Wozniak made it a point never to miss the biweekly meetings of the Homebrew Club. Not only did he have a chance to demonstrate his latest creations, but also he was exposed to work others had done. The members were a demanding bunch and had no compunction about telling their associates that they had created junk. Among this stellar group of computerphiles, Wozniak shone brightly.

One of the people Wozniak met was Alex Kamradt, who had formed a Mom and Pop company, minus the Mom, which was named Call Computer. Kamradt had been a physicist at Lockheed, become involved in computer programming, and had sold his home to start Call Computer. He had intended to use the minicomputer that was the heart of his operation to keep records of real estate transactions, but soon found himself in the time-sharing business, with customers linked by teletype machines.

The advent of the central processing unit caused a vision to unfold in Kamradt's mind. He believed that Call Computer could expand its operations if customers could have keyboard video terminals which they would either rent or buy from him.

Unfortunately, such a terminal was unavailable. Kamradt decided the best place to look for someone to design one was at Homebrew. He attended a meeting, asked to see the smartest engineer, and was introduced to Wozniak.

By this time Wozniak held a full-time job at Hewlett-Packard, but he agreed to form Computer Converser, a subsidiary of Call Computer, in the middle of 1975. Kamradt provided twelve thousand dollars in seed money, took 70 percent of the stock, while Wozniak agreed to design the terminal for 30 percent of the stock and free use of Kamradt's minicomputer.

Besides moonlighting, Wozniak had another reason for wanting to build a keyboard video terminal. He had visited Cap'n Crunch's home and seen such a device in the basement. Cap'n Crunch was still heavily into phone phreaking and the terminal helped him gain access to ARPANET, a nationwide computer network that linked universities and research facilities. Phone phreaks such as Cap'n Crunch had cracked the telephone access codes and were able to look into computer files around the nation. Sometimes they managed to look into the heart of a computer in Europe. Often they left weird messages in various computers or, if feeling devilish, would erase a file altogether. It was an idea that appealed to Wozniak's sense of mischief and presented a challenge to his intellect.

The idea behind Computer Converser was not to build an "intelligent" terminal, largely because that would have required using microprocessors, which were expensive. Rather, it was to create a terminal that could "talk" to a computer by means of a telephone hook-up. The keyboard would allow a user to type much the same as he would on a typewriter, with numbers and words appearing on a video screen. It was expected to be a faster way to communicate information through time-sharing than the cumbersome teletype machines that were in use.

Wozniak used the basic scheme that he had developed for his version of *Pong* and found the terminal easy enough to build. He tested it by tapping into the ARPANET system, was satisfied with the way it worked, and turned it over to Kamradt. Unfortunately, no one else could figure out how it worked. Wozniak was the only one who could make needed repairs and, since he had a full-time job, he was not always available. Kamradt concluded that Wozniak was a genius, but that he was unable to communicate his ideas so that others understood him.

Wozniak's father had wanted his son to follow in his footsteps and join Lockheed when he left Berkeley. But the excitement that had surrounded Lockheed in Wozniak's childhood had vanished. The company had acquired the patina of a staid, unexciting company that was no longer on technology's cutting edge. For a bright young man like Wozniak, Lockheed was out of the question. Instead, he worked on an assembly line at Electroglass, a company that was part of the semiconductor infrastructure. He remained for half a year, then joined Hewlett-Packard.

Hewlett-Packard was an unusual company. For one thing, it was home-grown, having been started by Bill Hewlett and Dave Packard, who had attended Stanford. H-P was known for the care and feeding of its employees, generous bonuses, and stock options. Both Packard and Hewlett believed that work should not simply provide a livelihood, but that the workplace ought to provide an atmosphere that allowed employees to grow personally and to share a company's prosperity. Employees high and low referred to Hewlett and Packard by their first names. Even today, long after both men have left active management, their influence is still reflected in Hewlett-Packard's corporate culture. Wozniak noted all that, and was also interested in H-P's reputation for creating high-technology scientific instruments and sophisticated calculators.

Wozniak came to Hewlett-Packard's attention through the good offices of Elmer Baum, who had joined the company following his graduation from college. Wozniak joined the company in 1973 as a technician, because he didn't have a college degree, but was promoted to the status of engineer within six months. He worked in the advanced products division, which manufactured pocket calculators. The company had gained the reputation for high-technology by introducing the HP 35 desk top calculator a year before Wozniak became an employee. Additional calculators became smaller and more sophisticated and Wozniak enjoyed his work, although he was not considered anything special. In fact, he was often the brunt of unkind comments because of his limited formal education. An engineer who worked with Wozniak on a calculator said that he was considered a competent engineer, but did not stand out. Wozniak was one of the few engineers who didn't have a degree and, when he applied for a transfer to a group that was rumored to be designing a small terminal for the handicapped, he was refused because officials didn't think he had the qualifications.

Hewlett-Packard encouraged the entrepreneurial spirit and allowed employees working on projects of their own to use the company's stockpile of electronics devices. Wozniak and Elmer Baum, who had joined H-P as a technician, took advantage of this. Wozniak built an HP 45 calculator for Baum and added features to convert Baum's HP 35, an earlier calculator, into an HP 45. He had also developed an interest in flying, which was to become a long-time addiction, and joined friends with airplanes during his lunch period for short hops.

All along, Wozniak retained a keen interest in phone phreaking. He began a dial-a-joke service and recorded ethnic jokes on his answering machine, poking fun at the Polish. Sometimes the telephone would ring while he was at home and he would answer it himself, calling himself Stanley Zeber Zenkanitsky and speaking in what he believed passed for a Polish accent. Wozniak discontinued the Polish jokes after receiving outraged letters from Polish organizations and abusive individuals. Rather than disband the service, he simply turned the Poles in his jokes into Italians, but still spoke in the same accent and identified himself as Stanley Zeber Zenkanitsky. It was through this mischief that Wozniak met his first wife, Alice Robertson. He answered the telephone one evening when Robertson called, chatted with her for a while, then told her he could hang up faster than she could and slammed the receiver down, presumably leaving Robertson dumbfounded. Nevertheless, she called back from time to time. The conversations between her and Wozniak became more frequent and longer, finally leading to a date. Thus began Wozniak's first important romance, culminating eventually, in his marriage.

During this time, Wozniak had more than a full-time job and a budding romance on his mind; he also was besieged by Alex Kamradt at Computer Converser. Dismayed at the inability of engineers to understand the terminal Wozniak had designed even after months of trying, Kamradt appealed to Steven Jobs, who had been hovering in the background, to use his influence to convince Wozniak to help. Wozniak, at the time, didn't realize how closely Jobs was following his work at Computer Converser. But Jobs always had a knack of being in the right place at the right time. Kamradt didn't have a particularly high opinion of Jobs. He said that Jobs agreed to take charge of the terminal project for stock and a salary. He sensed that Jobs resented him for having money. He also remembers that "Jobs was somewhat unscrupulous," and that he wanted all he could get out of the arrangement. While Jobs was busy with his negotiations, Wozniak was into other designs and had no idea how intensely involved Jobs was with Kamradt.

Jobs took charge of the terminal design and worked with Robert Way, who headed a small company that was part of the electronics infrastructure. Jobs wanted a printed circuit board, he wanted it fast, and he wanted it neat and clean as a whistle. Jobs and Way made arrangements to get the parts they needed and set to work. Jobs drove Way hard and was constantly critical. Way says, "Nothing was ever good enough for him." It wasn't the first time, nor would it be the last, that Jobs would be referred to as a "rejector." In this instance, the constant criticism of Jobs and his abrasive manner caused Way to drop the project.

While Way was aggravated by Jobs, whom he considered "one of the weirdest people I ever met," and fretted over the Computer Converser terminal, the ever-curious Wozniak was at work on his own computer. He spent hours examining the new microprocessing units and was ecstatic when he found that the basic laws of computer science hadn't been changed. In fact, he found them similar to the minicomputers on which he had performed surgery.

The advent of the microprocessor, however, presented intriguing problems and possibilities. Some of the old ways of doing things were not possible with the computer on a chip at

the heart of a machine. Instead, there was the challenge of linking the chip to various memory chips, then to a television screen,
and to a typewriter-like keyboard. Baum complained that the
restrictions made computer design more work than fun.

The cost of microprocessors was also a problem for engineers like Wozniak, who earned $24,000 a year at Hewlett-
Packard, a sum that allowed little money for extras after living
expenses in Silicon Valley. Elmer Baum discovered that Hewlett-
Packard, which was using a Motorola 6800 microprocessor, was
offering them to employees at a discount. For Wozniak, this was
manna from heaven. Wozniak bought the Motorola microprocessor and began experimenting with that, running contrary to
the center of attention at the Homebrew Club, the Intel 8080.
The Motorola chip was cheaper, but it had qualities similar to
minicomputers that Wozniak did not find in the 8080. Wozniak
used the 6800 to design a computer to create "intelligence" in a
terminal similar to the one that he had designed for Computer
Converser.

In Silicon Valley, microprocessing chips first introduced are
generally on the expensive side, then the price drops rapidly as
new manufacturing processes are developed and copycats make
similar versions. One semiconductor company official notes that
if cars dropped in price the way silicon chips do, the price of a
Cadillac would now be about five hundred dollars. This dramatic
drop in price continued as Wozniak worked on his computer and
he eventually dropped the Motorola chip for a 6502 microprocessor developed by MOS Technology. It sold for just twenty-
five dollars. He experimented with the new chip and wrote a
program in BASIC, a computer language that would operate on
the 6502.

Wozniak's tackling of programming emphasized the need
for software to make computers perform various logic functions.
There was little or no software at the time except for those that
allowed a person to play video games. He was the first person at
the Homebrew Club to write a BASIC program for the 6502.

Wozniak was also in a personal quandary. He could not
decide whether to marry Robertson or not. After much soul-
searching, he decided on a solution. He would toss three coins

in the air and, if they all came up heads, he would propose. If not, he would go his merry way as a bachelor. The first toss of the coins was indecisive. In fact, Wozniak continued throwing the coins until they all came up heads.

With affairs of the heart settled, he was able to press on with his computer. He used a computer at Hewlett-Packard to test his program and found that it worked. Wozniak credited his success with spending time working with computer language when he should have been studying mathematics at college. All of Wozniak's work on the computer was based on knowledge he had painstakingly gained all by himself, over the years, but he had never had the means to test it. As it turned out, he had been on the right track all along.

Wozniak completed his computer language, then began designing a computer that was based on the circuitry he had designed to use with the Motorola microprocessor. He discovered that, even using the MOS 6502, his computer worked except for minor changes that were needed in the timing of electrical currents. He didn't have to change a wire.

The Cream Soda Computer was history, but Wozniak drew upon what he had learned while working on it in Bill Fernandez's garage, and he also incorporated the experience he had gained while designing the terminal for Computer Converser. The new computer was much more sophisticated than the previous two. The Cream Soda Computer contained rows of switches and blinking lights, while the new design incorporated a typewriter-like keyboard and a video screen to display information that had been entered. That was similar to the Computer Converser terminal except that, instead of being a "dumb" terminal that couldn't perform logical functions, the new computer contained a microprocessor and other components that made it "intelligent."

Wozniak was also scrupulous about the way the circuit board should be laid out. He had no use for sloppy work. He insisted that the various chips be painstakingly cut and soldered together instead of the faster, and messier method of wire wrapping that was popular at the time. Wire wrapping created a maze of incomprehensible wiring, whereas the circuitry that Wozniak used was neat and clean, and made it easier to spot trouble points in case of malfunction.

Wozniak tried to sell his computer to Hewlett-Packard, but was rejected because the company didn't see a future in making personal computers. Neither did any of the large, sophisticated high-tech companies in Silicon Valley. Robert Noyce of Intel says that any number of companies could have created a personal computer, but didn't have the vision that Wozniak had. There was no real market at the time other than computer hobbyists. Wozniak did not concern himself with such things as business and markets, and had no interest in being a businessman. He was an engineer and wanted to remain one. When Wozniak took his computer to the Homebrew Computer Club, it received little recognition because it used a microprocessor other than the Intel 8080. Nevertheless, a few enthusiasts were eager to snap up the schematics that Wozniak offered for free. He was about to sell the computer to Call Computer when Steve Jobs, who had been watching Wozniak's activities with growing interest, intervened.

Jobs had not attended many meetings of the Homebrew Computer Club, but he started going and noticed that members were eager to receive Wozniak's schematics. Wozniak, who was not interested in starting a business, was happy to give his schematics away free of charge. "Steve was the one who thought we could make money," he said. "I was the one who designed the computer. I was the one who had attended the Homebrew meetings and I had written the software, but Steve is the one who had the idea that we could sell the schematics."

Jobs convinced Wozniak that they could have printed circuit boards made and sell them to computer hobbyists. Jobs, remembering his days in the orchards with the Hare Krishnas, suggested that they call their business Apple. The two debated it for a while and settled on Apple for lack of anything better. The financial plan was nothing grand, but Jobs was thinking about profit. He calculated that the parts for each printed board would cost twenty-five dollars and could be sold for twice the price. Neither Jobs or Wozniak thought they would sell more than one hundred a year. They were also operating on a shoe string and agreed that each would contribute half of the $1,300 they needed to get started. Wozniak sold his coveted Hewlett-Packard calculator to help raise money for his share and Jobs sold his Volkswagon van.

Wozniak decided to make some modifications to his computer and Jobs often quarreled with him. "He wanted to make some changes, but he didn't have the background," Wozniak says. "We had quite a few arguments, but I made all of the technical decisions. He was basically a scrambler, looking for parts, and running the errands that needed to be done."

In the meantime, Alex Kamradt was still having problems trying to figure out the terminal Wozniak had designed for Computer Converser. He laid siege to him at every opportunity but Wozniak's attention had been almost totally diverted to the enhancement of his own computer. Wozniak was also embattled from the other side by the persistence of Jobs, who was pushing for Wozniak to devote all of his time to Apple. Wozniak, the very picture of patience, did not allow the tug of war to get him rattled. He considered selling the computer to Kamradt's Call Computer, causing Jobs considerable alarm and resulting in a prophesy of doom. No way, Jobs contended, could the computer ever succeed as part of Call Computer. To bolster his argument, Jobs enlisted the support of Ron Wayne, an Atari field engineer, who argued that Apple would have a much brighter future if the three of them formed a coalition.

In his early forties, Wayne was considerably older than Wozniak, who was in his early twenties, and Jobs, who was not yet twenty. Wayne had been around long enough to gain some practical business experience and had an almost religious belief in the role that engineers played in the shaping of society. He also believed that the world was on the verge of economic chaos and was investing in such things as stamps and precious metals to protect himself from catastrophe. Wayne did his best to convince Wozniak not to sell the computer to Kamradt, but Wozniak proved to be a tough customer even for Jobs, who had been accustomed to getting his way in most things. At the root of the disagreement was Wozniak's aversion to corporate politics, owning a business, and giving up his dream of being an engineer.

Neither did he want to leave his job at Hewlett-Packard, which paid a steady salary, and he feared that he might someday work on a project for H-P that would require him to use some of the things he had learned in building the Apple computer, resulting in a conflict of interest.

After long sessions of arguing late into the night, the three signed an agreement to form a partnership, delineating responsibilities. None of them could sign a check of more than one hundred dollars without another signature; Wozniak was in charge of engineering; Jobs was given responsibilities in marketing; Wayne would work with documentation. Even though he had invented the computer, Wozniak was not worried about stock splits. Wayne was given 10 percent of the stock while Jobs and Wozniak divided the remainder equally. Jobs had managed to become a major share owner of a small company with only one product—the computer Wozniak had invented.

"I don't think Wozniak ever worried about money," said Trip Hawkins, who worked with Apple later on. "He's a pretty happy-go-lucky guy. He's not the kind of guy who's going to spend his time worrying about money. I think he would have been just as happy if he had never become rich."

Wozniak, Jobs and Wayne signed their agreement on April Fools Day in 1976 in Mountain View. None of them, least of all Wayne, had any idea of the riches that lay ahead. Unfortunately Wayne sold his stock long before the company became a success, and he never shared in the pot of gold at the end of the rainbow.

CHAPTER 7

The Scrambler

Jobs became part of Apple without having done anything to develop its one product—Wozniak's computer. And even though Wozniak characterizes him in those days as a "scrambler," he was one of the best scramblers around. He had unflagging optimism and, characteristically, he had become obsessed with the computer. He used the money he and Wozniak had contributed to the cause to have artwork created for a circuit board so that it could be mass produced. Howard Cantin, who worked at Atari, succumbed to the power of Jobs's persuasive personality, and decided to draw the art work as a favor to Jobs.

The same month that Wozniak, Jobs, and Wayne signed their agreement, Wozniak and Jobs introduced the circuit board at the Homebrew Club. Wozniak spoke like a proud father as he described in detail the various technical aspects of the computer. He talked about memory, speed and other engineering features. Jobs, in his role as marketing manager, tried to convince people to buy the board and haggled with prospective customers over how much they would pay. In spite of the dual presentation, the

Homebrew members gave the computer a cold shoulder and only a few bothered to look at it. One who did inspect it was Lee Felenstein, who wasn't the least bit impressed. His remarks, however, hinted at more than a little jealousy. Felenstein said he thought Wozniak would fall flat on his face and added that he would shed no tears.

In the past, Jobs had avoided the Homebrew meetings because he wasn't interested in listening to members describe technical details of their creations. Since hitching his star to Wozniak's computer, he attended every meeting to scout for customers. Homebrew, at that time, represented the only concentrated pool of potential customers for the fledgling enterprise. Jobs began to seek out Homebrew members whose only interest in the meetings was to sell electronics parts. Paul Terrell was one of them. Terrell sold electronics components and computer kits. He had seen the enthusiasm that Homebrew members had for the Altair computer, and had managed to get a distributorship for Altair in northern California. Not long after that, he opened a store in Mountain View called the Byte Shop, and found engineers snapping up the Altair kits. He had a grand vision of opening a chain of stores around the country similar to those of Radio Shack and, before long, he had three stores.

Jobs viewed Terrell's outlets the way a hunting dog sniffs out a rabbit. He pumped himself for a presentation and launched a selling attack. Even though Apple was tiny and had an uncertain future, Jobs drove a hard bargain. He wanted Terrell to commit himself to buy several circuit boards and to pay a cash advance before delivery. Terrell was suspicious of Jobs. He had met him before at Homebrew meetings and pegged him as "a guy who could give you a hard time." So when Jobs arrived to show a prototype of the Apple, Terrell was cautious. Jobs made his pitch, but Terrell told him he had no interest in selling printed circuit boards at his stores because his customers would have too much additional work to do, and because the boards needed peripherals to make the computer work. Terrell wanted computers that were already assembled and ready to go. That wasn't what Jobs had in mind, but he quickly seized the initiative to find out how much Terrell would be willing to pay for that kind of product. Terrell dumbfounded Jobs when he said he would place an order for fifty computers, paying betweeen $489 and $589 each, and that he would pay cash upon receiving them.

Jobs was floored but quickly recuperated from his shock. The order far exceeded his expectations. He quickly calculated that the order would generate between $24,450 and $29,450. Jobs excitedly reported the offer to Wozniak who was similarly thunderstruck. Wozniak broadcast the news to his friends at Hewlett-Packard and they couldn't believe it. Looking back, Wozniak believes that was the greatest moment in the company's history. "Nothing in subsequent years was so great and so unexpected," he said. Jobs, having pushed himself into the company with nothing more than sheer force of persuasion, was earning his keep.

The order meant that an entirely new business plan had to be created. Now, instead of anticipated costs of $2,500 for one hundred circuit boards, their expenditure would be around $25,000 for a hundred assembled computers. Apple intended to fill Terrell's order for fifty computers, and build an additional fifty Jobs hoped to sell to other customers at Homebrew. The additional expense, manufacturing time, and prospecting for other customers sent Jobs into a wild scramble for parts. The partnership needed additional money to buy components to manufacture so many fully operational circuit boards. There would also be additional manufacturing expenses in assembling the computers.

Jobs looked everywhere for money. His appearance did nothing to encourage those he approached. Thin, somewhat grubby, with long hair, he ran around either in sandals or barefoot. It was not an image likely to instill confidence in money men accustomed to dealing with older people wearing ties, suits, and shoes. Jobs, never one to be intimidated, walked boldly into a bank in Los Altos, explained the situation, and asked for a loan. He was turned down on the spot. Jobs lost hope of getting a bank loan, figuring that he would meet with the same reception at all banks. Undeterred, he visited Haltek, where he had worked, and offered to exchange Apple shares for parts. Hal Elzig, the owner, turned him down. "I didn't have any faith in Apple," he said.

Jobs hit the bricks once more, this time visiting Al Alcorn at Atari, but Alcorn demanded cash for the parts Apple so desperately needed. In spite of the rejections, Jobs continued his pursuit of either money or parts so Apple could complete its order. At last Mel Schwartz, a Stanford professor who owned a small company with a credit line at an electronics distributorship, agreed to buy parts for Apple.

Encouraged, Jobs pitched Apple with several electronics distributors, asking for credit. He met with no success until Bob Newton, of Kierulff Electronics in Palo Alto, agreed to meet with Jobs and look at a prototype. Newton remembers Jobs as "an aggressive little kid" who did not make a good impression. But he was impressed enough with the prototype, backed by the order for fifty computers, to sell Jobs $20,000 in electronics parts on credit, and agreed to charge no interest if the bill was paid in thirty days.

Now that they had parts, Jobs and Wozniak faced the problem of finding a place where they could manufacture and assemble the computers. Renting space was out of the question because they could not afford it. They turned to Wozniak's crammed apartment, where his new wife, Alice, met the intrusion with a cool reception. She was more than a little upset about the entire venture because, in addition to moonlighting on the Apple, Wozniak still had a full-time job with Hewlett-Packard. Alice complained that, between Apple and Hewlett-Packard, she was seeing very little of her husband, and she did not like having stacks of electronics components that she was not allowed to touch piled on the dining room table. Jobs and Wozniak caved in under Alice's resentment and moved the operation to Jobs's parents' home, where Jobs was living. Paul and Clara Jobs were accustomed to their son's demands and had no compunction about letting the two use a spare bedroom, vacated by Jobs's sister following her marriage. Using chests of drawers to store components and assembling computers in the bedroom, they soon expanded the operation into Jobs's own bedroom.

The printed circuit boards made it possible for a family assembly line to go into action. Although the printed board made assembling easier, they still had to be stuffed with various electrical components. This task became the primary responsibility of Jobs's sister, Patty, who earned a dollar for each board she stuffed. She was able to complete four boards an hour while watching soap operas on television. Because of the television distraction, some of the delicate pins on semiconductors were bent and, occasionally, a part was put in backwards.

Jobs and Wozniak mulled over the price they would charge for the computers. Wozniak, never much impressed with money, thought Homebrew members should get the computers for a portion over what it cost to manufacture them. Jobs had no sentimental attachment to Homebrew, as Wozniak did, and argued against it, setting a retail price that was twice the cost of manufacturing. This, he argued, would allow dealers a 33⅓ percent markup, bringing the retail price to an appealing $666.66.

Then came the day when Jobs triumphantly made the first delivery to Terrell. Terrell had ordered fifty fully assembled computers for his Byte Shop. Instead, he was stunned to find that he had received nothing but circuit boards, which he had adamantly refused to buy in the first place. The boards required a considerable amount of work, by people who knew what they were doing, before they could function. There was no software, no video screen or keyboard. Terrell wasn't even able to test them. Even after the necessary peripherals were added, the computer still wouldn't work unless the customer knew how to program BASIC, which hadn't been included either on a chip or a cassette tape. The circuit board didn't even have a case. Terrell was disappointed, and more than a little irritated, but accepted them anyhow and, what's more, paid in cash.

Although he was young and inexperienced, Jobs exuded self-confidence, and his business instincts were on target. He wanted people to think that Apple was a solid, established company and not a business operating out of a house. Rather than having mail delivered to a residential address, he rented a post office box. He also arranged for a telephone answering service so that callers would be answered in a businesslike manner. Jobs also tried to recruit help to meet production deadlines. Bill Fernandez, who had been working at Hewlett-Packard, was looking for a job. H-P was transferring his division to Oregon and Fernandez had not been asked to go. Jobs interviewed Fernandez in a rather haphazard way and offered him a job with Apple. Fernandez had hoped that he would be an engineer, but when he became Apple's first employee, his duties consisted mostly of scutt work. He described himself as a "gopher."

Jobs enlisted the aid of Elizabeth Homes, a former college friend, to keep the books. She worked for four dollars an hour and stopped by Jobs's house once a week for pick-up and delivery. Homes thought that Jobs was working himself to the point of exhaustion because he put so much time into the business. Jobs' old friend, Dan Kottke, who had accompanied him to India and shared the infestation of scabies, moved into the house, sleeping on the living room couch, and helped with production.

Before long, Jobs's house was a welter of electronic components, circuit boards, and random drips of solder. Paul Jobs, ever eager to help his son get ahead, made a supreme sacrifice. He agreed to move the car he was renovating outside and let Apple use the garage. Besides being prompted by his unfailing generosity to help his son, Paul realized that his cars could stand outside weather, but that the computer components could not. It also made the inside living quarters more bearable without the organized confusion of electronics parts spread around.

Giving up his automobile restoration projects and allotting the garage would have been sacrifice enough for most fathers, but not for Paul Jobs. He renovated the garage to make it more suitable for the assembly of computers. He lined the garage with plasterboard, installed lights, and had another telephone line installed. He even built a "burn-in box" to test twelve circuit boards at a time under heat lamps. Steve Jobs scavenged equipment from wherever he could find it and, most of the time, he paid rock-bottom prices.

Clara Jobs pitched in, too. She inched her way around the garage workshop to do washing and managed to ignore computer parts that were still scattered on tables on the inside of the house. Even though she was recovering from gall bladder surgery, she took telephone messages from the answering service, and served coffee to salesmen or prospective customers who arrived at the house. Clara also donned the mantel of a marriage counselor and comforted Wozniak's wife when she made tearful calls regarding her husband's obsession with work. Inevitably, Wozniak and Jobs had arguments in the garage and Paul Jobs helped smooth ruffled feathers. The disruption of the household was more than most parents could stand, but they took it in stride and even made jokes about it.

Wayne was given the task of drawing schematics for the computer to be incorporated into a small manual to accompany the circuit boards. There was precious little money for publications, and the small business would soon come to regret scrimping on that important aspect of marketing. Wayne struggled with the manual and with the more creative task of designing a company logo. His first attempt showed Isaac Newton and a tree with one glowing apple. The legend read NEWTON—A MIND FOREVER VOYAGING THROUGH STRANGE SEAS OF THOUGHT, ALONE. It was rejected. Wayne also reverted to an old enemy of the new high-tech world, an IBM typewriter, to compose copy for the small operating manual. Jobs thought the manual would have a classier appearance if the paper were light gray. Wayne agreed, resulting in black type on gray that was next to impossible to read.

Outside pressures at play forced additional enhancement of the Apple computer. Paul Terrell, who had taken delivery of circuit boards for Byte Shop, was having trouble selling a naked computer that could do nothing without extensive modifications. He pressured Jobs for an interface that would load BASIC into the computer from a cassette tape. Jobs had no choice if he intended to keep the Byte Shop as a customer. Wozniak was so involved with other aspects of the computer that he refused to undertake the job. Instead, he offered a royalty to a Hewlett-Packard engineer in exchange for the interface. The end result was an interface that didn't work. Apple paid the engineer one thousand dollars for his trouble and cancelled the royalty agreement. Wozniak had never built an interface for information stored on cassette tapes, but he put himself to the task, trying for the simplest design possible. It proved to be less complicated than he had feared. The interface added a new dimension to the computer and was a customer incentive. For an additional seventy-five dollars, a customer could buy the interface circuit board and BASIC computer language. Apple touted this in advertising copy that read: "Our philosophy is to provide software for our machines free or at a minimal cost." The Apple slogan at the time, was BYTE INTO AN APPLE. The promotional material called it "A Little Cassette Board That Works." The advertisement did not mention that the computer needed a tape recorder that the user had to buy. Apple stretched the truth more than a little by stating that "The Apple Computer is in stock at almost all major computer stores."

Paul Terrell had covered the naked computer circuit boards with wooden cases he bought from a cabinet maker. Even so, the Apple was almost impossible to sell. Customers were more interested in the Altair and another computer made by a competing California company. While Apple wasn't selling, Terrell, himself, was on a very fast track. He had managed to open nearly seventy-five Byte Shops across the continent in just eleven months. He was strapped for cash because of the rapid expansion program. The new stores were each averaging sales of only $20,000 per month and he needed products with a short shelf life. He could ill afford to hold products that didn't sell quickly and was becoming discouraged with Apple.

Jobs made a tour of Byte Shops in California and met some of the store managers to make suggestions on how to sell Apple. The managers found his abrupt and abrasive manner hard to swallow, but Terrell, who initially had been suspicious of Jobs, had mellowed toward him. Jobs worried out loud to Terrell about the name he and Wozniak had chosen for their business, thinking that "Apple" was superfluous and no one would ever take the company seriously. Terrell understood his concern. When he had chosen the name Byte Shops, many people had mistaken his stores for delicatessens. He assured Jobs that the more unusual a name was, the more prone people would be to remember it.

The computer's price tag of $666.66 also brought telephone calls from fundamentalist Christians who believed that it was the "mark of the beast," and therefore evil. Jobs fielded many of the calls and invented a pat, if complex, rebuttal. He said that he had

73

taken the number seven, which, in some religions, has mystical significance, and subtracted the number one, another mystical number, to arrive at the altogether innocent $666.66 price.

Jobs was a whirlwind of activity, overseeing advertising, buying parts, and looking for new customers. The uncertainty of Apple's income, and the fear that he would be forced to pay 10 percent of the bills if Apple went bankrupt, forced Ron Wayne to leave the business. He was having problems with his stomach and admitted that he no longer had the energy to keep up with the frenetic Jobs.

Wayne was not alone in his doubts about Apple; Jobs and Wozniak had their own fears. They were afraid that Apple might die. Wozniak was not overly concerned because he had his salary from Hewlett-Packard to fall back on. He had never considered Apple anything other than a way to practice his hobby of designing computers and make extra money at the same time. But his marriage of six months was suffering because he was working fourteen-hour days, seven days a week, and had little time for his wife. Jobs had his doubts, as well, and often expressed them to Bill Fernandez on the long, late night walks that were becoming one of his trademarks. He seemed to suffer from insomnia because of his obsession with Apple, and wondered if he should give it up, claiming that he could always return to Atari. His arrangement with Atari, however, was highly questionable because of the trouble he had caused with other employees, and it was not all certain that he would be welcomed back.

As a garage operation, Apple predictably failed to get loans and the company was strapped for cash. At one juncture, it was Wozniak, rather than Jobs, who managed to persuade Elmer Baum's father, Allen, to loan the company five thousand dollars. The younger Baum was certain that the loan would be repaid, but his father was not so sure. He loaned the money as a favor to Wozniak, but had to negotiate the details with Jobs. Later, he said that Jobs made a strong presentation and, if he hadn't known Jobs, he would have considered him pretty good.

Jobs nursed a distrust for corporations and wondered aloud if forming a company was what he really wanted. He considered corporations disreputable because of politics, perks, and pay-offs for favors, and thought he would be better off in a Buddhist monastery. Ironically, in later years Jobs was to adopt the practices that he viewed with such disdain in those days. In fact, he never seemed to find a proper sense of balance between his search for enlightenment and his more practical side. He would preach human values over and over but, in practice, he treated people shoddily and gained a reputation for being arrogant, ill-tempered, mercurial, political, and somewhat unscrupulous.

"Steve will use anybody to his own advantage," Wozniak said. "He will say one thing and anybody who heard it would think that he was saying 'Maybe yes' or 'Maybe no.' You could never tell what he was thinking."

At this time, Jobs sought counsel from a Zen monk named Kobin Chino, whom he had met after returning from India. Chino had been a student of Suzuki Roshi and had been active at the San Francisco Zen Center. He was then at a Zen center in Los Altos. Judy Smith, Jobs's sweetheart, lived in a tent on the grounds. On several occasions, Jobs talked with Chino about his inner conflicts: to become a monk in a Japanese monastery or settle for being a businessman. Chino listened to Jobs with some amusement and finally advised him to stay with Apple, offering the off-beat opinion that there was little difference between the two choices that were causing Jobs so much inner turmoil.

Jobs took Chino's advice, but said he did it warily. He said he had a vision that Apple would become all-consuming and detract from his search for spiritual enlightenment. Judy Smith noted that Jobs was afraid of Apple: "He thought it would turn into a monster." It seems that Jobs may have recognized the darker side of his nature sooner than anyone else.

If Jobs nursed doubts about the future of Apple, he had good reason. There was no such thing as a personal computer market because there were no personal computers. Even larger companies such as Hewlett-Packard and Intel saw no possibilities for small computers other than the tiny market represented by computer hobbyists. Intel's Robert Noyce explains: "The whole computer business was an area we just didn't see in the beginning. It just seemed impossible that this phenomenal level of electronic sophistication represented by the microprocessor could ever be reduced enough in cost so that the consumer requirements could be met. The home and hobby microcomputer market was an area we really didn't see in the beginning, either, and so was the whole field of electronic games."

So Jobs and Wozniak were plowing unknown ground, and it is not hard to understand the trouble they were having. One computer analyst, who has followed Apple's development closely, says: "Jobs and Wozniak might have had more credibility with lenders in the beginning if they had been Stanford geniuses like Dave Packard and Bill Hewlett. But they were just a couple of guys working out of a garage. Wozniak was a college drop-out and Jobs was barely out of high school."

Even the manufacturers of minicomputers saw no benefit in getting into the microcomputer business. They continued making minicomputers, although these became increasingly smaller. Most companies had never heard of Apple and those who had considered it a fly-by-night operation that shouldn't be taken seriously. Computer hobbyists were leery of the Apple because of Wozniak's decision to buck the trend and use the 6502 Motorola microprocessor instead of the favored Intel 8080.

Jobs and Wozniak were fighting an uphill battle all the way. In the early fall of 1976, Jobs and Wozniak scraped together a few dollars, packed some circuit boards and advertising leaflets, and headed to Atlantic City to attend a computer fair. Wozniak carried a demonstration computer, which he and Jobs guarded like junkyard dogs. The fair was designed so that new companies, or individuals, could show off their computers. It attracted salesmen, hobbyists, engineers, and prospective customers.

Among those who would be competing for attention with the Apple was the Sol Terminal Computer, which was manufactured by Processor Technology. It was a neat little package, housed in a metal case, and included a typewriter keyboard as part of the integral structure. Representatives of Sol Terminal Computer were confident that it would blow competition out of the water. Lee Felenstein, who had envied Wozniak at Homebrew, was one of the people who had consulted with Processor Technology in development of its computer. He took a disdainful look at Wozniak's computer and was satisfied that it was nothing to be concerned about. Felenstein concluded that Jobs and Wozniak didn't know what they were doing.

What Felenstein didn't know was that, in spite of its unimpressive cosmetics, Apple computer had been improved considerably. At Homebrew meetings, members had asked Wozniak what he was doing and he told them, to their disbelief, that he was working on a computer that would have a color video display, using only a few chips. The claim was not taken seriously since it was generally thought that it would take at least forty chips to accomplish what Wozniak proposed. In fact, Wozniak was able to create color by *reducing* by half the number of chips used in the original computer. Furthermore, the computer was more powerful.

Wozniak was one of the first people to recognize the need for software, the programming that tells a computer what to do. At the time, most hobbyists believed that, at the very least, a computer or kit should come with software free of charge. Wozniak's work on programming had sparked heated debates at Homebrew meetings. Hardware enthusiasts argued against it, while those who were heavy into programming supported Wozniak. Bill Gates, who had helped develop BASIC for Altair, wrote in a Homebrew newsletter: "Without good software and an owner who understands programming, a hobby computer is wasted." Later on, software was to become a multi-billion dollar business.

Before the trip to Atlantic City, there was trouble between Jobs and Wozniak. In the original agreement among Jobs, Wozniak and Wayne, Wozniak retained all rights to any improvements he made to the Apple. He was not at all certain that he wanted Jobs to sell the color version and considered selling the whole thing to Processor Technology. Wozniak's guarded attitude toward Jobs was reinforced by his entire family, who considered Jobs as an interloper taking advantage of Wozniak's genius. Jerry Wozniak had grave doubts about his son's association with Jobs, expressing the opinion that Jobs wanted to start at the top without having to work to get there. But Steve Wozniak is a kind-hearted soul who softens easily, and he and Jobs had patched things up fairly well by the time they trudged to the East Coast.

Wozniak's computer aroused enough interest at Atlantic City to bring Commodore Business Machines knocking at Apple's door. The Commodore representatives believed that Wozniak's computer would allow the company to enter the microcomputer business. Commodore's interest was more than welcome because both Jobs and Wozniak were wearing themselves out. Jobs handled the negotiations with Commodore and asked for $100,000 plus salaries of $36,000 a year each for himself and Wozniak. Luckily for Apple, the sale didn't go through. Jobs was suspicious of Commodore and when he began checking the company, he didn't like what he found. For its part, Commodore thought the price was far too high. Irving Gould, Commodore's chairman of the board, decided it was absurd for the company to buy a business from two young men who were working out of a garage.

Commodore's interest served to chaff the raw feelings that existed between Jobs and Wozniak's family, especially when Jerry Wozniak discovered that the money was to be evenly split. Wozniak's father made no bones about how he felt. He lit into Jobs, telling him that he deserved nothing. He told Jobs that he had designed nothing, nor had he produced anything. To sum it all up, he added, "You didn't do shit." Jobs burst into tears on several occasions during this lambasting. He told Steve Wozniak that if they didn't split fifty-fifty that Wozniak could have it all. Jobs's proposal was never put to the test because Commodore changed its mind about buying Apple.

Commodore's interest, however, prompted Jobs and Wozniak to think that there might be other companies interested in buying Apple. Jobs offered to sell the business to Nolan Bushnell at Atari, but was turned down cold. Bushnell saw no future in microprocessors. Wozniak approached Hewlett-Packard, hoping to sell Apple, but received a similar reception. Hewlett-Packard told him it had no intention of getting into that rather dubious market.

Meanwhile, the Apple computer needed additional modification, including a power supply. Wozniak had not bothered to design one because it was not high-tech and held little interest for him. Power supplies used the basic laws of electricity and had not changed much in several years. But without proper regulation of power flowing through the computer, surges in electrical current could blow out chips and semiconductors. To complicate matters, Jobs insisted on a power supply that didn't need a noisy fan to cool the inner workings.

Jobs trooped to Atari and button-holed Al Alcorn to ask him to recommend an engineer who could design that kind of a power supply. The engineer that came to mind was Rod Holt, a middle-aged man whom Jobs described to Wozniak as the greatest designer in the universe. While Jobs was enthusiastic about Holt, Holt viewed Jobs with suspicion, and wondered if he would ever be paid for his work. Jobs assured him that it was no problem. Holt later recalled that the smooth-talking Jobs simply "conned" him into taking the job. So it was that Holt began working at the Jobs's garage on weekends and became an integral part of Apple for some time.

For all the work Jobs and Wozniak were doing, Apple occupied an unimportant place in what was still the unimportant world of microprocessors. Several companies making microprocessors had sprung up like mushrooms in Silicon Valley and were hanging on by their teeth. Nevertheless, some of them were much more successful than Apple. Jobs considered Apple's image and determined that they needed better advertising and public relations. He turned once more to acquaintances in the electronics field and was given the name of Regis McKenna and, after much persistance, was eventually able to get McKenna's agency to represent Apple. It was one of the most important associations the small company could have arranged.

CHAPTER 8

The Start of Something Big

Regis McKenna was a California transplant who moved to Silicon Valley in 1963 to work in public relations, advertising, and marketing for high-technology firms. He was an Irishman with a quick wit, hair-trigger temper, and ideas for promoting companies that seemed way out of kilter with the times. McKenna formed his own agency in 1970 and tried out his new approach to marketing and advertising. In those days, most advertising and press releases for high-tech firms dealt in great length with RAMS, bits, bytes and other technical information about products. "It was engineers selling to engineers," he says. The news releases were so boring and incomprehensible that they were almost guaranteed to go directly from an editor's hands into the nearest trash can.

McKenna's approach was to create an image for a company that would appeal to a broader segment of the marketplace. Instead of bits and bytes, he stressed the human values of a product and capitalized on important people within companies who carried a sheen of respectability. His approach to the press was also unusual. Rather than bombard the media with news releases, then sit back and wait for publicity, he stressed the importance of building relationships with the press. "If you have dinner or lunch with a guy, he's going to remember you," he said. "He won't remember a press release." McKenna believed that if you could get ten influential publications in your corner, the rest would follow like sheep.

McKenna spent hours with his client companies discussing the necessity of "educating" the press to the vagaries of high technology products. Chips, minicomputers and microprocessors were in their infancy and reporters covering the new industry were relatively naive. They found themselves boggled with information that was totally incomprehensible to them. McKenna took pains to educate them, had meetings where he shared industry gossip, and managed to hold the press in the palm of his hand. No one in Silicon Valley was more adept at getting favorable publicity for a client than Regis McKenna. So when Jobs telephoned the agency for help, he was turning to high-powered talent.

Jobs had little to offer when he approached the McKenna agency. He was, after all, just a kid working out of a garage with Wozniak. When Jobs called the agency, he was not transferred to McKenna, but to Frank Burge, an employee who helped screen potential clients. Burge was not impressed with Jobs and what he had to say, but to get Jobs off his back, he agreed to meet with him. Even with the appointment set, Jobs continued his telephone calls to Burge, leaving message after message. He knew that Burge received numerous telephone calls and was fearful that, if he didn't continue calling, his messages would fall into neglect at the bottom of the pile.

Burge was impressed with Jobs's persistence. Furthermore, he wanted to get the teenager out of his hair and, being of a kind nature, didn't want to hurt Jobs' feelings. But when Burge set out to meet with Jobs, he was already running scenarios in his head that would allow him to make a fast getaway without being rude. He considered the trip a waste of time.

His worst suspicions were confirmed when he arrived at the Jobs's household. Jobs emerged from the kitchen looking as he always did. All of Burge's courteous plans went out the window. All he could think of was escaping. Then Jobs started to talk and Burge found himself captivated by a man who, despite his raga-muffin appearance, was making an eloquent presentation. He says that within three minutes he was struck by two thoughts: "First, he was an incredibly smart young man. Second, I didn't understand a fraction of what he was talking about."

Clearly, Burge thought, this offbeat operation deserved a lit-tle more investigation and study. He contacted Paul Terrell, owner of the Byte Shops and a client of McKenna's, and asked him about Jobs's credentials and for more information about Apple. Terrell reported that the company was disorganized, over-extended, and that Jobs was not suited for marketing. The McKenna Agency didn't respond immediately. Several weeks went by as executives considered the pros and cons of Apple. A memorandum was written that was favorable. The memoran-dum noted: "Though he [Jobs] moved a quantity into retail dis-tribution, there is as yet no evidence that the retailer(s) are suc-cessful in finding customers." The hook that captivated the agency was a comparison between Jobs and Nolan Bushnell, at Atari, a company McKenna represented. The memo noted that Jobs was young and inexperienced, but so was Bushnell when he started Atari, and now Bushnell claimed a personal net worth of ten million dollars. The agency agreed to handle the Apple account, getting paid from a percentage of revenues.

The meeting that was eventually planned for Wozniak and Jobs to meet Regis McKenna, did not get off to a good start. McKenna was established and respected in Silicon Valley. By 1976, when the meeting took place, he had already represented scores of high technology clients. He had something of an ego, too. His business card read REGIS McKENNA, HIMSELF. One of the innovative ways McKenna had helped establish National Semiconductor was to print cards with pictures and highlights of some of National's luminaries, similar to baseball cards that were so popular with kids.

When he started off on his own, McKenna landed the busi-ness of Intel, a major manufacturer of semiconductors. McKenna had used public relations, rather than advertising, as the tool to catapault Intel into the limelight. He went beyond the usual publicity in trade magazines, struck at the heart of the national press, and was successful in placing stories in major magazines and newspapers. By the time he met Jobs and Wozniak, McKenna had some experience in promoting the small world of microprocessors and, by applying to himself those public relations techniques that were so successful with clients, he had created an image of polish and expertise that made the agency seem larger and more substantial than it really was.

Jobs, Wozniak, and McKenna were uncomfortable with each other at first. Wozniak was writing a story about Apple to be published in a trade magazine, and McKenna asked to look at it, emphasizing that it should not be filled with technical terms. Wozniak bristled and retorted that he didn't want a PR man to rework his copy. McKenna's Irish temper flared and he said, "Well, you better both get out." Jobs, alarmed at the way things were going, turned on all his persuasive charm and managed to calm the sudden storm. The meeting ended with the agreement between McKenna and Apple intact. Apple had less than one thousand dollars in its bank account at the time.

McKenna was not taking a big chance with Apple. The agency said it would consider other work only after reviewing the effectiveness of the first Apple advertisement it prepared. Nevertheless, it was an important agreement for Apple, and the first of many breaks that would come in rapid succession.

Apple had plans to expand, but it did not have the money. Jobs considered venture capital and asked Nolan Bushnell to put him in touch with people who might have investing interest in the young company. Bushnell talked to Jobs about the problems he could have with venture capitalists and warned him, "The longer you can stay away from those guys, the better." Apple was desperate for money and Bushnell told Jobs about Don Valentine, who had invested in Atari, and was still working as a venture capitalist.

Valentine was highly successful. His father had worked as a truck driver in New York, and Valentine had made it big by his own initiative and drive. He had a number of years of practical experience in high tech under his belt. He had been marketing

head of Fairchild and head of marketing for National Semiconductor before he formed Sequoia Ventures in Portland, Oregon.
His success was reflected in his expensive suits and the Mercedes
Benz that he drove from Portland to Silicon Valley to take a look
at Apple. The fact that Valentine bothered to make the trip to
see two young men in a garage was a tribute, helped along by
Regis McKenna, where Valentine sat on the agency's board of
directors. McKenna had telephoned Valentine about Apple. Valentine had not arrived at his station in life by letting himself be
beguiled by fast-talking young men like Jobs. He looked at cold,
hard facts and the potential to make money. He often said he was
not interested in helping someone unless they had big ideas and
an operational plan to get there. He wanted to invest in start-ups
where the entrepreneurs were talking in terms of billions of dollars instead of millions. "If a man comes into my office and says
he wants to be a millionaire, I'm bored to death," he said.

Valentine was not impressed with either Wozniak or Jobs,
and their scheme for Apple's future was almost patently designed
to lose his interest. Jobs and Wozniak explained that the market
for single-board computers was continuing to grow, as had been
predicted, and that they would be content with a small part of
the market. Valentine concluded that neither of the two young
men had any idea about the size of the market or how they
would go about positioning their product. The youngsters were
also thinking much too small to interest him. "Small thinkers
never do big things," he told himself, and lost interest in Apple.

In defense of Wozniak and Jobs, *no one* really understood
the potential of the microprocessor market. The market, so far,
consisted primarily of computer hobbyists. When Apple Computer finally came into its own, McKenna noted, it had to *create*
a market and an infrastructure to support it. These marketing
ideas helped assure Apple's success, which was just around the
corner, although no one realized it at the time of Valentine's
visit. Valentine kept his money, but suggested other venture capitalists who might be interested in making an investment in
Apple. One of them was Armas Clifford Markkula, who was
known as Mike because he despised both of his given names.

Markkula had worked with Valentine at Fairchild and, through taking risks, had become a millionaire by the time he was thirty. He was retired at age thirty-three when Valentine suggested that he meet Jobs and Wozniak. A native Californian, he had received both bachelor's and master's degrees from the University of California. One of the goals he had set for himself was to become a millionaire by the time he turned thirty. Markkula worked for Hughes Aircraft Company as an electrical engineer, went to Fairchild, then joined Intel.

Markkula was a straight arrow in Silicon Valley, preferring family life to the glitz and glamour of California's fast lane. At Intel, he was considered a competent employee, but no one saw him as a man who would create thunder and lightning. He disdained the hard partying and never really felt comfortable at Intel. Markkula borrowed heavily to invest in Intel stock and, when the company went public, he made millions. But in terms of Silicon Valley, where millionaires are a dime a dozen, he was considered a "small" millionaire. However, he enjoyed fancy clothes, houses, and cars and, when he visited Jobs and Wozniak, he arrived in a gold-colored Corvette.

The computer Wozniak had built struck a positive note in his engineer's heart, and he liked Steven Jobs. After a harmonious meeting, Markkula returned to Valentine for additional conversations to see what sort of a future Valentine saw for Apple. Valentine had turned Apple down because it didn't seem big enough for him, but his comments about the computer and potential market convinced Markkula that there was an opportunity to create a new business and earn a great deal of money.

Markkula, whose net worth was estimated at more than twenty-two million dollars, enjoyed his retirement and really didn't need additional funds to live luxuriously. Yet he saw an opportunity, not just for riches, but to make an indelible mark for himself in the business world. On weekends and evenings, he discussed Apple at great length with Wozniak and Jobs. He became more optimistic with each meeting, but he wanted to have his wife's support before he pledged himself to what he realized would be a hard struggle to make Apple a success. Markkula's wife offered no objections when he decided to devote four years to Apple and offered to underwrite a $250,000 bank loan to start a company and pay the cost of developing and manufacturing the Apple II.

After making his decision, Markkula telephoned Regis McKenna and received assurance the the agency would be tolerant of Jobs and Wozniak, neither of whom had business experience. Jobs, Wozniak, and Holt spent additional hours with Markkula, discussing Apple's future and the thorny issues of their salaries and how the stock should be divided. Markkula wanted to own a third of the company and Wozniak, who was still employed at Hewlett-Packard, openly questioned whether Jobs was worth the $20,000 a year salary that was offered. To Wozniak's surprise, Markkula rose to Jobs's defense. "He liked Steve," Wozniak says. "He saw him as a future executive." Holt had misgivings about Markkula, whom he viewed as being somewhat arrogant, "the way some people with money are." Markkula, for his part, was suspicious of Holt and checked his references as far back as high school.

Wozniak had doubts about the whole arrangement. He believed that Markkula's faith in Apple's future was pie in the sky and thought he would lose every cent of his investment. Neither did Wozniak want to leave Hewlett-Packard, where he had a bright future, to join Apple full-time. Wozniak's wife, Alice, also accustomed to regular paychecks, shared his doubts. Wozniak was due to be transferred to Oregon with Hewlett-Packard, but Markkula made his deal with Apple contingent on Wozniak working full-time with Apple. Wozniak was given a deadline to make up his mind, or else he was out. The problem facing Markkula, Jobs, and Holt was that Wozniak was indispensable.

Jobs began telephoning all of Wozniak's friends and relatives, asking them to put pressure on Wozniak to join Apple. He even visited Wozniak's parents, who still considered him a pushy young man who was taking advantage of their son, and asked them to help bring Wozniak around. They responded so vitriolically that Jobs left their home weeping.

"Mike Markkula said he would put in $250,000, but only if I left Hewlett-Packard," Wozniak said. "My feeling was that I had designed the Apple II, the BASIC and had done all of these incredible numbers of designs while moonlighting. I thought I could keep on doing that and keep a nice secure job at Hewlett-Packard. But Mike Markkula said, 'No. You've got to make a one hundred percent commitment.' That was where I thought it over for a few days and, on the ultimatum day, I said 'No.'"

"Steve got friends and relatives to call me, but I didn't want any part of running a business," Wozniak continued. "I was very much the young technical nerd and thought that companies and managers were all political bullshit. It's a game that I would never want to be near. Then one of my friends telephoned me and explained that I didn't have to be a manager or a businessman. He said I could still be just an engineer for the rest of my life even if I helped start a company and got rich. That made sense to me because I didn't want to be something I wasn't. It made all of the difference when I realized that I could be an engineer for my whole life."

Apple Computer Company was formed January 3, 1977, and less than three months later, bought the partnership for just $5,308.96. Markkula wanted to make certain that Ron Wayne would have no claim in the future against the company and bought his shares for $1,700. Wayne, who had seen no future for the company and had tried to bail himself out earlier by resigning and relieving himself of obligations for bad debts he envisioned piling up, was delighted with his settlement.

Markkula had no desire to run the business, and neither Jobs or Wozniak had the experience. Wozniak would not have been interested in any case, but Jobs, accustomed to having his own way most of his life, feared having a boss. He relished having power and a free hand, and wanted to keep it that way. Markkula convinced him that the most pressing issue was not power, but a company that was organized and well managed so that it could make money. Jobs liked money as much as he savored power and saw the wisdom in Markkula's assertion.

Markkula thought of Michael Scott as a man who might be persuaded to become president of Apple. His career path had often crossed with Scott's, and he had faith in him as a man who would watch the pennies. The two, who shared the same birth date a year apart, had become fast friends. They had made a ritual of celebrating their birthdays together, and it was at the February 11, 1977 get-together that Markkula proposed that Scott join Apple.

Scott was an engineer who had grown up in Gainesville, Florida, and had an interest in computing that dated back to his teenage years. After knocking around a bit, he joined Beckman Instruments Systems Division in California and busied himself with helping make ground support equipment for Saturn rockets. Scott, who hated corporate politics, left Beckman to join Fairchild, but found himself once more tangled in politics and joined National Semiconductor, hoping to leave corporate gamesmanship behind. By the time he was thirty-two, he was in charge of a semiconductor assembly line doing thirty million dollars in business a year. Making semiconductors is not a glamorous business and Scott was bored. He saw an opportunity to make a name for himself by being the president of a company he believed rightly would leave a mark in the corporate world.

Markkula knew he, himself, wasn't equipped by temperament to run Apple. He hated conflict and had a hard time saying no. His strengths lay in diplomacy, business planning, and market strategy. When he suggested Scott as president of Apple, Wozniak was delighted. He wanted no part of running the company and was pleased with Scott's obvious interest in computers. He was also glad to have somebody besides Jobs calling the shots. Even though Jobs had doubts about Scott, he was ambivalent about his own role at Apple. On the one hand, he didn't want to give up control and, on the other, he seemed to realize he didn't have the qualifications. Jobs was also aware that, in any showdown, he could unseat Scott if either Wozniak or Markkula backed him up. Scott's biggest concern was whether or not he would be able to get along with Jobs. "I wondered whether I could get anything done or whether we would be arguing all the time," he said. As it turned out over the years, his concern was real; he and Jobs were at odds with each other from the beginning and, in combination with one another, almost tore the company apart.

Nevertheless, everyone involved finally agreed, and Scott was hired as Apple's first president. As titular boss of the three principals, Scott was paid a salary of $20,001 a year, a dollar more than Markkula, Jobs, and Wozniak.

The four made up an unlikely alliance. The only real interest they shared was electronics. Wozniak had created the computer but wanted nothing to do with running a business. Markkula had come out of retirement because he saw an opportunity to add to his millions and to help create a new company. Scott joined because, bored and tired of semiconductors, he wanted to do something different. Jobs was there because he had no career goals and had grabbed onto Wozniak's coattails for lack of anything else to do.

Markkula's association with Apple had implications that far exceeded the money he invested in the fledgling company. He brought organizational skills, business experience, and a steadying influence over the mercurial Jobs, which he would have to exercise countless times in coming years. Although they all had high hopes for the new company, they had no idea that, just three years later, Apple would be worth two billion dollars and each of them would be worth hundreds of millions of dollars.

Steve Jobs.
Photo courtesy of Next, Inc.

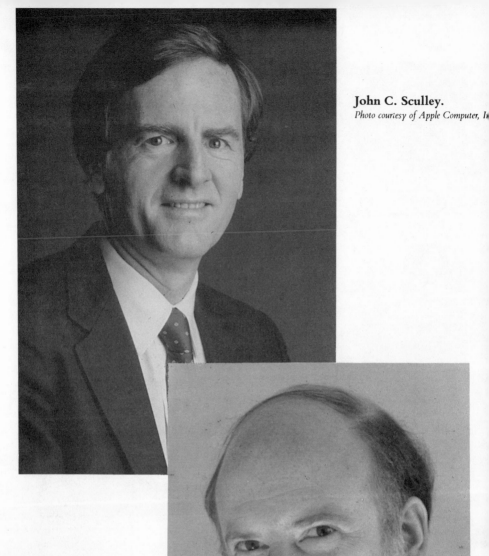

John C. Sculley.
Photo courtesy of Apple Computer, I

Jef Raskin.
Photo courtesy of Information Appliance, Inc.

H. Ross Perot.
Photo courtesy of Texas Business.

CHAPTER 9

Problems and Promise

Apple's situation began to change rapidly once it had professional guidance and a thin cushion of operating capital. The company moved out of Jobs's garage into a building located on Stevens Creek Boulevard in Cupertino, close to where Wozniak and Jobs lived. The quarters were small, and the technical area was separated from the rest of the company by a plasterboard wall. Mike Markkula began the difficult task of developing a business plan while Scott took care of day to day operation. Wozniak was involved, along with a handful of technicians and engineers who had been hired on a rush job to complete the Apple II in time for the West Coast Computer Faire, just months away. Jobs, who had no real responsibility within the company, flitted from project to project, desk to desk, ruffling feathers and generally making himself feared and unpopular.

Markkula was faced with an unprecedented challenge in developing a plan to make Apple successful. The established business practice of seeing a market, then targeting a share of it, was not applicable because the only existing market consisted of a relatively small group of computer hobbyists. Dozens of major companies had investigated the possibility of developing micro-computers but had abandoned it after deciding that the market wasn't big enough. Most computers in those days had no practical use. Markkula had to create a market where none existed. He and Scott looked beyond the hobbyist market and envisioned small businesses and professionals using personal computers if they were marketed properly. Tandy, which operates a string of Radio Shack stores around the country, had created a microcomputer and was thinking along the same lines as Markkula.

To help develop a business plan for Apple, Markkula turned to people he trusted and respected, and spent the first quarter of 1977 developing what he hoped would be realistic goals for Apple. A key consultant in Markkula's efforts was John Hall, a controller of a pharmaceutical company. They were not close friends but had considerable respect for one another. Through their casual acquaintance, Markkula knew that Hall had helped a number of small start-up companies set their goals. When Markkula asked him to help Apple, Hall took a fourteen day vacation to spend seemingly endless hours with Scott, Markkula, Jobs, and Wozniak to discuss the nuts and bolts of the operation.

The development of the overall strategy fell to Markkula, Hall, and Scott. They decided that Apple should try to capture the hobbyist market and expand it to include professionals and home users. The professional market would consist of physicians, dentists, accountants, and people who had small operations. They decided to stress the Apple computer's ability to operate automatic systems in a home, such as locking doors, regulating heat, and turning various appliances on and off. The market plan was the result of three months of work and, when it was completed, no one who had been involved in its creation believed in it. Hall's distrust of the strategy he had helped create was so strong that he refused Markkula's offer to join Apple as vice president for finance. He thought Apple was "screwy" and didn't want to get involved. Nevertheless, Hall seemed to have some confidence in the company because he asked that his consultancy fee be paid in Apple stock. Markkula refused and opted to pay Hall four thousand dollars in cash.

Markkula turned to other people he knew for the administrative help that Apple needed, but it was not an easy sell. He hired Sherry Livingston as Apple's girl friday, to do everything from answering the phone to running errands, but only after convincing her that Apple was a going concern. He accomplished this by showing her a drawer filled with purchase orders. Gene Carter, whom Scott had known at Fairchild, was out of work and in search of a job. Scott hired him to take on responsibility for sales and distribution. Scott also hired Gary Martin, another Fairchild acquaintance, to handle finances. Martin accepted the job with reservations and had an ace up his sleeve to cover his bets: "I knew I could return to Fairchild within thirty days." Martin had little faith in Apple's product. He inspected the Apple II, which was not yet completed, and wondered, "Who in the hell is going to buy it?"

On the technical side, there was no shortage of qualified people to work on the Apple II. The few technicians and engineers who were hired were confident of their ability to find other work if Apple went belly up. To a man, they were excited about creating a new product and being freed from the boredom of doing humdrum work to do innovative engineering.

None of the employees realized the pressure they would be under once they joined Apple. Computers had gained increasing importance in the market because they were capturing the interest of prospective customers outside of the hobbyist market. The Homebrew Club had been the original showplace for new computer products, but now computer shows were being held around the country. The attention these shows received attracted information managers from numerous companies, who stood shoulder to shoulder with the hobbyists. A product that caught the fancy of information managers could result in dozens of orders, making a start-up company successful overnight.

Not long after Jobs and Wozniak had pinched their pennies to tote their computer board to Atlantic City, a large computer show was planned in the spring of 1977 at the civic auditorium in San Francisco. The Homebrew Computer Club organized the show after being encouraged by the large numbers of people who trouped through the displays in Atlantic City. Homebrew's newsletter late in 1976 promised that a large number of computer enthusiasts and potential customers would attend what had been dubbed the First West Coast Computer Faire. It was imperative for Apple to be there, and Steven Jobs was one of the first exhibitors to reserve space to show off the Apple II, even though an enormous amount of work remained to be done on the computer.

Wozniak had already completed the technical work on Apple II, but he was a computer designer and not particularly interested in elegance. Jobs was able to envision a complete product. He thought that it should be elegant in appearance and easy to use. The crude, naked displays he had seen the times he attended Homebrew meetings left him cold. They were unappealing to look at and he realized that the Apple II had to stand out as a swan against the background of ugly ducklings.

"Steve had a great deal to do with designing the computer housing," Wozniak said. "I was more interested in making a small, powerful computer, and didn't think much about its case. He had nothing to do with the technical aspects of the Apple II, but he was very much involved in how it should be packaged."

The covering used by most microcomputers then was sheet metal, which was pliable and reasonably inexpensive. But Jobs believed that a plastic case would be more elegant and saleable. Opponents argued that computer hobbyists couldn't care less about a computer's appearance, but Jobs was adamant and believed rightly that an unattractive computer would not interest prospective customers outside the hard core hobbyists. He argued his point strongly enough to convince others at Apple that plastic was the way to go.

Jobs farmed out the job of designing the computer case to Ron Wayne, who produced several sketches and water color paintings. Wayne's design served the purpose of protecting the inner workings of the computer from spilled coffee, hair and other debris, but the sides were made of wood, not at all what Jobs wanted. He rejected Wayne's design and was guided to Jerry Mannock, who had been suggested by one of Wozniak's friends at Hewlett-Packard. Mannock had started out to become an electronics engineer, but found that he enjoyed design more than the esoteric workings of electricity. He had started a company that was barely providing him with a livelihood, and was eager for additional work when he met with Jobs. Jobs told Mannock he needed the cases in three months so the computer could be shown at the Computer Faire in San Francisco. Mannock readily agreed to produce the cases, but wanted to be paid $1,500 first because he had his doubts about Apple. He thought it was a "flakey" company that could easily go broke before he was paid. But Jobs tried to convince him that Apple was as solid as the Rock of Gibraltar.

The shape of the computer's innards, and their functions, helped establish the design for the case. Form had to follow function. The case needed a removable lid, had to be high enough to accommodate the mother board, and air space was needed inside to prevent heat from building up. It took Mannock only three weeks to present a drawing, which was the simplest he could conceive. Jobs like the drawing and, with a few modifications, including handles so that it could be picked up, accepted Mannock's design.

Jobs was also overseeing the development of the company's logo after deciding that the original design, with Newton leaning against an Apple tree, was too cerebral. The business plan called for marketing to a wider audience and Jobs wanted a simple logo that would have greater appeal. Rob Janov, an art director at the Regis McKenna Agency, worked closely with Jobs as they struggled with a concept. Janov started with the idea of an apple with a bite taken out of one side. The bite, to him, was symbolic of bits and bytes, and Jobs agreed. Janov then started to dress up the apple with colorful horizontal stripes to give it a jaunty touch of class. The colors were redolent of a rainbow, a symbolic sign of future good luck. Jobs firmly rejected any idea of separating the colors with thin strips to make reproduction easier. While most computer companies simply stamped their name on a plate and attached it to the computer, Jobs wanted to go first class. The multi-colored apple with a bite missing became the company's logo.

Jobs flitted around the company to help with details that had to be worked out in a short time. Holt was still working on a power supply for the Apple II and was trying approaches that had never been used in microcomputers. He decided to use a switching device which turned currents on and off so quickly that it guaranteed a steady flow of electricity to the computer, eliminating the possibility of a power surge that could blow out sensitive chips. Wozniak watched Holt's progress with more than passing curiosity and was surprised at the result. "I only had a vague idea of what a switching power supply was," he said.

Jobs also took charge of getting printed circuit boards for the Apple II. He turned to Howard Cantin, whom he had known at Atari, to do the work. Jobs made strenuous demands and insisted that the chips be connected by neat, straight solder lines. Cantin said that Jobs drove him up a wall, and he became so angry with the demands that he vowed never to work for Jobs again.

There were dozens of details that had to be cleared up, and Jobs scurried from one thing to another. Business cards weren't delivered until a few days before the Computer Faire was to open. Jobs also fretted about the color of the computer keyboard and decided that it should be brown. The color was the least of the problems with the keyboard, which went dead after less than a half hour of continuous use. The problem was traced to a faulty chip. Wozniak was also busy incorporating an abbreviated form of BASIC onto a chip and writing programs that would demonstrate the computer's power, plus its color and sound potential.

As the Faire drew closer, there was a frantic scramble to see that the housing, designed by Mannock, would be ready on time. A decision also had to be made on the most efficient way to have the housing molded. When the cases were removed from the molds, they had lumps and burrs and, for weeks, Apple looked more like a cabinet factory than a computer manufacturer as employees filed and sanded the casings until they were smooth, then painted beige.

The computer that evolved was the work of several people. Wozniak patented a microcomputer with a video display, while Holt received a patent for the important new switching system.

None of this went smoothly, and the fear Scott had harbored about whether or not he could get along with Jobs proved to be well-founded. Jobs insisted on being in the middle of everything. "Steve had no ability to manage people," said an analyst who has followed Apple for years. "He ruled by intimidation, yelling and screaming at people. People were terrified by him." Scott, who admired Jobs in some respects, seconds that analysis. "After you get something started, he causes a lot of waves," he said. "He likes to fly around like a hummingbird at ninety miles an hour."

Employees recall frequent shouting matches between the two. "Scotty was the only one Jobs couldn't intimidate," said an early Apple employee. "He would go into Scotty's office talking ninety miles an hour, not letting him get a word in edgewise. That was his style, just to run over people. Scotty wouldn't let him get away with it. He would hit Steve between the eyes with a two-by-four."

Jobs's ego also got in his way when Scott began issuing employee identification badges, which numbered the employees. Since Scott considered the technical aspect more important than administrative, he issued Wozniak badge number one. Jobs went rushing to Scott.

"Am I number one?" he asked.

"No. Woz is number one. You're number two."

"I want to be number one. Can I be number zero? Woz can be number one. I want to be number zero."

Scott, to keep peace, made Jobs number zero while Wozniak was number one.

Other employees watched Jobs and Scott go at it. "Steve had a lot of ideas, but he had no experience." one of them said. "Steve had ideas, but Scotty had the *right* ideas." And yet another said "You could hear them shouting at each other from one end of the building to the other. Scott would get so mad that he would turn beet red. Steve would often leave those encounters in tears because he was so hurt and frustrated. Scotty had to come down on him pretty hard to keep him in line."

Some of the squabbles were over petty things. When office partitions arrived, employees used creative arrangements to avoid monotony. Jobs and Scott fought over that, as well as what color the partitions should be. Another time, Jobs was signing purchase orders when Scott arrived and told him he wasn't authorized to do so. "I got here first, I'll sign them," Jobs said. Scott replied, "No, I've got to sign them." When Jobs insisted on signing the orders, Scott threatened to quit.

Jobs was also gaining a reputation for being rude and overbearing with outside people with whom Apple did business. He was furious when a typewriter arrived that wasn't the color he ordered, and scolded a representative of the office supply store that delivered it. Another time a telephone installer wilted under Jobs's abuse when the phones weren't the color he had approved. He didn't hesitate to attack employees of any of Apple's vendors, even those from much larger companies than Apple. "He was very obnoxious to them," another employee recalled. "We all wondered, 'How can you treat another human being like that?'"

Markkula, knowing that word of mouth was the best advertising, decided that anyone who owned an Apple I could exchange it for an Apple II. Among computer hobbyists, this kind of exchange was particularly significant. At the time, the Apple I computer was in eighth place among computers used by the 1,500 members of the Homebrew Club. The Apple II was expected to move Apple up the ladder.

Even with the internal turmoil, hurt feelings, and shouting matches, work on the Apple II progressed while Markkula contemplated how to show Apple in the most favorable light at the First West Coast Computer Faire. Thanks to Jobs committing them to exhibit early, Apple had been alloted a choice spot at the civic auditorium. Markkula knew that impressions were of paramount importance and turned to the McKenna Agency to help design the display booth.

Three Apple IIs were dramatically displayed in front of gray plexiglass, with the company's colorful new logo illuminated by a spotlight. A large television screen was in place so the computer's power could be shown to big audiences. The display was dramatic and professional, making it appear that Apple was a substantial company. In fact, the three computers on display were the only ones Apple had that were fully assembled. Markkula realized that Jobs's sloppy dress and sandals would not make a favorable impression and he ordered him to a San Francisco tailor where Jobs bought the first suit he had ever owned. Wozniak also spruced up.

The Computer Faire attracted an enormous crowd, and Apple's display, as prominent as it was, still could not compare favorably with larger booths. Commodore was showing its new microcomputer in an impressive booth, as was Tandy. Representatives of competing computer companies prowled through the auditorium, giving other displays an appraising and critical eye. Although Apple's booth was not as large as some, it was unmistakably different from those that had been established by computer hobbyists. The exhibit made Apple look classy and solid. Thousands of prospective buyers trooped through the auditorium and Markkula did his best to sell them on Apple.

Apple's new look drew a great deal of attention, and prospective customers who took printed leaflets describing the Apple II were surprised at its power. Hardly anyone could believe the radical new approach of housing a computer in a plastic case, and engineers were impressed that it could produce color video display with so few chips. Over the next few weeks, Apple received orders for about three hundred Apple IIs, which was one hundred more than the total number of Apple Is that had been sold.

As important as it was for Apple, the First West Coast Computer Faire could not contain the mischievious imp in Wozniak. It proved to be a perfect place for a prank that could have had serious repercussions for Apple. Wozniak wrote some copy, had it printed, and secretly distributed stacks of leaflets around the auditorium that described an amazing new computer that didn't exist. The leaflet read:

> Image a dream machine. Imagine the computer surprise of the century here today. Imagine Z-80 performance plus. Imagine BAZIC in ROM, the most complete and powerful language ever developed. Imagine the raw video, plenty of it. Imagine autoscroll text, a full sixteen lines of sixty-four characters. Imagine eye-dazzling color graphics. Imagine a blitz-fast 1200-baud cassette port. Imagine an unparalleled I/O system with full Altair-100 and Zaltair-

150 bus compatibility. Image an exquisitely designed cabinet that will add to the decor of any living room. Imagine the fun you'll have. Imagine Zaltair, available now from MITS, the company where microcomputer technology was born.

The leaflet also contained fiction about BAZIC, which was fiction in itself. "Without software a computer is no more than a racing car without wheels, a turntable without records, or a banjo without strings. The best thing of all about BAZIC is the ability to define your own language . . . a feature we call per-Zonality.TM." Nor was the fictional hardware without its luster. "We really thought this baby out before we built it. Two years of dedicated research and development at the number ONE microcomputer company had to pay off, and it did. A computer engineer's dream, all electronics are on a single PC card, even the 18-slot motherboard. And what a motherboard."

Wozniak had printed a company logo on the leaflet and a coupon offering a trade-in allowance on other computers. The representatives of MITS were frantic and rushed about, grabbing up the leaflets and stamping them with the word FRAUD. Even Jobs was taken in by the fictional computer. "Oh my God!" he exclaimed. "This thing sounds pretty good." Wozniak had also printed a comparison of other computers on the leaflet, comparing Zaltair with Sol, IMSAI and the Apple II. Jobs, noting that Apple was listed third, breathed a sign of relief that Apple had not fared badly in the comparison. Wozniak, realizing that his prank had gotten way out of hand, hauled the remaining leaflets away and dumped them.

As Apple set about gearing up to meet its commitments for the Apple II, order began to develop out of chaos. The older engineers didn't trust the younger ones and vice versa. There were only a dozen or so employees and no one worried much about rank in those early days. They had no compunction about calling one another names and there was no fear of authority. "We thought of ourselves as peers, not presidents and vice presidents," said one employee. Jobs and Scott continued with the

Scotty Wars, but at this time they were viewed with amusement and had little adverse effect on morale.

"Steve was really great in the early days," said Wozniak. "He didn't develop his abrasive style until later on. There was a strong sense of community at Apple."

Wozniak was viewed as a genius, but one who was interested only in solving complex problems. He would do the hard part, then leave the rest to other engineers and technicians. Holt discovered that the best way to make Wozniak produce was to constantly express amazement at the things he accomplished. Markkula discouraged programmers from tinkering around with programs for their own amusement, and arduously threw himself into the task of personally designing programs. Scott kept an eagle eye on finances, and tried to keep Apple's primary goals in perspective. He wanted to farm out as much work as possible, claiming that Apple's job was to create, educate, and market, and to manufacture as few parts as possible. He believed in letting subcontractors do the routine work.

Subcontractors made the printed circuit boards and, for stuffing them, Scott hired Hildy Licht, who had a small business in her home. When components were delivered to Licht, she tested them, farmed out the stuffing to neighbors, and tested the finished boards before taking them back to Apple.

Scott brought professionalism into some of the financial and administrative details necessary to a company. Bank of America handled the payroll, relieving Apple of the chore of establishing a complicated system that would include withholding taxes and social security. Scott arranged sixty days credit to pay vendors, while expecting payment from buyers within thirty days. A large accounting firm established Apple's fiscal year in September and saved it considerable taxes during 1977.

Like Markkula, who did tedious programming in addition to his other tasks, Scott pitched in by helping pack computers and even carting them to UPS for shipment. Apple was a closely knit community in those days. Employees came to work early and stayed until late at night, partly because they wanted to and partly because Jobs expected it. "Steve demanded total loyalty," said Tim Bajarin, an analyst who has followed Apple closely over the years. "He expected you to place Apple above your family, friends, and personal life."

This type of commitment extracted its toll in the personal lives of both Wozniak and Jobs. Jobs, Kottke, and Judy Smith, Jobs's girlfriend, rented a house together in Cupertino and furnished it in a make-shift fashion. Jobs brought a mattress and a cushion for meditation for the master bedroom, while Kottke laid his head to rest on a foam pad in the living room. Judy Smith was becoming increasingly restless and insecure, and didn't like living with two twenty year old men. She saw little of Jobs, who was burning the midnight oil, along with the rest of Apple's employees. She began calling him at work for advice on such trivial matters as changing light bulbs. She had fits of anger where she scrawled words on the walls with charcoal and knocked books from the shelves.

"I pulled into the parking lot once, and Judy was beating him on the head with her fists," Wozniak said. "I was dumbfounded. I just couldn't believe it."

At her wits end, Smith, who had become pregnant, moved out of the house. She claimed that Jobs didn't care that she was pregnant, a situation that would later result in a paternity suit. "I just had to get away from Steve and Apple," she said.

Wozniak was having his own miseries. He spent most of his time working at Apple and saw little of his wife. The two had one or two trial separations and Wozniak slept on a couch at work. Finally, they decided on a divorce. Wozniak was disturbed about the divorce, but he was further concerned about having to give his estranged wife Apple stock in a settlement. Markkula, who had become more or less the *pater familia* of Apple, advised him to give his wife 15 percent of his stock. Wozniak didn't like the idea of his wife having stock, but agreed to the arrangement. Years later, Jobs would turn to Markkula for advice in a paternity suit but, unlike Wozniak, he wouldn't follow it.

Jobs had always sought a role model to emulate and he tried to do the same at Apple. He saw traits in both Markkula and Scott that he admired, but he didn't want to be like either one of them. As was his habit, he had long walks and talks with people, outlining his hopes and dreams, and also seeking comfort for his

101

emotional turmoil. Holt said he sometimes felt like a big brother to Jobs, sometimes like a father.

There were business problems at Apple as well, although they were not particularly unusual for a new company. The cases that were mass produced for the computers often did not fit and the tops sagged. Part of the blame fell on Jobs, who had insisted on the most inexpensive form of production. By autumn, Apple was running behind in its orders because the tooling broke and the company started to get a reputation for not fulfilling its commitments. Since Apple couldn't ship fast enough, and demanded payment in thirty days, its threadbare coffers became even more depleted. A dark cloud hovered over Apple, which faced the possibility of no revenue for three months. Rumors spread that Apple was going bankrupt. Scott recalled, "It was life or death for us. We had a good product and couldn't ship."

Jobs found a company that made casings for computers and calculators and presented Apple's dilemma to Bob Reutimann, spicing his story with the success the company expected in the future. Reutimann listened cautiously, thinking, "Here's another guy with big ideas." Jobs's persuasive powers were never more elegant and he won Reutimann's confidence, helped along by a promise of a one thousand dollar bonus for each week the mold exceeded the target date.

Jobs also had the notion of sending a complete operational manual with each computer, but the technicalities proved to be too much. Scott decided on a simple data sheet, which he had favored over Jobs's polished manual, to go out with each computer. It contained only the bare bones of the computer, listing codes and instructions for getting it hooked up. A few weeks later, he decided that more complete instructions were necessary. These were typed at Apple, printed at a quick-copy shop, and stuffed into the packaging with the computer. Often these instructions were inadequate for the buyers and, at Wozniak's insistence, a complete technical package, known as the *The Wozpak,* was available to those who requested it. Wozniak remembered the days when, as a youngster, he had received complete specifications from microprocessing firms, and wanted the same opportunity made available to owners of the Apple II. But the initial instructions on the Apple II were wholly inadequate. An information package with a *Star Trek* program simply said COO.FFR.LOAD.RUN.

Whenever anyone walked in off the street and handed over $1,200 for a computer, it was cause for celebration. One man who appeared was Cap'n Crunch, the phone phreak, who had just been released from the minimum security prison to which he had been sentenced for making more than $50,000 in illegal telephone calls. Cap'n Crunch approached Wozniak with a circuit board that, when connected with a computer, would make automatic telephone calls. The board would call a telephone number over and over until somebody finally answered. Wozniak was interested and even started to make modifications on the board, but Scott, Markkula and Jobs didn't want someone with Cap'n Crunch's unsavory background associated with Apple. "They were chickenshit about having me on the premises," Cap'n Crunch explained. A few months later, having taken an Apple computer and his automatic dialer out of state, he was once more arrested and put behind bars.

Jobs's perfectionism, compounded with the woe in his love life, made him even more difficult to please. He became known as the Rejector because he routinely turned everything down because it wasn't good enough. Jobs was finding it much more difficult to produce computers in a factory, with some two dozen employees, than to oversee a small garage operation. It was hard for him to deal with people and retain even a semblance of normalcy in the relationship. Jobs bullied and overwhelmed others while other aspects of the business overwhelmed him.

For one thing, Jobs began to realize that computers and software could not be created in days, perhaps not for months. He didn't understand the technical aspects of programming, but he argued with those who did, trying to make them hot-foot it with their projects. When Wozniak was writing a form of BASIC, Jobs tried vainly to intervene. "Steve was not an engineer," Wozniak said. "If you have a hardware man there, Steve can't talk hardware. If you have a software man, Steve can't talk software. He can help design computer cases." Jobs's unwillingness to accept his own limitations did not prevent him from getting involved in things he didn't understand. People working on projects started to dread seeing him around.

In spite of his flaws, Jobs made some significant contributions. He was by far the most dominant personality in the company, even though Scott often hammered him to his knees. Jobs had more of a vision for Apple than either Markkula or Scott. He began to think in terms of selling hundreds of thousands of computers and millions of dollars in revenues when the company was barely limping along. Jobs overcame Markkula's objections and won a battle to put Apple's colorful logo on its tape cassettes. Jobs also wanted a one year warranty on the computer when the rest of the industry guaranteed them for only three months. Scott was beside himself, thought it was a ridiculous idea and told Jobs so in such harsh language that Jobs broke down in tears. Jobs was so upset that he had to be taken for a long walk to soothe his bruised ego. In the end, he won the argument and had his way.

Scott, whose disputes with Jobs were shouting matches rather than discussions, was delighted to discover one of the methods Jobs used to refresh himself. Jobs would go into the rest room, sit on the toilet tank, plunk his bare feet into a toilet bowl, and flush. It gave Scott no end of pleasure but, if Jobs was embarrassed at having this quirky behavior discovered, he never once showed it.

Markkula was a moderating influence on the company. He tried to keep Jobs and Scott from unsettling employees with their volcanic outbursts. His style was so easy going it seemed almost casual. If two programmers had a dispute, he would simply tell them to work it out between themselves. He was so smooth that one employee said, "You couldn't find anything to blame him for." One reason Markkula may have been less frantic than Jobs and Scott is that he had already made a fortune. His future security would in no way be affected if Apple failed. On the other hand, Jobs and Scott were depending on Apple for their present livelihood and their hope for future wealth.

The year 1977 had all the appearance of being prosperous for Apple. The marketplace was starting to give the company serious attention, but things were not as good as they seemed.

"Everybody thought we were going great guns," Wozniak said, "We were really struggling."

The situation was so bad at one point that it appeared the company was going to fold. Failure was prevented only because Markkula and Scott underwrote a $250,000 loan to replenish Apple's thin cushion of cash. Markkula realized that Apple needed some heavy-duty investments from respected venture capitalists. Not only would solid investors give Apple the money it needed, reputable venture capitalists would help get Wall Street's stamp of approval. Markkula was already looking toward the day when Apple would become a public company.

CHAPTER 10

Apple Grabs a Lifeline

Apple suffered many problems during 1977, but the major crisis was the threat of bankruptcy. The computer company was building an inventory of Apple IIs, paying its creditors, but sometimes having to wait months before receiving payment from customers. Apple's revenues were inadequate to meet its expenses.

Markkula, however, remained optimistic about the company's future. Reports from satisfied buyers of the Apple II verged on the ecstatic. People were astounded to take it from its packaging, plug it in and discover that it actually worked. At the same time, Apple was working on incorporating a disk drive into the enhanced Apple II and promised to have it completed by the end of 1977, a deadline it didn't meet.

A disk drive represented a radical departure in the budding microprocessor industry. Disk drives had been used in mainframe computers for years, but they were large and required a computer about the size of a cabinet to accommodate them. A disk drive, however, offered great advantages over the cassette tapes being used on the Apple II to store information. With tape, a user had to wait several minutes while the cassette tape raced forward or backward to find information. Just loading a cassette tape with BASIC could take ten minutes. And sometimes the tape would tangle or break, losing all the information it contained.

The floppy disk offered many advantages. The disks were small and spun continuously at a rapid speed while a floating "reading" head could find information in seconds. Wozniak's cassette design was a subject of concern as the new disk drive technology was being developed. A software company wrote to Jobs to complain about the cassette: "The cassette subsystem is particularly frustrating. I used two different recorders and found them both equally unreliable . . . I must consider the backup storage subsystem as low-end hobbyist grade."

With Apple wanting to expand its market, the "hobbyist" comparison was not what it wanted to hear. A concerted effort was made to connect a disk drive to the enhanced Apple II. The major effort was undertaken by Wozniak, who studied disk drive circuitry made by IBM. Wozniak procrastinated and didn't get into high gear until near Christmas of 1977. Scott, always impatient to ship the product out the door, was frantic. He complained that Wozniak always waited until a crisis point before he would start to work in earnest. "He seemed to need that to get his adrenalin flowing," Scott said.

Once Wozniak immersed himself in the project, he didn't stop until it was finished. He was at Apple all hours of the day and night, skipping meals, and taking cat naps. Eating and sleeping seemed secondary to completing the disk drive.

When the Consumer Electronics Show opened early in 1978, Apple displayed the disk drive and drew a considerable amount of attention from engineers and prospective buyers. The disk drive met with the same enthusiasm when it was exhibited at the Second West Coast Computer Faire. Wozniak considered it the best design of his life, and other engineers greeted it with equal enthusiasm. One of Wozniak's harshest critics, Lee Felenstein, says, "I almost dropped my pants, it was so clever." Felenstein gained immediate respect for Wozniak and warned others that Apple had become a major force in the personal computer industry, one that could bowl over the competition.

Several other companies, such as Commodore and Tandy had been working on disk drives, but Apple won the race and hit the market first. The advent of the disk drive changed Apple's fortunes considerably. Unsold inventories suddenly started to sell and Scott pushed hard to ship as quickly as possible. The rush to ship was so frantic that many of the disk drives were shipped without an operating manual telling how to use them. Customers who received a disk drive without an operation manual were unhappy and let Apple know it in no uncertain terms. One irate customer concluded his letter with the curse, "I hope your dog dies."

Markkula, in the meantime, concentrated on keeping Apple afloat and building its reputation as a stable company. He knew the importance of appearances, which was reflected in the way he dressed, and set out to court respected venture capitalists to invest in Apple. The prestige of the "right" venture capitalists would bring a sheen of solvency to Apple that would be at least as important as the necessary influx of money. Markkula had made several investments as a venture capitalist, but was not familiar with how to deal with them. Markkula had hoped to wait until 1978 before turning to venture capitalists, but financial pressures forced his hand late in 1977.

Luckily, Markkula knew some heavyweights in the world of venture capital. One of them was Hank Smith, who had worked with Markkula at Fairchild and Intel. Smith had left industry to become a general partner in Venrock, which invested Rockefeller money. Venrock not only had money to invest, it was one of the most respected venture capital firms in the nation. Markkula made his first pitch to Smith early in 1977 and created a favorable enough impression for Venrock to begin watching Apple closely. Partners in the firm met several times with Apple representatives to discuss its business prospectus and visited Cupertino to see the operation at work. Markkula's friendship with Smith was the only reason Venrock looked at Apple, Smith was to say later on.

Markkula's sales projections for 1977 were considered high when they were first conceived, but Apple actually exceeded them. He had long meetings with Scott to develop a prospectus that would be realistic yet optimistic enough to interest investors. There was little solid information to guide the way because the personal computer market was in its infancy, and the projections were often stabs in the dark, based on intuition rather than fact.

Markkula had also been twisting the arm of Andy Grove, who was executive vice president of Intel. Markkula not only wanted an investment from Grove, he wanted to have Grove's guiding hand on Apple's executive board. Grove bought fifteen thousand shares in Apple, but decided against serving on the board. He said his plate was already full at Intel and he didn't have time to devote to Apple.

The most important venture capitalist came to Apple out of the blue. Arthur Rock, who was reputed to have a Midas touch, had seen Markkula give a demonstration of the Apple II and was impressed. Rock had a long list of successful investments to his credit, making millions for himself, his clients, and the companies in which he invested. Hearing Rock express an interest in Apple was as if the heavens had suddenly opened and God had smiled. Rock had invested in Fairchild Semiconductor and in Scientific Data Systems, which was sold to Xerox for $918 million, earning Rock sixty million dollars. Rock also invested $300,000 of his own money when Intel started and helped get an infusion of another $2.2 million. He was not only a wise investor, he was a canny businessman who had a reputation for offering invaluable advice in helping start-up companies succeed.

So when Rock telephoned, Markkula was ecstatic. He and Scott burned the midnight oil to prepare a prospectus designed to whet Rock's interest even more. Rock was not a casual investor, but a hard-nosed businessman who made only two or three investments a year. When it came to sniffing out success, Rock had a nose like a bloodhound.

Don Valentine, who had initially shunned Jobs and Wozniak for thinking too small, saw Apple gathering steam and made known his interest in a rather unorthodox way. Valentine was dining at a restaurant when he saw Markkula, Jobs, and Smith, sent them a bottle of champagne, along with a note that read, "Don't lose sight of the fact that I'm planning on investing in

Apple." Riding high on the interest of important investors, Markkula and Jobs were not so enthusiastic about Valentine's change of heart. Apple was on the brink of becoming an important company and Jobs viewed Valentine as a man who simply wanted to latch onto the company's coattails.

The final arrangements for financing were completed in January 1978. Papers were signed, money exchanged hands, and shares were distributed. Apple was valued at three million dollars. The financing resulted in a total of $517,500 in new capital, with Venrock investing $288,000. Valentine shelled out another $150,000 and Arthur Rock opened his wallet for $57,600.

These new investments spurred further interest in Apple and whetted the appetites of other venture capitalists. Investors from Chicago's Continental Illinois bank approached Markkula when the Apple II was being exhibited at the Consumer Electronics Show and asked to buy $500,000 in shares of Apple. The shares had tripled in price during the past six months. Venrock, unhappy about the increased cost of shares, invested again and wound up owning 7.9 percent of the company. Valentine considered the shares over-valued and refused to up the ante for additional stock.

About the same time, Scott was astonished to receive a telephone call from venture capitalist Henry Singleton, who was a close friend of Rock's and chairman of Teledyne, Inc. Singleton was not only one of the initial investors in Teledyne, he served as chairman of the board for the two billion dollar corporation. Teledyne was poles apart from Apple, both in size and in product. Teledyne was a conglomerate that sold life insurance and various kinds of non-computer related hardware. Singleton was not a casual investor and he was known to foreclose in a wink when his investments went sour. Scott was not only interested in getting Singleton to pump money into Apple, but to have him serve on the company's board of directors. Arthur Rock thought it was an impossible prospect because Singleton had his hands full with Teledyne.

Scott, however, did not abandon his dream and, when Apple's disk drive was completed, he personally delivered one to Singleton's office. There, he was surprised to find that Singleton had an Apple II in his office and another at home, and that he was busily writing programs for them. The lunch date turned into an all-afternoon affair, with Singleton consequently investing $100,800 in Apple and agreeing to serve on the board.

By late 1978, Markkula had succeeded in attracting the kind of investors to Apple who would get the company attention on Wall Street. The respectability and experience these investors brought to Apple were at least as important as the cash. All of them had been involved in starting new companies and understood the twists and turns of fate, the ups and downs of business. They had experienced such problems before with start-ups and had overcome them. Markkula was counting on this know-how to guide Apple through the turbulence of becoming a major public company. Because such luminaries had made an investment in Apple, amounting to a strong vote of confidence, the company began to be talked about in important business circles.

The personal computer business had hardly been created when Apple captured the practiced eye of Ben Rosen, who was one of the most powerful Wall Street analysts. He had been watching the electronics industry for years, traveling around the country to attend trade shows, visiting companies, digesting all the information he could, then making predictions that were printed in a newsletter. He was often quoted in such important business publications as *The Wall Street Journal, Forbes* and *Business Week.* A favorable analysis by Rosen could make a company; one that was unfavorable could break it.

Rosen had met both Markkula and Scott on the rounds he made to various companies in Silicon Valley. When Rosen visited Intel, he gave Markkula instructions on how to operate a new calculator. Apple treated Rosen like a king when he bought an Apple II in 1978 and, when he had questions, Rosen was able to telephone Scott, Markkula or Jobs at home. Apple also revealed to Rosen some of the projects it planned to develop, sometimes two or three years into the future.

Rosen's influence with the press was largely due to the thoroughness of his research and his impartiality. Reporters trooped to his New York office because they knew they could count on him for straight talk. He became one of Apple's best salesmen simply by stating facts. Rosen sponsored a lunch where Regis McKenna was introduced to reporters from *Time,* and which would later pay off in a favorable story about Apple.

Meanwhile, Apple's investors were talking with growing excitement about the company and making it sound like a big winner. This word of mouth was one of the important ways that Apple gained a reputations as a strong, solid company on the way up. Arthur Rock also contributed greatly to generating analysts' interest in Apple. Barton Biggs, an analyst for Morgan Stanley, met with Rock and Rosen in San Francisco to talk about Apple and came away with glowing reports about the company. He summarized his meeting in a memo that was liberally sprinkled with hyperbole: "Arthur Rock is a Legend with a capital 'L' like Ted Williams or Fran Tarkenton, Leonard Bernstein and Nureyev . . . In his line of business he is a player who is several orders of magnitude better than anyone else who has ever been in the game. . . . The people running this company [Apple] are very bright, very creative and very driven."

Apple's early publicity, advertising and marketing plans have been described in business lore as being unfocused. In fact, they were very carefully orchestrated.

Regis McKenna says that when Apple Computer Company formed in 1977, the climate could not have been better. The personal computer industry had not yet been created, although there were a few companies starting out, and Apple positioned itself well. By 1977, Americans were starved for homegrown success stories. The economic news around the nation was bleak. The American automobile companies were in the doldrums because of foreign competition, particularly from the Japanese. Silicon Valley's semiconductor industry was also under seige by Japanese firms, which were able to manufacture cheaper products. The newspapers around the nation were filled with chilling stories of how foreign competition was undermining American business.

Apple, with the help of the Regis McKenna Agency, capitalized on this environment. Rather than emphasizing its technical advances, Apple positioned itself as a bastion of hope for American free enterprise. "Most people don't know about the technical aspects of a computer," McKenna said, "and furthermore, they don't want to know." The American public had become fascinated with entrepreneurs to the point of according them heroic adulation. They loved to hear about success stories, and who were better examples of the rags to riches story than Steven Jobs and Stephen Wozniak?

Apple began to play up the story of how two threadbare teenagers, pinching pennies to buy parts, managed to create a personal computer company after starting in a garage. The press was eager for such stories, and "The Two Steves" began to appear regularly in magazines and newspapers. During the course of this publicity campaign, some facts became twisted and have since become accepted as fact. Jobs was described as "a computer whiz kid turned executive" and was hailed as an electronics genius. The stories made it appear that he was the one who had actually built the Apple I and Apple II. Jobs did nothing to discourage that and, in later years, was often quoted about the problems *he* overcame in designing the computer. Many people associated with Apple think that part of Jobs's problem was that he started to believe his own publicity.

"Steve was pretty much of a hanger-on," Wozniak says. "He was a quick study and learned as he went. Everyone thought he had designed the computer and he tried to pass himself off as an engineer. The early publicity left the impression that Jobs was the dominant person in designing the computer. But he was the right one to get the publicity because he had gone into management. It was sort of implied that he was the designer and that we had both been Hewlett-Packard engineers, which was inaccurate. But I didn't mind. I never felt slighted."

The publicity made both Jobs and Wozniak cult heroes, not only among computer devotees but among a wider national audience. Apple Computer, Steve Jobs and Steve Wozniak became household names. The favorable publicity was invaluable when Apple began to grow and needed additional engineers and technicians. The best and the brightest beat a path to Apple's door, lured by the living legend of the "two Steves."

The publicity was not easy to get and was the result of planning and hard work by the McKenna Agency and Mike Markkula. McKenna's philosophy about company publicity did not revolve around news releases, which had a better chance of going into an editor's wastebasket than into print. He encouraged all of his clients to build personal relationships, believing that a journalist would remember them and be more amenable to printing future public information releases. One year, Jobs and Markkula spent weeks both on the West Coast and in New York visiting newspaper and magazine offices, lugging an Apple computer around to demonstrate its capabilities. That early publicity trek did little to gain Apple immediate media exposure, but it established relationships that were invaluable in the future.

Because of the constant flux in the personal computer market, the McKenna Agency, which had helped Wozniak and Jobs in their days in the garage, was reluctant to take Apple on as a fulltime client. There was doubt as to whether Apple would survive, and no one at the agency believed that Jobs or Markkula had the necessary marketing experience to make it succeed. A number of people at the McKenna Agency considered both of them "flakes." McKenna, however, believed in the computer Wozniak had created, and it was the product that finally convinced McKenna to accept Apple's business.

McKenna had protected himself in the days when Apple operated out of a garage by accepting a share of revenue for payment and not committing to further advertising until there were positive results. He hedged once again, after accepting Apple, by taking on another personal computer company called Video Brain. If one or the other failed, McKenna would still have his foot in the door of the emerging personal computer market. As it turned out, Video Brain was the company to go out of business.

In accepting Apple as a client, McKenna had to consider the possibility of being stuck with a big debt if the company flopped. Advertising agencies normally pay the cost of developing an advertisement, shell out the cost to the publication for printing it, then collect later from its client, adding on costs and a commission. That can run into thousands of dollars and McKenna worried about it. He wanted Apple to spend no more than $300,000 on advertising, while Markkula insisted on a budget of $600,000. Markkula wanted to present an image of Apple as a strong, vibrant company and was convinced that it would take a major advertising budget to do it. In the end, Markkula won out.

Apple's advertising was designed to position it as a personal computer that was not only fun, but practical. Apple II's first advertisement capitalized on that by depicting a domestic scene. A wife worked at the kitchen while a husband sat at an Apple computer placed on the kitchen table. The text read in part: "The home computer that's ready to work, play and grow with you . . . You'll be able to organize, index and store data on household finances, income taxes, recipes, your biorhythms, balance your checking account, even control your home environment." Aware of the computer hobbyist market, the advertisement also listed some of the Apple II's technical aspects.

Apple also displayed marketing sophistication in the publications where the advertisements appeared. It advertised in technical publications but, more importantly, the Apple advertisements were also placed in *Playboy*. Other personal computer companies had not advertised in the popular press, and Apple's bold stroke helped establish Apple as a computer that would be fun and useful to people who had little or no technical inclinations. Smaller advertisements attempted to create an image of the company rather than the computer. The copy on one read: "A is for Apple. It's the first thing you should know about personal computers."

The message that came across in Apple advertising caused some concern among the users. With the personal computer market expanding, a group of other new industries was being created, now called the personal computer infrastructure. A computer by itself is almost useless. It needs software, the intelligence fed into a computer, to tell it what to do. This software ranges from games to complicated graphics today, but in the late 1970s the availability of software was meager, at best. The Apple advertisements led some people to believe that software could be purchased or that it could easily be programmed. This was not the case at all. Software was scarce and programming was something that only the most avid computer devotees could accomplish. In late 1977, a representative of Digital Research, who had criticized Apple earlier, wrote to Apple:

"From our earlier discussions I believe you want to address the consumer market . . . The Apple advertising is somewhat misleading . . . The Apple II is not a consumer computer and, even though I have had 'previous computer experience,' I had some difficulties getting parts together, and making the system operate. . . . Further, commercial appliance and manufacturers do not advertise products which do not exist . . . Your advertisement implies that software exists (or is readily constructed) for stock market analysis and home finance handling. Do these programs exist? Secondly, a floppy disk subsystem is promised by the 'end of 1977.' Where is it?"

The personal computer infrastructure, which includes software companies, was just starting. There was no need for it, obviously, until the personal computer became popular in homes and in the office. Because of Steve Jobs's decision to keep the Apple computers secret, and to insist on systems that accepted no peripherals that were not created by Apple, this early complaint was a harbinger of a controversy that would eventually contribute to his downfall.

CHAPTER 11

The Enfant Terrible

Apple Computer's internal structure was designed by Mike Markkula to be similar to that of Hewlett-Packard. H-P was a company that offered key employees stock options and created an atmosphere at work where people felt useful and happy with themselves and what they were doing. Hewlett-Packard lavished praise upon employees who were doing a good job and made the work force feel as if each individual was a key element in the company's success. Employees were stroked so much that they purred like kittens and, consequently, Hewlett-Packard workers didn't look upon work as merely a necessary means to economic survival. Rather, the company was an integral and satisfying part of their life experience.

Jobs would later claim credit for creating the same "corporate culture" at Apple, but his actions seem to indicate otherwise. On the one hand, he would take long walks with employees early in the morning or late at night, talking about his hopes and dreams for Apple. He would tell them how much he cared about the employees. In reality, Apple never was a comfortable place to work, in spite of Mike Markkula's efforts to make it so. The major reason was Steve Jobs.

Not long after Apple moved from a garage into a two-story building in Cupertino, Jobs became unpredictable. He was often tyrannical, sometimes praising, but always mercurial. Part of the reason may have been that he had been accustomed to having his own way and, with the strong-willed Scott at the helm, Jobs no longer had total freedom.

Jef Raskin joined the company while it was still in its infancy. Raskin was a modern day Renaissance man who had written music and conducted several musical companies, in addition to having experience in computers. He joined the company in 1977 and, because he had considerable knowledge about computers, he said that Jobs befriended him. "In the early days of the company, we would take long walks together and he would tell me about his problems and try to use me as a confidant and counselor." Raskin said. "We were sort of friends, and he had all of these big ideas and dreams about how a company should work, and wanted to know how I thought it should work. He wanted to talk about his love life, which seemed to be pretty terrible, and I tried to discourage him from confiding his personal problems to me because I didn't want to get involved."

Raskin had approached Apple in the hope of becoming a consultant because he didn't want to be involved in what was starting to become a corporate bureaucracy. "I didn't want to join the company as an employee because I've always been an independent sort and working at a company didn't appeal to me," Raskin said. "Steve kept making more and more offers and finally offered me I don't know how many thousands of shares of stock. So I finally agreed and bargained myself into a tolerable good stock position."

Raskin was one of the people Jobs desperately wanted and he used charm and wit, along with promises of wealth, to lure Raskin to Apple. The two men started off being friendly, but they parted as bitter enemies, with Raskin feeling that Jobs had stabbed him in the back. "He was a megalomaniac," Raskin said. "He had to know more than anybody. What he was good at was initially charming people and getting them excited. But you never knew what to expect of him from one minute to the next."

Other eager employees who were interviewed by Jobs did not have it as easy as Raskin. Often, Jobs would throw his dirty bare feet up on a table and attack them mercilessly. Sometimes he would interview them at lunch, usually at The Good Earth Restaurant, not far from Apple's headquarters. On more than one occasion he made interviewees feel uncomfortable because of his behavior.

"He would take one look at the food, then look at the waitress and say, 'This is garbage. Take it back.'," said Trip Hawkins, an early Apple employee. "He could shatter people. Most people came away from their first meeting with Steve completely blown away."

Raskin said that Jobs, who still didn't have a clearly defined job at Apple, alienated people with his overbearing attitude. "He would try to push himself into everything," said Raskin. "No matter what you were doing, he had to have something to do with it. Nobody at Apple wanted him involved with their projects. I had started the Macintosh team and we didn't want him either."

Bana Witt, who was Apple's software librarian, said that her relatively low position in the corporate hierarchy was no haven from Jobs's attacks. "He could reduce me to tears in a minute," she said. "He would walk up to my desk, stare at me and ask, 'What do you do here?' I would tell him that I was the software librarian, and he would give that cold look and say 'What the hell is a software librarian? Is it important? Do you know what in hell you're doing?' He was so used to having his own way that he didn't care about how other people felt. When he was charming, he was *so* charming and when he was crazy, he was really terrible."

"He was exceptionally immature for his age," Witt said. "He can be really sadistic and, if he feels the least bit threatened at all, he's so smart that he can turn the tables on anyone. What he does then is attack, attack, attack. I don't think Steve is wicked, like a lot of people do who considered him the *enfant terrible.* I just think he's spoiled. His parents worshipped him and

119

would let him get away with anything. He was their golden boy."

Witt joined Apple in 1978 and saw Jobs in wild mood swings that he did little or nothing to conceal. His fights with Michael Scott are still legendary. "They would constantly scream at each other," Witt said. "You could hear them yelling from one end of the room to the other. They had these really horrendous, childish fights. It was just awful."

Even when he met employees outside of the company, Jobs could have a devastating impact on them. He ruined a Christmas party for Witt with a single observation. "I had married [Bruce Tognazzini, a senior programmer] and become an Apple wife, so I was a little higher up in the echelon," she said. "I had just bought this beautiful new fox coat and wore it to the party. Steve looked at me with disgust and said, 'Well, how many foxes died for that coat?' I just laughed, but it cut me to the quick. Why would he have to say a thing like that? What made it worse was that part of me felt that he was right."

At the other extreme, Jobs had the ability to charm people. He was viewed wihin Apple as a consummate corporate politician. He had proven his persuasive powers time and again when Apple was working in a garage and he scrambled for parts, credit, and investors. Once Apple moved out of the garage and became a company, Wozniak noticed a change in him.

"You couldn't believe anything the guy said," Wozniak remembers. "He would say one thing and do another. He was also very political and would talk in such political terms that you never knew for certain what he was thinking. You could listen to him and it would mean one thing to me and another thing to somebody else. Steve will use anybody to his own advantage. He wasn't like that in the early days."

Witt blames Jobs's temper tantrums and personal attacks on his own self-doubts. "I think he's very insecure," she said. "He also had an uncanny ability to look at people and spot their weaknesses. He would zero right in on that."

Jobs quickly gained a reputation among Apple employees as a person who couldn't be relied upon for consistency from one day to the next. "He would walk by somebody's desk, look at

what they were working on, and say 'This is a piece of shit,'"
said one employee. "The next day he would walk by the same
desk and say, 'This is great!' The terrible thing about it all was
that he was saying it about the same thing."

Bruce Tognazzini was often at odds with Jobs, as was almost
everyone. "He would demoralize Bruce by telling him that his
work was shit," Witt said. "He had been working on a program
for a year and Steve would shoot him down. He did that to
everybody. Bruce would just come home and cry after his fights
with Steve. They were at war. When Steve took over the Macintosh Division, he tried to get Bruce to come and work for him,
but Bruce refused. He didn't want anything to do with Steve
Jobs. Steve really liked to exercise his power."

Raskin said that the stories circulating about Jobs running
roughshod over people "are all true, unfortunately. He has never
put himself in anybody else's shoes. He acted as if everybody else
was irrelevant except to achieve his ends." An analyst who has
followed Apple for years also spoke of Jobs's singlemindedness:
"He ruled by intimidation but, at the same time, he demanded
absolute loyalty, even to the exclusion of your family."

Raskin agreed with Wozniak's observation that one could
never tell what Jobs was going to do, regardless of what he said.
As an example, Raskin tells the story about "The Pipe Organ
Incident," which is now legendary at Apple.

"I always loved pipe organs and decided to buy one," Raskin
said. "I didn't have a house big enough to put one in, but I had
a chance to buy and rebuild an old one. It cost about fifteen thousand dollars and that was before any of us at Apple had much
money. We had a building with a huge room, so I said to Steve,
'Let's set it up here and we'll control it with an Apple. It would
be a great demonstration.' Steve said 'Great!' That was before he
began to change and I didn't realize that, if you didn't get something in writing, what he said didn't count."

"I made plans to get the organ, then went out and bought
it," Raskin continued. "When the truck arrived to deliver it,
Steve said, 'No, you can't put it here. I changed my mind.' I said,
'Well, okay, but I think Apple should at least help pay for the
storage charges until I find a place to put it.' Steve said, 'No way.

I never agreed to anything like that. I never agreed to have a pipe organ put in.' The amazing thing about it is that he said it in front of my father and other people who worked at Apple. They told him they had heard him promise, but he said, 'No, I didn't' and that was it. So I ended up having to sell it and losing about twelve thousand dollars."

Raskin and Jobs had continuing disagreements, culminating in Raskin quitting in disgust after Jobs took over a project that Raskin had conceived. This eventually resulted in a bitter split within the company that Jobs consciously nursed along.

Trip Hawkins said that working with Jobs in the beginning was a "fabulous" experience. "Most of us who were attracted to the company at that time were delighted to have an opportunity to develop such an exciting market with such an exciting product," he said. "There were some really bright people there with a lot of vision and creative approaches to business."

"Steve can be a very charismatic person," Hawkins said, "but he's extremely ambitious, almost to the point of megalomania. He's such a perfectionist that people can never please him, and that caused a lot of trouble with morale. He doesn't have much tolerance and he's very judgmental about people. He would make snap decisions about people. If he thought you were smart and that he could learn something from you, he'd put you on a pedestal. But most people weren't good enough for him and would really be in a state of shock after encounters with Steve."

Hawkins once asked Jobs why he would verbally assault people, particularly those interviewing for work. "He said, 'If they can't stand up to me man to man, I don't want them.' I think it was kind of a test he put people through. I think some of it was deliberately calculated, but for the most part, I think that's just the way he was. He rubbed almost everybody the wrong way." Jobs seemed to be aware of the effect he had on people. In fact, during meetings, he sometimes mentioned his lack of popularity in an almost self-deprecating way.

Hawkins said that Jobs's volatile personality was always at its worst when he had to deal with Michael Scott. No one in the company escaped the consequences of "The Scotty Wars." They would scream at each other so much, Hawkins said, that all of the employees would be terrified.

"Scotty had a tyrannical side," Hawkins said. "There were situations where Steve would come up with a really crazy idea. His style of trying to get what he wanted rubbed Scotty the wrong way. Steve would yell and scream, rant and rave, and try to intimidate people. He would just try to overpower them by talking fast and out-flanking them. Scotty wouldn't have anything to do with that."

Jobs also acquired a reputation among the company's vendors and distributors for making unreasonable demands. "If we weren't selling enough computers, he'd threaten to pull them out," one dealer said. "If we sold a competing product, he'd say we had to get rid of it or we couldn't handle Apple."

Apple relied on a number of third party companies to create the electronics components and hardware that went into making its computers. Most people, inside and outside of Apple, believed that Jobs was often irrational. "He would get on the telephone and rant and rave at them," one former Apple employee said. "He would be insulting. He gained a reputation for being arrogant and tyrannical."

Michael Scott was so disgusted with Jobs that, when Jobs had his twenty-third birthday, Scott sent him a funeral wreath decorated with white roses and a card that read: R.I.P. Scott was so pleased with what he had done that white roses became his personal trademark. When Apple became more successful and started having large parties, he would have a white rose for each woman who attended.

In 1979, when Apple was the leading personal computer company in the world and on the verge of going public, Judy Smith, Jobs's old girlfriend, sued him for child support for her daughter, Lisa. Jobs denied that he was the father and would have nothing to do with it. At the time, Apple was conducting a drive for the United Way to sponsor a disabled child.

"They were really putting the pressure on us to give," Hawkins said. "We were supposed to support this disabled child in a wheelchair. One day a poster of a baby in a wheelchair appeared in the office, reading 'Hi. My name is Lisa and I can't even get child support.' Jobs saw it and tore it down, but the next day, posters were plastered all over the place."

But if Jobs had his dark side, he also had a gentler nature. "He's like most creative people," said Raskin. "He has lots of ideas, and some of them aren't any good, but a lot of them are. He could charm the pants off of anyone. The only trouble was he could be Mr. Lovey-Dovey one minute and a screaming maniac the next."

Bana Witt, who had been the victim of Jobs's verbal onslaughts on more than one occasion, also found that he could make her feel like a queen. "We were at this party one time and, for some reason, he lavished attention on me," she said. "He had the ability to make you feel like you were the most important person in the world. He also had a sweet side, the hippie part of him who had gone to India soul-searching, and he brought a lot of that sweetness with him. One time he had an old friend visit Apple who played sitar, and he followed Steve around the company all day playing music. In spite of everything, I still like Steve."

When Bruce Tognazzini was stricken with cancer, Jobs paid for him to have a private room and paid all of the medical expenses. He visited Tognazzini every day that he was in the hospital and made certain he had everything he wanted. Jobs arranged for Tognazzini to have a private nurse and told the people in the hospital to treat him like a super star. "It was incredible how Steve was so supportive of him and me when he was sick," said Witt, who was married to Tognazzini at the time. "I was so touched. I just couldn't believe anybody could be so nice."

After Judy Smith left Jobs, in a huff and pregnant, Jobs met another woman who won his heart, at least for a few years, by greeting him with rudeness. Frances Nelson, who was half Asiatic and half Anglo-Saxon, was a beautiful young woman who worked at the McKenna Agency. "She was the most beautiful and intelligent woman I've ever met," said Witt. "She was just startling."

"When Frances joined the McKenna Agency, people kept saying to her, 'You've got to meet Steve Jobs! You've got to meet Steve Jobs!' They were just dying to have the two of them get together. Frances finally went to his office, stared him coldly in the eye, put a hand on her hip and said, 'So you're Steve Jobs.' She wasn't impressed. She was kind of disdainful. Steve ate it up and they ended up falling in love and living together. She used to love to tell me how rude she was to him. I guess the fact that she wasn't impressed got his interest."

Jobs and Nelson lived together after Apple started to make money. He bought a beautiful home in Los Altos, but furnished it very sparsely. "He couldn't make up his mind to buy furniture," Witt said. "Whenever people came over for dinner, they had to borrow chairs from the neighbors. They had this beautiful home and it was almost empty. But Steve had his lighter side. We were eating dinner there one time and, suddenly, Steve stuck a piece of cauliflower in his ear and started making funny faces and noises. It was so out of character that we all cracked up."

Nelson lived with Jobs for several years, but the relationship eventually broke up. "I could tell some really juicy stories about Steve and Frances," Witt said. "But I think that's all kind of private. They really had their problems because they both had dark sides. When she left Steve and went to work at Stanford, Frances was anorexic."

Jobs worked for several years in torn blue jeans and sandals, or else went barefoot, in spite of Markkula's efforts to encourage him to dress better. "He started going to a fancy men's store in San Francisco and buying clothes," Witt said. "The store was meticulous. They tailored everything, but all of Steve's clothes were too long in the arms and legs. It drove me nuts. I asked Frances why he dressed like that and she said, 'He demands that his clothes are too long.' I can't believe the tailors would let him go out looking like that, but he was so combative about everything that he probably *forced* the tailors to do it his way. He likes to exercise power at *any* level."

By 1979, Apple was working on several different products and Michael Scott, backed by the company's executive board, decided to create divisions within the company. Jobs was not included among the new divisional managers. He was furious and hurt.

"I don't know why I can't be a manager," Jobs said to Scott.

"Steve, you don't have the experience or the temperament," Scott replied. "Besides we need you to help with the public offering."

Stung, Jobs angrily left the building with an employee for one of the inevitable long, soothing walks. "He was really hurt and angry," said an Apple insider. "He felt like Scott, Markkula, and the whole board had stabbed him in the back."

There was no way Apple's board could have realized it at the time but, by making Jobs essentially a man without a company, it had set the stage for a future power play that would split the company in half, result in a threat of mass resignations, and create a situation where Apple lost the good faith of the all-important personal computer infrastructure, which had become a multi-billion dollar business. At the root of all this would be the unyielding iron will of Steven Jobs.

CHAPTER 12

Instant "Zillionaires"

There had never been any question that Apple would eventually become a public company. Markkula had quietly set the stage by wooing investors whose financial stake in Apple was guaranteed to have other money men frothing at the mouth. Key employees at Apple had been lured to the company partly because they were offered stock options that could eventually make them rich. It was the dream of every new "techie" in Silicon Valley to get a job with a start-up and get rich overnight when the company succeeded.

There was a great deal of discussion at Apple about who received what in terms of shares. As the dream of going public grew closer to becoming a reality, there was a mad scramble among employees to get stock. One engineer was reputed to have mortgaged his house so he could invest in Apple. Some people who had been given shares were envious of those who had more than they did and, those who had none were boiling angry. There was considerable hostility within the ranks.

When Apple first started operations as a company, stock options were sometimes given instead of salary increases, causing considerable grumbling among some employees. Their attitudes changed drastically because, by 1979, the stock had split three times. These who kept "founder's shares" had an opportunity to make a killing. Anyone who owned 1,420 shares in Apple was worth 1 million dollars after the company went public in December 1980.

Stock options were used as bait to attract the best employees. More seasoned employees, who had been around long enough to know about riches that had come to others in Silicon Valley, bargained hard to get as many options as they could. Others who were less worldly insisted on higher salaries, innocently unaware of the intrinsic value of the stock option opportunity. Apple's executives were given opportunities to buy stock but hourly employees were shut out. This created rancor, especially in the technical departments where engineers held stock, while technicians who worked alongside them, did not.

Dan Kottke, once a good friend of Jobs's who had made the trip to India with him, was one of Apple's first employees, but received no stock because he was a technician. Jobs didn't care. Wozniak believed this was unfair, because Kottke had been with the company so long, and told Jobs he would match any stock Jobs gave to Kottke with an equal amount. Jobs replied, "Great! I'll give him zero."

Elmer Baum, whose father had loaned Jobs and Wozniak money when they were about to go bust during their garage days, was rudely turned away when he wanted to buy shares in Apple.

Employees at Apple took delight in revealing how much stock they owned, causing waves of discontent throughout the company. Bill Fernandez claimed there was no rhyme or reason to the way shares were distributed. Some senior people who joined Apple were furious to learn that many of their subordinates owned more stock than they did.

It was frequently much easier for well-connected people outside of Apple to invest in the company than it was for employees. The money men, who often tipped each other off about good investments, spread the word among themselves about Apple, and venture capitalists were able to make significant buys. All of this did nothing to dampen the flames of resentment among Apple employees who wanted to buy shares but could not.

Apple shares were selling for $10.50 each in the middle of 1979. Apple raised more than 7 million dollars by selling shares to sixteen venture capital firms. Jobs and Markkula both sold one million dollars in shares and Wozniak sold stock to three well-connected friends. The largest buyer was Fayez Sarofim, a friend of Arthur Rock, who purchased 128,600 shares. Dan Valentine bucked the trend of accumulating Apple stock and sold all of his shares for what he said were tax reasons.

Not all of Apple's managers were keen on the idea of its becoming a public company. Jobs was afraid of losing power and having to answer to stockholders; Scott shared the same sentiments. From the beginning, Scott had wanted to manage a large, private company and was dismayed at all of the legal requirements that were necessary when the decision was made to take Apple public at a board meeting in August 1980. A frantic scramble began to prepare the reams of reports necessary to meet the requirements of the Securities Exchange Commission and other regulatory agencies. Regis McKenna cancelled an Apple advertisement in *The Wall Street Journal,* fearing that it might violate SEC regulations.

In 1980, Apple dominated the personal computer market, which was growing by leaps and bounds. It had sold some 170,000 computers during its short life and the future looked even brighter. Because of its leadership in the market and the sheen that widely respected venture capitalists had brought to the company, the public offering promised to be one of the most spectacular in history. Underwriters courted Apple for an opportunity to handle the offering because of the huge commissions that were anticipated. Apple finally decided on two underwriters, one from each coast. Hambrech and Quist of San Francisco was selected on the West Coast, while the plum on the East Coast was plucked by Morgan Stanley. Morgan Stanley's underwriting of Apple marked a major shift in priorities for that company. The firm dropped its association with IBM, long established as a business leader, signaling new emphasis in the world of personal computers.

Both Scott and Jobs disdained the underwriters, but Scott was almost obsessive about it. Once he showed up at a meeting wearing jeans and a cowboy hat. At another meeting, he and two other Apple managers wore baseball hats, black armbands (to signify mourning) and T-shirts stenciled THE APPLE GANG. The financiers had to stretch their imaginations to envision Scott as the president of Apple.

Apple experienced the slings and arrows of all exciting new companies that plan to go public. Although law prohibited Apple from publicizing itself during the time it announced its intention to make a public offering, the press did its own work. Apple had assiduously courted the press in the past, and the story of "The Two Steves" had made the company appear very special. Journalists wrote their own stories about the public offering and speculated on how spectacular it would be. People with newsletters offering investment information mentioned Apple and urged people to buy shares, if they could. *The Wall Street Journal* reported: "Every speculator in hot issues wants a bite of Apple—Apple Computer, Inc.—but most will be lucky to get even a bit." The company received an avalanche of letters from people asking where and when to buy stock and the telephones rang constantly in Apple's Cupertino offices.

Potential investors smelled money and went into a frenzy. Old friends of Apple employees suddenly made appearances after having disappeared for months or years. Major investors were chomping at the bit to buy Apple stock, including the Hewlett-Packard pension fund—which boosted the prestige of Apple even more.

The intense interest in Apple stock fanned the smouldering resentments among the company's employees. Wozniak saw what he thought were inequities and tried to correct as many of them as he could. He created the Wozplan, where by employees he thought deserved stock could buy some of his shares. Wozniak sold the shares for $7.50 each, three dollars below the 1979 value. Some 36 people quickly snapped up the 80,000 shares that

Wozniak decided to sell. The buyers were questioned by the California Commission of Corporations, which feared insider trading, about their stock purchases, but all were able to give the Commission satisfactory answers. Wozniak also unloaded 25,000 shares, at a bargain price, to the owner of a racquet club where Apple had a corporate membership.

Jobs watched all of this with bemusement and concluded that Wozniak gave stock to the wrong people. "Woz just couldn't say no," Jobs said. "A lot of people took advantage of him."

Jobs, on the other hand, was hanging on to as much of his own stock as he could. What he released, he sold at top dollar. The stark contrast between Wozniak's generosity and Jobs's tight-fistedness did not go unnoticed among employees at Apple.

"All along, Steve Jobs had been talking about such high ideals for Apple," said Trip Hawkins. "He talked about being generous and fair to employees and creating an atmosphere where they could share in the company's success. But in the end, it was Woz, not Jobs, who put that into practice. It really elevated Woz in my estimation and it made Steve look pretty bad."

When Wozniak had gotten divorced, he had gone to Mike Markkula for advice and, although he resented giving his former wife Apple stock, he had followed Markkula's suggestion and given her several thousand shares in the settlement. During the time Apple was getting ready to go public, Jobs's old girlfriend, Judy Smith, filed a paternity suit against Jobs for the support of her daughter, Lisa. Jobs denied all responsibility of parenthood. Jobs had met with Smith shortly after the child was born and helped select the name "Lisa," even though he refused to admit that he was the father.

Smith had held a variety of menial jobs to support herself and her baby since she had left Jobs. The suit she filed asked for a twenty thousand dollar settlement. Jobs, like Wozniak, went to Markkula for advice, but was aghast at what Markkula said. Markkula suggested that Jobs up the ante to eighty thousand dollars to be fair to both Smith and the baby. Jobs refused and even stopped making the meager child support payments that he sent voluntarily. Whenever Smith threatened to get a lawyer involved, Jobs would once more start sending money for Lisa's upkeep.

Jobs, to the amazement of many people, finally agreed to have a blood test to settle, once and for all, the question of paternity. The test was conducted at the University of California and the result did not please Jobs. The university reported that the probability of Jobs being Lisa's father was 94.4 percent. Jobs saw it differently, and angrily announced that all the test proved was that nearly seven percent of the men in the United States could be Lisa's father. Jobs finally agreed to a court-ordered settlement, but says he gave in only because he was under such a strain. Considering the stock Jobs held in Apple, and what it would be worth within a month, his settlement with Smith was meager. He agreed to pay $385 a month in child support, provide health insurance for Lisa, and to reimburse public assistance for the baby in the amount of $5,856.

One of Apple's computers is named Lisa but, contrary to popular belief within Apple, it was not named after Judy Smith's daughter. "We named it after the daughter of one of our software managers," Wozniak said.

Meanwhile, the Apple juggernaut continued to roll and the price of the stock climbed. People took bets on how high it would eventually go. The price of the stock increased so rapidly that the state of Massachusetts temporarily stopped people from buying it. Apple had done nothing wrong, but speculation on the stock had pushed its price over the company's required book value. In August, when the company announced it was going public, stock sold for a little more than five dollars. The stock was selling for twenty-two dollars per share the morning of December 12, the day the company actually went public, but that was still not the peak. Before trading closed on the first day, the stock had risen to twenty-nine dollars per share.

There was little else going on at Apple on December 12, 1980 except the frenzied excitement of watching the performance of the company's stock. Computers in the Cupertino offices were connected to the Dow Jones ticker and people whooped and cheered with excitement as the stock performed beyond all expectations. Some of the excited Apple managers wanted to erect a giant thermometer outside to show the world Apple's astounding success. And it was an incredible success. Apple's stock offering was by far the most successful public offering since Ford Motor Company went public in 1956. By the end of the day's trading, Apple had reaped $82.8 million from the public offering. The company reached the list of the Fortune 500 faster than any company in history. The stock market placed the value of Apple at $1.778 billion, which was larger than Ford Motor Company, four times more than Lockheed, and twice the combined value of United Airlines, American Airlines, and Pan American World Airways.

Robert Noyce, no stranger to instant success, was startled when he attended an Apple celebration party and noticed that everyone in the room was at least a millionaire. He felt as if the world had shifted. Markkula's Apple stock was worth $239 million. Wozniak had stock valued at $135.6 million. Scott's tally was $95.5 million. Wozniak's former wife, who had been given Apple shares in the divorce settlement, held stock worth $42 million. Steve Jobs, the largest stockholder with 15 percent of the outstanding shares, was worth $256.4 million. He was twenty-five years old.

The instant riches brought about radical changes in the way most of the new millionaires lived. For one thing, they discovered that they couldn't sell their stock immediately because of legal requirements. But that did not prevent them from borrowing against it. Some did that and started to live the ostentatious kind of life so prevalent among Silicon Valley's nouveau riche. They built fancy houses and bought exquisite automobiles. Others worried because the local newspaper had printed a list of how much their shares were worth and built fences around their homes, installed elaborate alarm systems, and hired security guards.

Markkula bought a used Learjet, repainted it, and decorated it with the Apple logo and skittered from continent to continent in luxury while listening to music on an expensive stereo system he had installed. Others held on to their options, then sold them at an opportune time and retired in their twenties or thirties. Those who sold their stock found themselves under attack by

Jobs, who considered it an act of disloyalty. One of those he accosted was Jef Raskin, who had been bullied by Jobs for almost a year, and knew he would probably leave the company. When Jobs accused him of being disloyal, Raskin replied, "I found myself looking at the stock market pages every day to find out how I was doing. I didn't want my life to revolve around the stock market, so I sold."

Jobs did not change his lifestyle radically, in spite of becoming a multi-millionaire overnight. He had thought about buying the Learjet with Markkula, but decided that it was too ostentatious. His money, however, brought an avalanche of invitations to social events, and streams of charities hounded him. One thing that changed was his wardrobe: in the past, he had worn jeans and sandals, but his wealth turned him toward tailored suits. He had a house built in Los Gatos and drove the contractors to distraction with his demands for perfection. When his latest girlfriend moved out, he remained there, living almost like a monk. He had never been able to make up his mind about what kind of furniture to buy and his luxurious home remained sparsely furnished. The beat-up automobiles that Jobs had driven over the years were replaced with a Mercedes. He bought a motorcycle and engaged in the dangerous hobby of riding it along winding mountain roads when he could find the time.

The millions of dollars did not bring him happiness, however. Instead, he fretted over whether or not he would be able to live up to the expectations he thought people would have of him. At Apple, his personality began to change. "He would spend hours, sometimes staying up all night, figuring out how he was going to present something," Wozniak said. "He would talk at a very high, political level, so that you never could pin him down. He liked to give the impression that he was always a very sophisticated executive, but that wasn't the case. He started to change in 1980."

Wozniak's millions did not change him, but allowed him to engage in the pursuit of happiness as he never had before. He spent money lavishly. He had never been careful with money, and having millions of dollars made no dent in the haphazard way he dealt with finances. The kind-hearted Wozniak remained approachable and was an easy mark for anyone with a sob story.

Wozniak was generous with his family and friends, as well. He gave his parents and siblings four million dollars in stock and doled out another two million dollars worth to various friends. Wozniak bought a Porsche for himself and once his father found uncashed checks totaling $250,000 inside the car. Wozniak bought a theater in San Jose, and had the money to engage in his long-held desire to become a pilot. He received his license, bought an airplane, and crashed during take-off, receiving only minor injuries. Undeterred, he promptly bought himself another aircraft.

Apple's rise had been meteoric, even by Silicon Valley standards. It started as a garage business in 1976, with assets under six thousand dollars. When the company was formed, it was valued at three million dollars. By September 1980, three and a half years after the Apple II was introduced, revenues rose from $7.8 million to $117.9 million and profits increased from $793,497 to $11.7 million. There were more than a thousand employees on Apple's payroll.

In 1980, Apple dominated the personal computer market, but the phenomenal success of the stock offering did nothing to quell the internal strife within the company. Apple was split in half, Jobs became even more dictatorial, and a tyrannical streak emerged in Scott. Apple, having gone public, began to have problems recruiting top-notch engineers because the chance of getting in on a big score with a start-up was gone. Apple had become a major success, zooming upward in the financial heavens like a rocket. It was a temporary trip to paradise, because the company's problems were just starting.

CHAPTER 13

Problems

In 1979, Jef Raskin had a brilliant idea for a new computer that was radically different from anything that Apple, or any other personal computer company, was manufacturing. He called it the Macintosh and it was to be targeted toward business users. The Macintosh, when developed, would have increased power and use an instrument called a "mouse" to make it easier to operate. With the mouse, a user simply had to point at data and the information would be recorded on the computer and appear on the video screen.

"Jobs hated the idea," Raskin said. "He ran around saying, 'No! No! It'll never work.' He was one of the Macintosh's hardest critics and he was always putting it down at board meetings. When he became convinced that it *would* work, and that it would be an exciting new product, he started to take over."

After Apple organized into divisions in 1979, Jobs was left with no operational role, a situation that rankled him. He held the title of vice president for new products and, in that capacity, flitted in and out of the different divisions, criticizing and cajoling. Jobs had always been hard to get along with, but some people say he became even tougher because he felt that Scott and the executive board had demeaned him. He desperately wanted a role in operations. He tried to use his influence to become involved with the development of the Lisa computer, but was told in no uncertain terms that he wasn't wanted. With nothing else to do, he became a corporate gadfly, zooming in and out of various divisions and generally making people uncomfortable.

"No one appreciated him at any level," Wozniak said.

Raskin had convinced the executive board that the Macintosh was at least worth pursuing, in spite of Steve Jobs's opposition. Raskin had been authorized to start working on the Macintosh and was given a handful of engineers and technicians to help. Raskin had written a four hundred-page document, giving detailed descriptions of what the Macintosh should be. As time went by, it became more apparent that the Macintosh could be something special. Steve Jobs, at that point, stopped his naysaying and moved in. He saw an opportunity to become involved in operations, even though the Mac group was small.

"He was dead set against the Macintosh for the first two years," Raskin says. "He said it was the dumbest thing on earth and that it would never sell. When he decided to take it over, he told everybody that he had invented it."

Not only was Jobs unwelcome in Apple's other divisions, the people involved with the Macintosh tried to keep him out. "He was persona non grata in our group, too," Raskin says. "We didn't want him any more than anyone else did, but he had the power to muscle his way in. The way he did it was by presenting false information at executive staff meetings. He would say, 'Hey, this is a great idea, but it's a real disaster. I've made it into a great idea, but if you don't let me take it over it's going to collapse because Raskin doesn't know what he's doing.'"

Raskin had been one of the people with whom Jobs had spent hours talking about his hopes and dreams for Apple and his personal life. He had considered Jobs a friend and confidant before Jobs turned on him.

Raskin was no stranger to computer design. He had worked on Lisa, another powerful Apple computer, and influenced the way it functioned. "Lisa was originally started as a character generated machine, like the IBM PC," Raskin says. "I was the one who changed it to being a bit more graphic. I changed it singlehandedly to a graphics computer connected to a Xerox machine to make the print-outs. I was the one who put it all together, but Jobs told everyone that he had done it. It made me very annoyed because it took me two years to negotiate that deal with Xerox."

Raskin created the concept of Macintosh because he believed that the Apple II, which had achieved such success, still bewildered a lot of people unless they were computer devotees. His idea was to create a computer that would require no great expertise. The Macintosh Raskin envisioned would not require hours of learning commands to make the computer perform its assigned tasks. At first, he called it Everyman's Computer because it would be so easy to use.

Regis McKenna claimed that Raskin's computer would "never have seen the light of day" if it had not been for Steve Jobs. McKenna, an avid Jobs fan, admits that Jobs was "a man without a company" and was not welcome in Apple's other divisions and that he "jumped at the chance" to become involved in operations. The Macintosh group was small enough so that Jobs was able to convince Mike Markkula to let him run it, even though he was far from being a technical star, and had proved time and again that his management style was disastrous. Jobs's dictatorial management didn't change, but he was able to learn enough technology to get along by assaulting engineers with the vigor of a grand inquisitor.

"The standard way he operated was picking your brain," says Raskin. "He would immediately poo-poo the idea, then a week later, he'd come back and say, 'Hey, I've got a great idea!' The idea that he gave back to you was your own. We called him the Reality Distortion Field."

Jobs's takeover of the Macintosh group shows him as a consummate corporate gamester. Since 1980, he had been unofficially managing the division. Then one day in 1982, he walked over to Raskin and said, "Hey, I'm taking over the hardware."

"Fine," said Raskin.

A few weeks later, Jobs told Raskin, "I'm taking over documentation." Raskin, who had no choice, agreed.

Not long after that, Jobs approached Raskin again. "I'm taking over software," he said.

"Fine," Raskin replied. "I quit."

Raskin was ready to storm out the door, but Jobs, who had not anticipated this reaction, was alarmed. Raskin was too involved in Macintosh details for Jobs to lose immediately. Frantic, Jobs asked Raskin to stay a while longer. Raskin was unmoved by Jobs's pleas until Jobs brought in Markkula, Apple's peace maker. Raskin said he had been pushed around enough, but agreed to remain a month longer before leaving Apple. This was in 1983 and Macintosh had grown from a handful of people to become a full-fledged division with Steve Jobs in total command. There were six hundred people in the Macintosh division and Jobs was fond of telling them, "This is the cream of Apple. This is the future of Apple."

From the time Jobs took over Macintosh and made it into a division, there was a horrendous split in Apple. Regis McKenna and others say that Jobs, in effect, made Apple into two separate companies that were bitter rivals. Jobs made it no secret that he believed Macintosh was the best and brightest division in the company and he showed it in numerous ways. The Macintosh division had the best of everything: it had the biggest parties, highest salaries, and more stroking from Jobs than the other divisions. He was fond of saying that he had created a "metaphorical garage" where ideas would flow freely with the spirit of entrepreneurism in full bloom.

In reality, there was little spirit of the entrepreneur in Macintosh after Jobs began managing it. He ran it dictatorially, especially after he became a multi-millionaire in Apple's public stock offering in 1980. "The money turned Steve into kind of a monster," said Trip Hawkins. "He thought he was a little bit better than anyone who ever lived. He would engage in ferocious, dynamic interactions with bright people around him. He didn't have much technical training, but that was the way he learned. His success went to his head and he made people grovel around him."

Apple was struggling to find a way to market its products so that they would not cannibalize each other. Apple had the highly successful Apple II, the Lisa and the Macintosh under development, but it was essentially a one-product company. The Apple II contributed most of the computer's revenue, but Jobs hated the computer because he considered its design "inelegant." While other top Apple executives struggled to find distinct markets for each product to keep them from competing with each other, Jobs had no interest in finding market niches. Hawkins, who worked on both the Lisa and Macintosh said, "Steve's approach was that we should let the free market decide. He would go into the board meetings and say, 'Hey, let's just go out there and compete on the open market and, hopefully, we're going to blow your brains out.' Steve could get away with that because people like Mike Markkula, Henry Singleton, and Arthur Rock were his buddies and mentors. Steve had a very good rapport with the board of directors for a long time. But I think his ambition and competitive urges were sometimes at odds with what was really in the best interests of the company."

During development of the Macintosh, Jobs doused the entrepreneurial spirit he boasted about creating in his metaphorical garage. He would set timetables for certain projects, then, when they were finished, he would reject them. "It didn't matter what you brought in to him, he would reject it," says one engineer who worked on Macintosh. "After a while, we knew he was going to reject whatever we did, so we stopped paying attention to timetables." People at Apple called him The Rejector as well as the Reality Distortion Field.

People in the Macintosh division did nothing to help morale at Apple. They were puffed up with their importance and the fact that they were favorites of Steve Jobs. They would wander into the Apple III and Lisa divisions and openly scoff at the work that was being performed.

As the company grew and became more of a corporate bureaucracy, Jobs's inexperience in management created a host of other problems. He would leap-frog back and forth among various projects, dictating design, with little or no knowledge of whether or not the technology even existed to make his ideas work. Whenever engineers balked, he used Wozniak's name like a weapon. "I'll bring Woz in if you can't do it," he would threaten. His threats only worsened the morale problems of a company that was struggling mightily to bring out its first product, the Apple III, that was not almost exclusively a Wozniak design.

Hardly anything went right in the design and production of the Apple III, which was intended to bridge the gap between the Apple II and the forthcoming Lisa computer. Both Jobs and Apple, as a company, were flushed with the success of the Apple II and had unrealistic ideas for development of the Apple III. Wozniak had created the Apple II, but the Apple III was designed by committee. It was as if a host of mischievous gremlins had been loosed inside the company. There were miscommunications between marketing, engineering, and the all-important personal computer infrastructure. Jobs, having had no experience in building a computer, believed the Apple III could be developed more quickly than the computer Wozniak had designed in a garage.

Fear that the market for the Apple II would collapse at any moment prompted a frantic scramble to complete the Apple III. The marketing experts at Apple were constantly predicting doom and gloom for the Apple II. Pressure also mounted because the prospectus Apple included when it filed for a public stock offering promised delivery of an Apple III. Jobs added additional pressure to the production schedule by passing out posters that read: THE DECISION YOU'RE MAKING NOW HELPED SHIP 50,000 APPLE IIIS IN 1980.

There was little software for the Apple III. In fact, Apple's programmers didn't even see the computer until nine weeks before it was supposed to be shipped. The timetable was so tight that programming and operational manuals were reviewed by the various departments on the same day that the mechanicals were sent to the printer. The Apple III had been publicized as a computer that would use the same software as the Apple II, but the difference between the two machines left major gaps. Jobs was obsessed with secrecy and revealed as little as possible about the Apple III to outside software and hardware developers. This made it impossible for third parties to design computer enhancements and software that would provide the "intelligence" for the Apple III to perform a wide variety of functions.

Jobs's penchant for guarding computer development at Apple alienated the all-important computer infrastructure. The Apple II had been a novelty and newspapers, fascinated by this new area of computing, published stories by wide-eyed reporters about how it could be used. The computer was not just a video game; it was used by various small businesses around the country. The computer could handle anything from accounting problems to helping a dairy farmer run his operation more efficiently. But, before a computer can perform any of a wide variety of tasks, the software telling it how to operate must be available.

Another problem facing Apple was the number of copycat computers that were being manufactured. Many of them allowed for additional components to be added that expanded the basic computer's power and versatility. Jobs kept the Apple computers "closed geographical systems" that would not accept any outside peripherals. When you bought an Apple computer, you bought a machine with severe limitations.

"Jobs didn't care what the market wanted," said a computer analyst. "He thought he knew more than they did. He would just take what Apple developed and shove it down their throats."

The Apple III was introduced at the National Computer Conference in 1980 and, although Apple generated considerable hoopla, the company knew it had laid an expensive egg. When orders were taken, the manufacturing problems became an almost intolerable nightmare.

Jobs's insistence on elegance of design made it difficult to cram the working parts inside his approved casing. The company was also lax about testing components and completed units, with the result that some of the chips used in the computer failed after short use. So much attention had gone into an elegant appearance that electrical lines were crammed too closely together, causing short-outs. The engineers raised a howl about shipping the computer without new boards, but were overruled by the marketing department. The metal cases housing the computer were heavy and cumbersome, making it almost impossible for the assembly-line workers to handle them. Some of the screws that held the casing to the innards punctured cables on the inside of the machine. Apple found that, to seat the components properly, the computer had to be raised a few inches, then dropped. This method was later replaced by a system of pounding on the cases with rubber mallets. Wozniak was totally disgusted. "I strongly disagreed with the direction the company was taking relative to displacing the Apple II with the Apple III," he said. "I saw a lot of inside stuff that almost no one on the outside knew anything about. I thought it was very wrong. It was deceptive and misleading. I never spoke up, because I didn't want to be political, but you could always more or less assume what my position was."

Although sales of the Apple III reached one hundred million dollars by 1983, less than three years after its introduction, the marketplace considered it a loser. People who had used the Apple II expected at least the same quality of performance on the Apple III but never received it. The computer was not reliable and users could not find software. They were also angry because it was a closed system that could not be expanded with add-on components.

"Apple was getting a reputation as a company that couldn't meet its commitments," an analyst said. "It didn't deliver what it promised."

The Apple II remained the company's most important product, even though Jobs snubbed that department. "It was Mac this and Mac that," said Wozniak. The bitterness between the Apple II division and the Macintosh division grew even stronger as years passed. After it became a public company, Apple began using shareholder meetings as a forum to hype new products. These meetings resembled old time revivals where Jobs, playing the role of corporate evangelist, whipped the audience into frenzies of excitement. Key members of the Macintosh division were given front row seats while Apple II managers sometimes were seated in a separate room where they listened to Jobs promote the Macintosh through a speaker system.

"You never heard the Apple II mentioned," Wozniak says. "We were generating most of the company's revenue and the

Apple II was the best-selling computer in the world. All of us felt slighted."

Jobs's fanatical devotion to the Macintosh division almost resulted in a mass walk-out of Apple II employees. Wozniak relates the story: "You would go to shareholder meetings and hear the Macintosh pushed and pushed. You'd come away from a meeting with a whole different impression than what was reality in the company. It was a very phony treatment. I mentioned this to my family and some friends and, when they went to a shareholders meeting, they came back to me and said, 'Hey, you're right.' Some of the Apple employees saw a meeting one night on TV and, when I came to work the next morning, there were a bunch of people ready to resign. They had already typed out their resignation letters. I managed to talk them out of it."

Jobs had unrealistic expectations of the Macintosh from the time he took over the division. "He originally believed that the company could sell five million Macintoshes in the first two years," Hawkins said. "That's such a crazy number that it's ridiculous. No one has ever done that with any machine, and yet he would use that point to drive home his arguments." Not only did Jobs grossly overestimate prospective sales for the Macintosh, he was wrong about how much it would eventually cost a buyer.

"One time we had an argument about pricing," Hawkins said. "He thought the Macintosh could debut at $1,500. I said, 'Steve, your parts costs are way too high for the company to make a reasonable profit. You'll have to bring it out at $2,500.' Steve said, 'No, no. Our parts costs will be much lower than that because we're going to be buying parts by the millions.' That was preposterous, but he was basing that on his ludicrous projection of sales."

Jobs was not entirely to blame for his unrealistic expectations for the Macintosh computer. Regis McKenna held numerous strategy sessions with Jobs and other marketing people. These were brainstorming sessions to determine where the market would be for the Macintosh. Apple reached the decision that it would target a group of people it called "knowledge workers." A less flattering description used to delineate them was "spread sheet junkies." Apple believed there were twenty-five million knowledge workers in the United States who could benefit from using a Macintosh.

This is how Apple described this market: "Knowledge workers are professionally trained individuals who are paid to process information and ideas into plans, reports, analyses, memos, and budgets. They generally sit at desks. They generally do the same generic problem solving work irrespective of age, industry, company size, or geographic location. Some have limited computer experience—perhaps an introductory programming class in college—but most are computer naive. Their use of a personal computer will not be of the intense eight-hour-per-day keyboard variety. Rather they bounce from one activity to another; from meeting to phone call; from memo to budgets; from mail to meeting. Like the telephone, their personal computer must be extremely powerful yet extremely easy to use."

Apple believed that of the twenty-five million knowledge workers it targeted, five million were in small businesses that had less than five million dollars in annual sales. Five million others were seen to fill slots in *Fortune 2000* companies, with the remainder in medium-sized businesses, colleges and in homes. McKenna said that Apple thought it would be "relatively easy" to sell the Macintosh to the knowledge worker market.

Positioning the Macintosh so it wouldn't compete with the successful Apple II was another problem, not one that concerned Jobs or other division managers. Because of the rift in the company, the divisions were operated like separate kingdoms and divisional managers were more interested in competition than cooperation. The divisional managers refused to sit down with one another and resolve conflicts.

Apple's marketing department started talking about the Macintosh as an "appliance." McKenna and others at Apple had reservations about the description but, gradually, the concept jelled. Mike Murray, who was the marketing director for Macintosh, solidified the marketing stance in a memorandum: "Think of Mac as an appliance. A thing applied as a means to an end. Like a Cuisinart in the kitchen, one could live without a Macintosh on the desk. Yet the increased personal productivity combined with the opportunity for personal creative expression will hit hard at our customers' psychic drives. Perhaps only 15–20 percent of a person's working time will be spent using a Mac, but as with the Cuisinart, it will make all the difference in the world. Our customers will find it very difficult to return to the 'old way' of doing things. Macintosh will become an integral part of life at a desk. In fact we would like to see the day when a freshly hired product manager for a *Fortune 500* company walks up to his new desk and finds a telephone, a couple of pens, a tablet of paper, a company magazine, and a Mac."

As the debate went on about how to position the Macintosh, Apple was gaining a poor reputation in the market. Apple's early success not only affected Jobs, but the company as a whole. Managers began making what many of their vendors considered unreasonable demands. Michael Scott once sent a funeral wreath covered with white roses to a supplier, with a card that read: "Here's what I think about your ability to meet your commitments." The word most often associated with Apple before 1984 was "arrogant." Apple had always been hard on its vendors, but success made it become even tougher. Jobs told a meeting of Macintosh employees, "We're going to have to come down harder on our vendors." Apple was also a stern task master with its distributors, dictating what computers they could or couldn't sell if they wanted Apples on their shelves. Apple forced one distributor to change the name of his store before he could sell Apple products.

Apple was in disarray, a company divided against itself. Jobs had alienated most of the personal computer infrastructure and created deep divisions within the company. Soon after Apple's enormously successful stock offering, it was so flushed with success that it failed to recognize the importance of a new competitor in the personal computer market: IBM, the giant from Armonk, New York.

CHAPTER 14

"Welcome, IBM. Seriously"

In 1981, IBM announced that it was entering the personal computer market. The announcement should have sent shivers of fear through Apple, but it did not. IBM had a long, successful track record as a leader in high-technology office machines, a heritage that gave it instant credibility in the marketplace.

Rather than being intimidated, Apple looked at IBM with condescension and arrogance, much the way it looked at suppliers, retailers, and the personal computer infrastructure. Jobs placed a full page advertisement in *The Wall Street Journal* with the headline: "WELCOME IBM. SERIOUSLY." The advertisement was representative of the puffed up arrogance that Apple and Jobs wore like a panoply in the first blush of success. In 1980, Apple had 80 percent of the personal computer market in its pocket and company executives believed its position was impregnable.

They should have known better. Regis McKenna, who was Apple's marketing and public relations adviser, had told them repeatedly that the market's perception of a company was all-important. IBM had the leadership and track record to make its entry into the personal computer market instantly credible. IBM was immediately recognized as a leader, not because it had developed a personal computer, but because it was sheened with a patina of success and leadership accumulated through the years.

Although Jobs seriously underestimated the threat posed by IBM, other personal computer companies shivered in their shoes. They were intimidated because they realized the power of IBM. Their fears were soon justified when they began losing market share to Big Blue. Some personal computer companies were driven out of business. Apple, while it failed to recognize the threat posed by the giant company, soon found that it was in serious trouble.

But at the time IBM made its intentions known, Apple was surprisingly ignorant, which was no doubt the result of its almost instant success. Apple's complete advertisement read: "Welcome IBM. Seriously. Welcome to the most exciting and important marketplace since the computer revolution began 35 years ago. We look forward to responsible competition in the massive effort to distribute this American technology to the world."

Markkula, as well as Jobs, failed to see that IBM would be a formidable competitor. Markkula took an almost ho-hum attitude when asked about it by the press. He said IBM's entry into the market was nothing out of the ordinary and that Big Blue had no competitive edge. He said that Apple had been waiting for IBM to enter the market, but stated emphatically that, "We're the guys in the driver's seat." Markkula emphasized that Apple had the advantage in every area of personal computers: in software, in hardware, distribution, and market share. His most grievous underestimation of IBM was illustrated by his contention that IBM would have to do more reacting to Apple than acting, and that IBM had no idea about how to sell personal computers. Markkula added that "Nothing short of World War III is going to knock us out of the box." To which Jobs added, "We're going to out-market IBM. We've got our shit together."

Markkula's condescending thoughts about IBM were no doubt influenced by conventional business wisdom, which held that young companies could move more quickly than older, established corporations in creating new technology. What Markkula and Jobs failed to realize is that IBM was one of those stodgy old businesses that could adapt quickly to circumstances, and that it had the ability to give customers what they wanted.

IBM had an impressive record of success. When it first entered the mainframe computer field, it was insignificant compared to such giants as General Electric and RCA. Even smaller companies had an edge on IBM in the mainframe computer market. Yet IBM capitalized on its reputation as a leader in technology, with a reputation for outstanding marketing and service, and, by 1956, it had captured seventy-five percent of the market.

In not listening to what customers wanted and forcing them to accept what he thought was best for them, Jobs had created an untenable position for Apple, and IBM capitalized on it. The company sent some one thousand representatives into the field to find out what features customers wanted in a personal computer. IBM formed strategic alliances with third party companies to build peripherals for its computers so their power could be expanded. Having found out what the end user wanted, IBM set about the task of incorporating those features into its computers. The company gained immediate support of the infrastructure. IBM relied on its one thousand strong sales force to sell its products, but made arrangements with computer dealers and other retailers to sell its personal computers.

IBM's ability to produce a computer that met user needs startled new computer companies such as Apple. Apple had struggled for a long time to bring out the Apple III and, having completed it, had a computer that was a failure. IBM, seen as a lumbering, slow-moving giant, mobilized itself and created a computer, complete with software and, more importantly, able to accept add-on features, in just thirteen months.

For Apple's first three years, the personal computer had been seen as a machine that could stand alone, performing tasks that need not be communicated to other computers. But when IBM entered the market, personal computers were no longer viewed in such a simplistic light. Information managers became increasingly wary of letting department managers buy their own computers which could not communicate with a hodge-podge of other computers bought by other department heads.

When computers sold for $2,500, the problem was not so severe. But Apple's Lisa, which was not shipped on time, had the hefty price tag of about ten thousand dollars, and it could not communicate with other computers because of Jobs's insistence on it being a closed system. IBM computers, on the other hand, had the ability to "talk" with other computers and could readily accept peripherals to increase their power and capability. Apple's Lisa, on the other hand, had severe limitations, the worst being that it could not be connected to IBM personal computers. By 1983, the key words in the personal computer industry were "IBM compatible." Information managers balked at allowing unilateral decisions by department managers to spend ten thousand dollars on Apple's Lisa, especially when it had such limitations. They began to take control of purchasing personal computers.

Information managers might like the Lisa and commend Jobs for bucking the IBM trend, but when it came down to putting up their money, they opted for IBM. "No one ever got fired for buying an IBM product," an information manager said.

Apple also lost ground to IBM because it failed to meet its shipping deadline for the Lisa. There were manufacturing problems as severe as those that bedeviled the Apple III, all aggravated by the severe internal conflict within the company. Jobs insisted on putting his personal mark of approval on every Apple product, rejecting design after design. When Apple failed to deliver Lisa on time, it only added to the market's perception that Apple could not meet its commitments. The company was losing its credibility. A joke began to circulate throughout Apple:

Question: What are the two biggest lies in the world?

Answer: The check is in the mail and "Welcome IBM."

IBM was a trusted name, both for the reliability of its products and service. It also had good relations with the personal computer infrastructure, whereas Jobs had alienated it. IBM was able to sell personal computers by the hundreds to the corporate market. Apple couldn't get its foot in the door. The Apple II was still a viable computer, but it was not powerful enough to compete with IBM and the Lisa was too expensive. The Apple II, because Jobs was unwilling to form strategic alliances with the personal computer infrastructure, suffered from a lack of software and peripherals.

Once IBM got started, it rolled over the competition. In 1982 it had 18.4 percent of the personal computer market, but zoomed to a 30 percent market share in 1983. IBM was causing tremors in the personal computer market with rumors about a personal computer called Peanut that would sell for about $500. Because of IBM's respectability, the Peanut was a winner before it ever saw the light of day. The prospect of such a low cost computer from IBM had a devastating effect on other personal computer companies, forcing their stock to fall. Apple's long-awaited Macintosh, which was Steve Jobs's pet project, did not even seem to be in the running with a price tag of $2,500, compared to a five hundred dollar computer from IBM waiting in the wings.

Less than two years after IBM entered the personal computer field, it was recognized by customers and analysts as the technological leader, toppling Apple from the top of the mountain.

Apple was not only having a hard time competing with IBM, it was suffering from continuing internal turmoil. The Lisa and Macintosh were aimed primarily at the same markets. Instead of looking for ways to cooperate, Apple's divisions fought like cats and dogs, seemingly intent on destroying one another. The cauldron continued to bubble and trouble festered between the Macintosh and Apple II divisions. Doomsday predictions were made for the Apple II, which the company's marketing experts inexpertly considered an obsolete machine. They believed the Apple II, which was the company's primary cash producing product with five hundred million dollars a year in sales, faced extinction. If that happened, Apple would be in deep trouble because it was, in effect, a one product company and that product was the Apple II.

The Lisa was introduced in 1983, which started out as a banner year for Apple, even though the company was in turmoil. Lisa was seen as an advanced product, although expensive and not IBM compatible. But the marketplace in the early part of

1983 was still strong for personal computers. Atari, Osborne, Commodore, and other personal computer companies were doing a booming business. Apple's stock rose to sixty-three dollars per share in 1983, making Jobs's holdings worth about $437 million. The Apple II sold a record of 700,000 personal computers, which was 400,000 more than it had in 1982. The personal computer market was so exciting that, by the end of 1982, *Time* magazine, instead of naming a Man of the Year, extended that honor to the personal computer.

Personal computing companies such as Apple had been riding high on a brand new and expanding market, but in mid-1983, all of that changed radically. Not the least cause of the shift was IBM, which had, in a short time, captured a large share of the market, not just for personal computers, but for software and peripherals. Information managers at large companies asked a key question before buying a computer: Is it IBM compatible? Apple was not and its sales began to slide, along with a devastating market belief that Apple could not compete. Although Apple had sold Lisa computers at a breathtaking pace, the market began to view it as a loser because of its limited software and peripherals and inability to communicate with other personal computers that might be in an office.

The radical shift in the market drove several personal computer companies, such as Osborne, to bankruptcy. Companies such as Texas Instruments lost hundreds of millions of dollars. Apple, once the uncrowned king of the personal computer industry, suffered a loss in quarterly profits for the first time ever and there were alarming signals that something had to be done.

Adding to Apple's problems were the increasing costs of producing the long-awaited Macintosh, which Jobs had envisioned as selling for about one thousand dollars because he believed Apple could market them by the hundreds of thousands, thereby getting parts cheaper and cutting down on manufacturing expenses. It became clear that the Macintosh would have to debut for between $2,000 and $2,500 at the same time IBM was rumored to be bringing out the Peanut at five hundred dollars.

The Apple IIe, a further refinement of Wozniak's original Apple II, was the company's hope of survival. Apple's marketing managers belatedly began to see that the computer, far from becoming obsolete, was a continuing success. Even with IBM growing increasingly stronger in the personal computer market, sales for the Apple II continued to grow every year, confounding everybody, especially Jobs.

While Apple II and the Macintosh had originally been viewed as competitors for the same market, the two products began to differentiate themselves. Jobs had vowed that they should compete on the open market, and was confident that the Macintosh would blow the Apple II away. Fortunately for Apple, he was dead wrong in his feelings about Apple II, and the cannibalization that could have occurred without market divergency was avoided. And, while the cost of the Macintosh was steadily increasing, the price tag on the Apple II continued to drop.

Apple II's market was growing vertically and, because it was a machine that had been on the market for a few years, software companies had been able to program a large variety of software the machine could use, increasing its flexibility. The marketing people came to believe that Apple II's growth would continue and not compete with the Macintosh, which they believed would grow horizontally.

The future for the Macintosh began to look brighter when IBM, which had performed almost to perfection for the past few years, began to make mistakes. The Peanut, officially known as the IBM PCjr. when it was released, was a totally inadequate machine. Apple managers, who had ordered one of the first built, hooted with derision when they saw it. The PCjr. had a toy keyboard that made it difficult to use and the computer had a memory so small that it was totally inadequate to perform tasks business users demanded. The failure of the IBM toy computer embarrassed IBM and the company lost credibility, much the same as Apple had with the Apple III. IBM, which had gained a reputation for leadership, had to grit its teeth and retrench in an effort to regain its previous luster.

When the door closed on IBM, it opened once more for Apple. No longer did it have to worry about unfavorable comparisons between the IBM PCjr. and the Macintosh. The two computers weren't even in the same category.

IBM had also made some strategic mistakes with the computer infrastructure. The company had given software developers and retailers the jitters when it decided to expand its own software development and do more direct selling through its own distribution system. Some retailers had depended on IBM for 75 percent of sales and, when IBM added more product centers and expanded its sales force, distributors were worried about losing profits. Analysts predicted that IBM's own organization would account for 60 percent of its retail sales. This would leave retailers, who depended on IBM sales, cut off from more than half of their market.

Part of IBM's business strategy has always been to create fear, uncertainty, and doubt (FUD) about its competitors. Those negative perceptions turned 180 degrees so that IBM became the target of FUD. IBM had used FUD successfully against its competitors for years and, although the personal computer infrastructure still wanted to do business with Big Blue, companies were wary of becoming too dependent upon it. IBM made the same mistake Apple had made, as well, by keeping its product so secretive that second or third parties could not supply the necessary software.

IBM's trouble was an opportunity for Apple, but it was already clear that the company could not take the necessary steps under its present leadership. Jobs had alienated most of the infrastructure with his arrogance and demands, but Apple's board of directors did not target him for the headsman's axe. He was considered too valuable as a heroic figure in the minds of the general public or, as one board member put it, the "heart and soul" of Apple. Helped along by Jobs and the Scotty Wars, the board of directors turned unfriendly eyes toward Michael Scott.

Scott was the first employee hired by the triumvirate of Markkula, Jobs, and Wozniak when Apple first became a company. He was a tough-minded, practical president who acted as a tempering influence on the plans of Markkula, which were often wild and impractical. The only way Scott knew how to cope with Jobs's strong-arm methods was to verbally club him into submission, which was never an easy task. "Trying to have a conversation with Steve Jobs," said former Apple advertising manager Fred Hoar, "is like trying to take a sip from a fire hose." Scott, who was Jobs's first experience with unyielding authority, earned the latter's everlasting enmity.

Scott's role in the early days was as the voice of restraint that was sometimes able to put a damper on the polemics of Steve Jobs. He watched the company's coffers like a hawk and made certain that the company did not grow as fast as Jobs and Markkula would have liked. "Scotty was the moderating influence in the company," said Trip Hawkins. "If we had done all of the things Markkula and Jobs wanted to do, we would have grown so fast that we wouldn't have met our commitments. Scotty kept the company in a realistic perspective."

In spite of Scott's efforts, Apple grew at a breathtaking pace. By 1978, the company had outgrown its original two-story building and moved into a building that had fifteen times more space. Just three months later, Apple expanded into several more buildings in the immediate area. There were ninety employees by the end of 1978 and the company urgently needed more to meet its demands. A hiring spree, known within Apple as The Bozo Explosion, resulted in scores of new hirings. There was little or no order to it: Apple raided other firms for some and paid executive recruiters to find others. Things were happening so quickly at Apple that Scott had little time to organize. Such things as pay raises were given haphazardly. To try and keep control of manufacturing, Scott installed a computerized inventory system, but many important aspects of company operations fell through gaping cracks because of Apple's extensive growth.

The Bozo Explosion brought together engineers and technicians who had come up through the ranks, as well as fresh-faced young college graduates. The younger engineers viewed their older counterparts with disdain, complaining that most of them should have been in Cary Grant movies. For their part, the older engineers shook their heads with dismay at some of the wild ideas presented by the newcomers to the computing field. Jobs, who had his pets among both groups, compounded the enmity that already existed by stroking one and then the other, and, in the process, accidentally insuring that the battles never ceased.

Scott had a terrible time maintaining control during this period of growth. Part of the reason was that Jobs took every opportunity to wrest power from his hands. Trying to manage Jobs took up a major portion of Scott's time while he was attempting to bring order to the company. The more Scott tried, the more difficult Jobs became. Scott was trying to organize a rapidly growing company while Jobs seemed intent on creating anarchy.

Scott attempted to bring a semblance of order to Apple in 1980 by organizing the company into divisions. It proved to be a major miscalculation because the department heads, spurred on by the mercurial demands of Steve Jobs, grabbed for one another's throats. Instead of cooperating with one another, the department heads became adversaries and Apple engaged in a bloody civil war. Because of internal turmoil, Steve Wozniak found himself reluctantly embroiled in corporate politics. "I was lucky to find two hours a day to devote to work," he said. As for the newcomers, they turned up their noses at the Apple II, which was the backbone of the company. The younger engineers said, "The Apple II isn't a computer, it's a joke."

The divisiveness and bitterness between divisions was never more apparent than when the pressure came to meet targeted projections. "The national managers said, 'We're going to ship this sucker, to hell with the customer,'" said one former Apple executive. Apple's purported corporate philosophy had originally been influenced by Hewlett-Packard, which was a generous employer and good corporate citizen. At Apple, that philosophy fell by the wayside. Jobs endorsed it vocally, but did not adhere to it in practice. Secretaries were underpaid, it was difficult for women to be promoted, and the company was notably parsimonious in its charitable and civic contributions. Apple's early chauvinistic attitude toward women was underlined by a crude riddle Markkula presented at a manager's meeting.

Question: Why did God invent women?

Answer: Because sheep can't type.

There was chaos in every nook and cranny of the company. Although dress was casual and managers were called by their first names, there was never any doubt about who had the power.

Jobs, Markkula, and Scott could create instant fear simply by appearing in a work area. Stephen Wozniak, after serving a short stint as secretary to the board of directors, refused to accept a management position at the company he co-founded. He was to say time and again, "I don't want any part of that corporate bullshit." With friction between the various departments so rampant, there were frequent fist fights in the company parking lot.

Scott had joined Apple because he wanted to make a name for himself as an important company executive. At the same time, he had wanted to keep Apple small, and was one of those who resisted taking the company public. When he formed divisions, he was actually waving the flag of surrender to forces that were greater than his own desires.

"As Apple continued to get bigger, it almost necessitated more of a bureaucratic type of management," said Tim Bajarin, vice president of the microcomputer research group for Creative Strategies in San Jose. "Neither Jobs nor Scott were capable of managing it. Jobs had been able to make almost unilateral decisions and, at that point (when divisions were formed), he was hamstrung. He began to poke in every aspect of the business and alienated everybody because he tried to rule by intimidation. In the early days, he and Wozniak had been friends, but that friendship exploded as management became an issue."

Frequent memorandums started to appear from Scott. Jef Raskin has preserved a file drawer filled with memos from his days at Apple. One started with the bold warning: YOU BETTER READ THIS. The legal department chastised employees in a memo about the way they used the corporate name. "The legal name of the corporation is Apple Computer, Inc. (note the comma). Please don't hamstring our efforts by casually misusing the corporate symbols." Memos appeared urging frugality, the importance of closed-circuit television classes, shuttle bus schedules, and of the necessity to use up all of the stationery on hand before ordering more. There were even memos explaining the importance of memos.

The bureaucratic maze was so complicated that an anonymous author posed a hypothetical question: "How many Apple

employees does it take to change a light bulb?" Then he
answered:

One to file the user input report for the bad bulb.
One to revise the user interface specifications.
One to redesign the light bulb.
One to build the prototype.
One to approve the project.
One to leak the news to the press.
One area associate to coordinate the project.
One project manager.
Two product marketing managers.
One to write the light bulb product-revision plan.
One to analyze the light bulb's profitability.
One to negotiate the vendor contract.
Seven to alpha-test the light bulb.
One to revise the light bulb operating system.
One to obtain FCC certification.
One to write the manual.
One to do the foreign translations.
One to develop the light bulb product-training pack.
One to design the artwork.
One to design the package.
One to write the data sheet.
One to write the self-running light bulb demo.
One to copy-protect the light bulb.
One to write the ECO.
One to forecast use.
One to enter the part number in the computer.
One to place the order for each light bulb.
One to QC the light bulb.
One to distribute the light bulb.
One to seed vendors with the revision.
One to organize the product introduction party.
One to make the press announcement.
One to explain the light bulb to the financial community.
One to announce the light bulb to the sales force.
One to announce the light bulb to the dealers.

One to train service.
And one service technician to swap out the light bulb.

Raskin said that the bureaucratic structure all but killed good ideas before they had a chance to be fully considered. "It was like standing in front of a train and trying to pull it with a rope," he says. "It wouldn't move." Regis McKenna noted that the bureaucratic structure became so cumbersome that an employee had to plod through layers of people before getting an appointment with a person he used to deal with on a personal basis.

The bitter rivalries within divisions caused inefficiency, waste, and animosity. A manager in the production division said people there were afraid to deal with those outside the division. Worse yet, he said that managers outside of production "didn't give a damn" about production. The executives in the company, he complained, seemed to be at odds with the lower echelons. In an effort to create an idea of what the corporate culture was all about, Apple's executives issued a lengthy bulletin: "Apple values are the qualities, customers, standards, and principles that the company as a whole regards as desirable. They are the basis for what we do and how we do it. Taken together, they identify Apple as a unique company."

The bulletin proceeded to list Apple's mission, which was almost as detailed as a Papal bull:

Empathy for customers/users (We offer superior products that fill real needs and provide lasting value. We deal fairly with competitors, and meet customers and vendors more than halfway.)

Achievement/Aggressiveness (We set aggressive goals and drive ourselves hard to achieve them. We recognize that this is a unique time, when our products will change the way people work and live. It's an adventure, and we're on it together.)

Positive Social Contribution (As a corporate citizen, we wish to be an economic, intellectual and social asset in communities where we operate.)

159

Innovation/Vision (We accept the risks inherent in following our vision, and work to develop leadership products which command the profit margins we strive for.)

Individual Performance (We expect individual commitment and performance above the standard for our industry. Each employee can and must make a difference; for, in the final analysis, individuals determine the character and strength of Apple.)

Team Spirit (Teamwork is essential to Apple's success for the job is too big to be done by any one person. It takes all of us to win. We support each other, and share the victories and rewards together.)

Quality/Excellence (We build into Apple products a level of quality, performance, and value that will earn the respect and loyalty of our customers.)

Individual Reward (We recognize each person's contributions to Apple's success, and we share the financial rewards that flow from high performance. We recognize also that rewards must be psychological as well as financial and strive for an atmosphere where each individual can share the adventure and excitement of working at Apple.)

Good Management (The attitudes of managers toward their people are of primary importance. Employees should be able to trust the motives and integrity of their supervisors. It is the responsibility of management to create a productive environment where Apple values flourish.)

Markkula attempted to create an egalitarian atmosphere by encouraging people to come to him directly with any gripes they had about the company. On the other end of the spectrum, the doors of Scott and Jobs remained tightly closed. Neither of them had the ability, or the inclination, to deal with people on a personal level. So far as the long list of corporate policies was concerned, all but a few of them were ignored. For example, there was never any cooperation or goodwill between division heads or department managers.

Raskin found Jobs impossible to swallow, even before the latter finally stripped all control of Macintosh from his hands.

He was fond of saying that Jobs "would make an excellent king of France." This quotation was picked up in a *Time* magazine article. "On New Year's Day, he telephoned me at seven o'clock in the morning," Raskin recalled. "You don't call *anyone* that early after New Year's Eve. My wife answered the phone, woke me up and told me it was Jobs. I wasn't quite awake, so I answered, 'Good morning, your majesty.' He didn't make any comment about it. He just accepted it as if it was his due."

Raskin also wrote a long memorandum to Scott that was titled "Working for/with Steve Jobs," and suggested that Jobs be given management training before being allowed to manage. He also noted the vast difference between what Jobs claimed as his management philosophy and his real actions. "While Mr. Jobs's stated positions on management techniques are all quite noble and worthy, in practice he is a dreadful manager. It is an unfortunate case of mouthing the right ideas but not believing in or executing them when it comes time to do something. . . . Jobs regularly misses appointments. He does not give credit where due. Jobs also has favorites, who can do no wrong—and others who can do no right. He interrupts and doesn't listen. He doesn't keep promises. He is a prime example of a manager who takes the credit for his optimistic schedules and then blames the workers when deadlines are not met."

Raskin was formerly one of Jobs's closest confidants, but that friendship deteriorated into animosity. Many people who were friendly with Jobs, at one time or another, found that those bridges had been burned. "People used to say terrible things about how he uses people and intimidated them," said Trip Hawkins. "Unfortunately, all of that was true."

Scott, constantly under siege by Jobs and by the pressure caused by a company in explosive growth, started to change. He always had a temper, but the polemics were generally confined to his encounters with Jobs. Gradually, his darker side began to emerge with the fiasco of the Apple III computer. Apple had increased its work force to make the computer, but found itself top-heavy when the computer failed. Scott received authorization from Jobs and Markkula to fire forty-one people just a few months after the company went public. Rumors of the firing preceded the fact and fear swept through the company. Fred Hoar noted that the high tone of the notice stressing Apple's corporate values went out the window. "In its place we had ruthlessness," he said.

Before the actual firings, Scott asked department managers for their recommendations on who should get the axe. He received a list of eighty some names, then recirculated it and asked that it be reduced to forty-one. The day the firings occurred was dubbed Black Wednesday and the gloom of a dreary overcast day matched the mood at Apple. The unlucky employees were summoned to Scott's office and let go. Employees who survived the purge claimed that Apple did everything it could to avoid making severance payments. Scott held a company meeting that same afternoon to try and reassure the remaining employees, but he failed. In the weeks following Black Wednesday, he appeared to take malicious delight in hinting that the blood-letting might not be over. The employees at Apple, who had felt safe aboard the good ship Apple, were suddenly jolted into the reality that their jobs were no more secure than they would have been at any other corporation. Worst of all, there often seemed to be no good reason for firing those who were dismissed. One embittered employee, who had not been fired, cornered Jobs and told him this was not the right way to run a company. Jobs seemed to be as confused as everyone else, and asked, "How *do* you run a company?"

Some weeks after Black Wednesday, a memorandum appeared on Apple bulletin boards, authored anonymously: "We are forming the Computer Professionals Union (CPU) so that we can keep Apple's management in line. The thing they fear most is concerted employee action; the tactics they use are divide and conquer, and threats of economic reprisal. They can't get away with it if we unite! Apple was once a good place to work; management preaches to us about the 'Apple Spirit'; let's show them what a little bit of real spirit is like and ram it down their throats."

Management had kept Apple a union-free company, except in its Ireland plant, and wanted it to stay that way. The memo was a veiled threat that never materialized. Jobs was particularly

opposed to unions and vowed that the day Apple became union-
ized, "I quit."

Scott had become unofficially known as "the tyrant president" long before Black Wednesday. Much of the reasoning
behind this lay in his knock-down and drag-out fights with Jobs.
When Apple was just getting started, with a handful of employees, most of the Apple corps was composed of young people who
identified with Jobs rather than the more mature Scott. They
held Jobs in awe because he was co-founder of the company
while Scott was merely an employee. Being closer to Jobs's generation than to Scott's, the early employees were more suscepti-
ble to the influence of Jobs than they were to Scott's. At least a
few key employees considered Scott's reputation as a tyrant to be
the product of a whispering political campaign many believed
was initiated by Jobs.

"I think the 'tyrant president' thing was the result of Jobs's
behind-the-back politicking," said Trip Hawkins. "Both Markkula and Jobs were somewhat idealistic. If they had been
unchecked by Mike Scott, Apple would have grown too fast,
spent too much money, or simply run off the cliff. Scotty was a
very strong person who was capable of keeping both of them
from going over the edge."

But Scott never recovered from the damage done to himself
by Black Wednesday. The employees resented him and he was
under pressure from the executive board to pull the company out
of the abyss into which it had fallen with the failure of the Apple
III and the thundering entry of IBM into the personal computer
market. He also suffered from a severe eye infection that doctors
believed might lead to permanent blindness, and he was still
besieged by Jobs, who was struggling for power.

"I think he just sort of came unglued," said Trip Hawkins.
"The company grew too fast and outstripped his management
capabilities. He also had the company go to a divisional structure,
which works at some companies, but obviously didn't work at
Apple."

Whatever the reasons, Scott gained a reputation for being
ruthless, at least with the younger employees. Some of the older
hands, nearer to his age and closer to him in business philosophy,

thought of him as kind of a guardian angel for a while, but his behavior after Black Wednesday lost him even that support. Scott was never patient with menial problems in management meetings and bristled when debates erupted about whether employees should be offered both regular and decaffeinated coffee. He blew up because executives flew first class instead of economy and because salesmen drove full-size cars rather than compacts. To prove he was the boss, he would put off signing checks that were urgently needed and, once, he even asked that all vice presidents abandon their titles.

"Scotty just had more than he could handle," said Trip Hawkins. "I didn't always agree with him, but I respected him. He was just in over his head."

Scott had fired the vice president of engineering a short time before Black Wednesday and was running that department, as well as shouldering his other responsibilities. Stretched to the breaking point, his darker nature made him a brooding, ominous figure who mumbled almost gleefully about the firings that were to come. Never patient, he started to snap at people and would stop at desks, peer coldly at the occupant and ask, "Are you working your ass off?"

The employees at Apple feared him. The whispering campaign rippled throughout the company and found its way to the board of directors. "The company started to outstrip the capability and experience he had," said Trip Hawkins. "He started to act kind of strangely. At that point, Scotty alienated himself from pretty much everyone else in the company. People put a lot of pressure on Mike Markkula to do something about it."

Markkula was in a dilemma. By 1981, the four years he had pledged to the company were drawing to a close and he was looking forward to resuming his interrupted retirement. Already he was spending weeks away from the company, distancing himself from the day to day operations. But Scott caused so much dissension that he was forced to take action. The way Scott was ousted was a masterful stroke of corporate politics. While Scott was vacationing in Hawaii, the executive board removed him as president and demoted him to vice president. Markkula reluctantly stepped in as president, knowing full well that he did not have the expertise to do the job. Markkula, who had served as chairman of the board, became vice chairman and Steve Jobs, who had sought power, was elected chairman. The readjustments were explained in a memo that circulated throughout the company stating that it was part of a grand plan to keep management flexible. But, in reality, Scott had been done in. He went along with the pretense for a while, then fired off an angry letter of resignation that denounced "hypocrisy, yes-men, foolhardy plans, a 'cover your ass' attitude, and empire builders."

Scott was so depressed that he shut himself up in his home, with the drapes pulled, and stayed inside for weeks. People at Apple worried about him. Jobs mentioned that he was afraid he would learn that Scott had killed himself each time the telephone rang.

The end of Scott's career at Apple created a mixture of joy and fury, depending on what the employees thought of him. Hardly anyone realized the monumental task he had performed by holding Apple together during a period of explosive growth, despite throat-cutting divisional managers, the alienation of the personal computer infrastructure, and the constant problems he had with Jobs. Scott's ouster marked a victory for Jobs. Although Scott had the managerial experience, Jobs was able to outmaneuver him politically. The young Jobs, with a paucity of experience in both technology and management, had become the chairman of a two billion dollar corporation.

With Scott out of the picture and Markkula sitting in as president, Apple faced a host of problems, not the least of which was finding a new president. The company paid an executive search firm sixty thousand dollars to find a president, without success. Then the board began to feel out an energetic man in his early forties who had made a name for himself in marketing. That man was John C. Sculley, the president of Pepsi Cola.

CHAPTER 15

The "Courtship"

John C. Sculley, the man Apple's board of directors wanted to be its president and chief executive officer, was in almost every way the antithesis of Steve Jobs. Sculley had worked his way up through the ranks at PepsiCo to become president of Pepsi Cola USA, a division of that company. Steven Jobs had started out with no experience and became chairman of the board of a two billion dollar company.

Sculley also believed in strategic alliances with other businesses, while Jobs put Apple in an adversarial relationship with the entire personal computer infrastructure. Sculley had been an outstanding student in high school. He had both undergraduate and graduate college degrees while Steve Jobs, not able to keep interest in classes, did not even finish his first year of college, opting intead to seek enlightenment from such groups as the Hare Krishnas.

The son of a Princeton educated lawyer, Sculley had been the president of his class for six consecutive years at St. Mark's School, an exclusive prep school in Southborough, Massachusetts. He was captain of the school's soccer team and, when he was fourteen, he applied to patent a cathode-ray tube only to discover that someone had beaten him to it by just weeks. When he was graduated from St. Mark's, he was hailed as "the senior boy who did the most for his class."

Sculley was a romantic artist at heart and, when he finished high school, he enrolled at Brown University where he studied art history and architecture. He was a slight, energetic young man who did well. Sculley met Ruth Kendall, stepdaughter of PepsiCo chairman Donald M. Kendall, while he was at Brown and, during his junior year, they were married. Although Sculley's dream of being an architect remained unchanged, Kendall started a subtle campaign to get the young man into the business world.

"Since I was a child, I wanted to be a builder," Sculley said. Jerry Roach, the executive headhunter who made initial contact with Sculley on Apple's behalf, said, "Kendall convinced John that corporate architecture was more fun than physical architecture."

Sculley did not abandon his dream immediately and, to cover the bases, he majored in both architecture and business on the graduate level at the University of Pennsylvania, his business courses being conducted at the respected Wharton School. Destiny would lead Sculley to PepsiCo, but not before he worked for a while as an industrial designer, then pulled a stint as an advertising account executive. He was an intense man who attacked his work with an evangelical zeal that became his trademark.

Sculley eventually joined PepsiCo, but by that time, he and Ruth were divorced. It was a mark of confidence in Sculley's ability when Kendall retained a close personal friendship with Sculley. "We were able to separate business from our private lives," Sculley recalls.

One of Sculley's first assignments was to head PepsiCo's snack division in Sao Palo, Brazil. The product was potato chips, and the business was housed in a three-story apartment building. Sculley oversaw all of the operations, wanting to be involved in everything. Sometimes he helped peel potatoes in a room filled with their starchy odor, or he would watch women stirring the chips in huge vats of cooking oil. He was a tireless worker who believed in granting the maximum freedom to his staff. Within three years, Sculley increased sales of the snack division from one million dollars to forty million dollars a year, then he was called back to the United States to work for Pepsi Cola, USA.

However favored he was, Sculley was not ensconced in an executive office when he first reported to Pepsi Cola. Instead, he was put to work in the bottling plant where he worked on the loading docks to learn the business from the ground up. Sculley attacked the job with characteristic zeal and even helped load heavy cartons of soft drinks onto delivery trucks. "It wasn't required of the job," said Charles V. Mangold, a PepsiCo senior vice president who was Sculley's boss at the time. "But he wanted to make good. He wanted a total background." Sculley was small, but he kept fit by rising every day and running for five miles. In the evenings, he reported religiously to the YMCA, where he lifted weights so he would be more productive in loading the heavy soft drink cases.

His rise through the ranks was rapid and, within a few years, he was president of Pepsi Cola and on the board of directors for PepsiCo, the parent company. He earned a reputation as a cool-headed boss. "I do my very best work when I'm under pressure and times are toughest," he said. "I didn't have as much fun at Pepsi when things got easy. I have an intense ability to concentrate and switch from subject to subject like a computer changing programs. Stress doesn't bother me. If I can't control something, I don't worry about it. The only time I feel stressed is if I think my thinking is fuzzy."

Sculley's most notable achievement at Pepsi Cola, and the one that brought him to Apple's attention, was his innovative way of marketing during the "Cola Wars" between Pepsi and Coke. Rather than advertising Pepsi Cola as a product, he made a bold stroke and began to emphasize image. He was the father of the "Pepsi generation" concept, which eventually forced Coca Cola to change the formula it had used in its soft drink for one hundred years.

"Fifteen years ago, I and a few others broke away from the classical school of marketing, that of the brand name," Sculley said. "New industries like soft drinks, beer, and TV networks needed a different set of marketing ground rules." Sculley saw Pepsi and Coke as products that differed very little. Since the difference was so slight, he conceived advertisements that concentrated on image rather than product. It worked better than he or anyone else could have imagined. Now Coke advertises image, following Pepsi's lead.

As president of Pepsi Cola, Sculley had a plethora of corporate perks, including a large, ornate office filled with expensive paintings, and a private corporate jet. When he stood before an audience, the intensity radiated from him, and he was able to hold them in the palm of his hand. "I have great confidence on stage because I believe in ideas," he said. "I'm driven by ideas. I lead through presentations and use that as a way to communicate strategy. I'm a very visual person. I don't write more than two or three memos a year."

This was quite the opposite of what was happening at Apple, where memos circulated like snowflakes in a blizzard. Sculley also was active in business and civic functions: he was a member of the board of directors for Keep America Beautiful, and lectured weekly at his alma mater, the University of Pennsylvania's Wharton School. Although he was a visible public figure, he kept his private life strictly personal. "Look at Michael Jackson," Sculley once said. "He's extremely shy." The implication was clear: shyness has nothing to do with success.

Sculley's style of leadership was also diametrically opposed to that of Apple's Steve Jobs. "Leadership is far more important than management," Sculley said. "I like a decentralized organization where you give the best people as much authority as possible and let them run it. I'm basically a romantic who got sidetracked into business."

Sculley was a nationally recognized marketing whiz, with the ability to guide large companies toward profitability, when he was approached by Apple. He was a powerful executive at a major company, with prospects to go even higher. The tentative feelers from Apple were met with caution. Sculley knew, as did most other executives in corporate America, that it was next to impossible to have a compatible working relationship with Steve Jobs. His major concern, when he started to consider the offer, was whether or not he could get along with Jobs. "I knew my going to Apple would never work unless Steve and I had a good relationship," he said.

In retrospect, that may have been a moot point. Some of the hard-headed businessmen on Apple's board of directors, such as Arthur Rock, were well aware that many of the company's staggering problems were caused directly by Jobs's style, not just within the company, but with the entire personal computer infrastructure, which was becoming increasingly important to the health of the whole personal computer industry. "The board was willing to fire Jobs to get Sculley," said an Apple analyst. "They told John that, but he decided it would be better if he could simply manage Steve Jobs. Everyone was hoping that Steve would finally grow up."

To allay Sculley's fears about Jobs, Apple's directors arranged for several meetings between the two men over a period of four months. They met on several extended visits on the East Coast, where they walked through Central Park and visited museums. They dressed casually in blue jeans and corduroys and did not talk about computers. Sculley talked about art while Jobs, recalling his hippie days, spoke of philosophy and poetry.

When it became clear that Sculley would join Apple, the corporate public relations machine, which had been so instrumental in popularizing the story of "the two Steves," proved once again that it hadn't lost its touch for creating a favorable image. The reports on how well Jobs and Sculley got along reeked of superlative good will. The press was told that the two men met so often "to make sure the chemistry worked," a point that was hammered home time and again. Sculley was quoted as saying, "We just spent a lot of time in blue jeans getting to know one another." Jobs added, "I hired someone I could learn from." Flattery accepted, Sculley replied with his own, "There are a lot of things Steve is learning from me and that I am learning from him."

The press releases reported that the two men had an immediate closeness, a relationship that was sometimes brotherly,
sometimes like father and son. "We would finish each other's
sentences," Jobs said. According to Apple's corporate propa-
ganda, which was aimed as much at uneasy Apple employees as
to the general public, they were twin souls who created instant
harmony. In view of what was to happen just two years later, it
appears that these "goodwill" meetings were more like two bull
elephants cautiously and stealthily circling one another, looking
for strengths and weaknesses.

After a courtship that lasted four and a half months, Sculley
agreed to become president and chief executive of Apple. "I
decided to change my life and come to Apple because of my
admiration for Steve and what he had done," Sculley said. "Like
many people, I fell under the sway of Steve's charisma."

Sculley was most certainly helped in making his decision by
the golden carrots that a desperate Apple Computer, Inc. dangled
in front of him. Sculley was given a $2.5 million bonus for sign-
ing on, guaranteed wages and bonuses of $330,329 in 1983 and
a salary of two million dollars in 1984, not including bonuses
that would bring his total cash compensation in 1984 to $2.2
million. Apple also agreed to buy Sculley's home in Connecticut
for $1.3 million, (eventually losing $378,000 when it was resold)
and another two million dollars to help buy a house in the foot-
hills surrounding Silicon Valley. It was a package that would
have taken a very strong will to resist.

The Apple grapevine was whispering about Sculley long
before he arrived to become president and chief executive officer
in 1983. The word was that he was a "cold fish" who would
bring a pinstripe mentality to the renegade world of Apple. His
arrival was awaited with trepidation and mistrust because Apple
employees generally hated professional businessmen and disdained anyone who read *The Wall Street Journal* and actually
enjoyed it. The ironical part about the latter fear is that most of
the Apple people who held stock read the *Journal* avidly to see
how their stock was doing. Some even went so far as to post
bulletin boards so they could see at a glance the vagaries of the
stock market.

Sculley was shrewd enough to realize that Apple was peopled with employees who seemed to think their mission was to change the world for the better. He arrived at Apple wearing a plaid shirt, casual slacks and deck shoes. "John would never think of addressing Apple employees in a business suit," said Sue Espinosa, an Apple manager. "He'd do a wardrobe change. He's not spontaneous, but he is intuitively calculating." Sculley often popped into the offices of various managers to chat about their projects and, unlike Jobs, he listened carefully. There was a noticeable lack of fireworks.

"There was a lot of talk and fear before Sculley arrived," said a long-time Apple manager who has been with the company since the early days. "Ever since Black Wednesday, Apple was a particularly terrible place to work. We were all hanging on to trees and anything else to keep from being blown away. Sculley showed up in khakis, but I thought it might be window dressing. It took me about six weeks to realize that the guy wasn't going to screw things up even worse than they were."

Sculley had little knowledge of high-technology, but spent long hours studying it. He made some notable gaffes in staff meetings when talking high tech. Once he drew snickers and snide whispers when he mentioned in a staff meeting that the Apple III, with its new enhancements would have a 150 megabyte memory, which would have made it as powerful as a mainframe computer. But within months he was able to talk about personal computer technology with the best of Apple's engineers. He even hired a young software whiz to tutor him in computer programming. He attacked his job with the same zeal that led him to load cartons of soft drinks when he was a young executive with Pepsi Cola.

Apple held Friday afternoon beer busts and Sculley made it a point to attend them, dressed just as casually as everyone else. He chatted amiably, getting to know people, and letting them get to know him. Soon he was speaking with the same kind of evangelical zeal that fired the imaginations of other employees. "Here at Apple," he said, "we have a chance to change the world." It was exactly the kind of statement that was dear to the heart of Apple zealots. "When Sculley arrived, he was analyzed under a microscope," said Joanna Hoffman, an Apple marketing manager. "But he has managed to blend in well."

In spite of his seeming informality, Sculley got down to business. He had walked into a hornet's nest of problems. All around him were disarray, bitterness, envy, and dissension. Apple division managers were at each other's throats, while the Macintosh division, headed by Steve Jobs, irritated and angered everyone outside the group. Jobs flaunted the high-flying Macintosh division, which had yet to create a product, by hoisting a skull and crossbones at division headquarters. Apple employees were lax in their working hours and attention to timetables. Employees had no set hours, so long as they got their work done, and schedules had gone by the wayside because Jobs routinely rejected each and every design.

Sculley began to set an example. He arose every morning at 4:30, jogged five miles, and was at his desk by 7:30 and didn't leave until after the dinner hour. Employees began to take notice, especially when he started to classify them as A, B or C players. He warned staff meetings that there was no room at Apple for those who fell into the B or C categories. He began to reorganize the company, slowly at first because of his innate fear of changing too fast, and created small groups who focused on particular problems. Within a few weeks after Sculley's arrival, he had replaced three division heads and was making long-term plans for even more sweeping changes. When sales of Apple III slacked off, he quickly fired four hundred employees. He saw considerable overlapping of responsibilities in the various divisions, which were at odds with one another.

The year that Sculley arrived started out to be one of Apple's best years. Apple's stock reached $63.75 a share and the Lisa was finally introduced at the 1983 shareholder's meeting. The Lisa, as mentioned previously, had serious flaws. There was frightening talk that IBM was driving Apple into bankruptcy or that it would be merged into another company.

Sculley moved quickly. He slashed the price of the Lisa so that various models were available at prices ranging from $3,495 to $5,495. It has been estimated that this maneuver cost Apple some fifteen million dollars in short-term profits, but prevented Apple from being knocked senseless in the business arena.

Sculley noted, "We will sacrifice short-term profits for long-term stability." From the beginning, Sculley considered his major job one of teaching Apple how to market its products and to educate Steve Jobs on how to manage and market. Marketing Apple products was particularly important. The year that had started out so well ended up in near disaster. In the latter part of 1983, the bottom dropped out of Apple's stock, which reached a low of $17.24, down from a high of $63.75.

The presence of IBM in the personal computer market was also taking a heavy toll, and there was real fear that Apple might not survive through 1984. Apple's Lisa, although recognized as a technologically innovative machine, was a dud. "It was a great machine," said Bruce Tognazzini, a senior programmer at Apple. "We just couldn't sell any."

IBM had also announced the Peanut, and Apple's sales faltered in the face of this new entry into the marketplace. Worse yet, IBM announced that it intended to spend five hundred million dollars in 1984 on its personal computers. Apple's attempt to establish a beachhead on the corporate battlefield had failed miserably. IBM's market share grew from 18.4 percent in 1982 to 30 percent in 1983, while Apple's share dropped and profits faltered.

Apple's profits were far below expectations. Income fell to $5.1 million on sales of $273.2 million in the last quarter of 1983, down from $18.7 million on sales of $175 million during the final quarter of 1982. By the same token, IBM grabbed a higher share of the worldwide market, growing from 3 percent in 1981, when it entered the personal computer battleground, to 38 percent in 1983. The presence of IBM shook Apple's foundations. The threat of bankruptcy was very real at Apple.

Management at Apple, before Sculley, had also been a disaster. "There was chaos at the top," said a senior Apple manager. "No one knew what they were doing. The amazing thing about it is that, with all the fear we had of IBM, we were still shot through with arrogance. We looked down our noses at IBM, even though they were driving us into the ground. We thought we were a whole lot better than anyone else. Sculley brought us down to earth. He brought a different perspective."

Sculley had a back-breaking job in front of him. Apple's very survival as an independent company was at stake and he realized that the organization had to be made into a unified company, the rift with the personal computer infrastructure had to be mended, and that a new focus had to be achieved in marketing. Drastic measures were needed if the company was to survive and remain a viable force. The result of his drastic moves would eliminate 1,200 jobs and create a major rift with Steven Jobs.

CHAPTER 16

Undoing The Damage

When Sculley met with Jobs before he signed on with Apple, he told Jobs that he would continue running the company in unconventional ways. It took Sculley only weeks to learn that the untraditional management at Apple had created bickering, and had alienated customers, dealers, and the entire personal computer infrastructure. Sculley scrapped his plans for untraditional management, which obviously hadn't worked, and began making sweeping moves that were distinctly traditional.

"The divisional structure works at some companies, but it obviously didn't work at Apple," said Trip Hawkins. "People realized that it hadn't been as effective as they hoped. There are all kinds of explanations as to why it didn't work, but the truth is that the divisions did everything they could to hurt each other. It was crazy, but that's the kind of atmosphere Jobs fostered."

Sculley was committed to bring order to a house divided against itself, and to re-establish rapport with the entire computer infrastructure, which was in tatters. "A company the size of Apple needs not just to have great concepts, but to be aware of marketplace wants," Sculley said. "The different parts of the organization have to be well-tuned to each other. Apple's biggest competition has been itself. We have to find ways to work as one company. The industry is too tough to use up our energies on each other."

Sculley was as good as his word. Apple's organizational structure was so loose that it was unraveling, and he was determined to tighten it up and end the internal warfare. His initial plan in 1983 called for merging the company's nine highly decentralized divisions, most of which had broad responsibility for product lines, into an organization structured according to business functions such as engineering, marketing and manufacturing. One marketing group would handle advertising and promotion for all Apple products.

Within three months, Sculley consolidated Apple's nine cut-throat divisions into three. Previously, the divisions had operated like fiefdoms and had been more interested in competition with one another instead of cooperation. Under Sculley, the new structure *forced* cooperation.

Under Jobs, Apple had an almost maniacal focus on new products, and he was fond of describing "insanely great" new computers that Apple would manufacture. Sculley realized that, with the drastic market shift in the latter part of 1983, to simply dazzle potential customers with new technology was not enough to guarantee sales. The failure of the Lisa, which incorporated the latest in new technology, was a dismal example of this. Instead, Sculley started to focus on marketing and advertising to create an image that would once again make Apple appear to be the technological leader in personal computers or, at least, on a par with IBM, which was beating Apple's socks off.

Sculley discovered that Apple's advertising for the Lisa made the company appear schizophrenic. On the one hand, advertisements were aimed at the corporate market, where Apple was attempting to secure a beachhead in its war with IBM, while other advertisements were targeted toward the home user. The Lisa was also aimed at the same market as the Macintosh, which was to be introduced in 1984, and used essentially the same technology as the Mac. Confusion reigned. Sculley revamped the advertising and scaled it down through 1983, awaiting a big push for the long-awaited Macintosh in the coming year.

Sculley also tightened the corporate belt. He stopped profit sharing, which created grumbling and morale problems throughout the ranks, and announced that Apple would pay no dividends for 1984. Although the company had a hefty four hundred million dollars in cash reserves and no long-term debt, Sculley believed Apple needed the money to generate products, to increase advertising and to improve manufacturing. Sculley also placed a freeze on hiring. Wall Street analysts and other Apple watchers cast a favorable eye on Sculley's battlefield tactics, but they were still wary because Apple was bogged in a quagmire of problems.

The *San Jose Mercury News* noted that Sculley brought "accountability to brainy, brash computer hackers, who were ruled by gonzo management."

Apple had hired Sculley because of his market-driven approach to business. He had earned a reputation for promoting products and making big companies profitable. Apple had finally realized that the radical shift in the personal computer market demanded a new approach. In a nutshell, it meant that Apple had to recognize the fact that their personal computers would eventually have to become IBM compatible, or at least be able to accept peripherals manufactured by the infrastructure. The needs of the end user also had to be considered in developing personal computers.

The shift in the personal computer market made it almost identical to the mainframe computer industry, and there IBM was the leader. McKenna warned Apple that a company that didn't respond to the marketplace could be engineering its own downfall. McKenna noted that Apple's most dangerous competitor was itself. "When people develop an air of omnipotence and believe they can't fail . . . when they are unwilling to listen, then they are unwilling to change . . . they are competing with themselves."

It was particularly ironic that McKenna, who was retained by Apple for advertising and marketing advice, held "relationships" as being among a company's foremost business strategies.

He preached it over and over, noting that relationships pay off in the long run. Jobs did not heed the advice. McKenna noted, "Steve seemed to be listening only to himself."

Sculley had fences to mend with the personal computer infrastructure. He stayed on the road at length, sometimes making three or four speeches a day to stock analysts and dealers. He also pledged that Apple would seek strategic alliances with third party companies. He was dedicated to cooperation, whereas Jobs had aggravated, insulted, and frightened many of them off. "Apple wants to have cooperative relations," Sculley said. "We want companies building products for us and co-selling agreements. Expect to see that."

This was refreshing news to the computer industry, and to Wall Street, all of whom had long since grown weary of Jobs's single-mindedness and brash manner. Sculley also recognized the shift in the personal computer market long before Jobs did.

IBM pounded Apple in the marketplace because it listened to what people wanted and it had strategic alliances with the personal computer infrastructure. Big Blue, long noted for its service orientation, devoted considerable attention to the needs of the market before it introduced new products. These products had to enhance what was already there. There were also dozens of companies producing software that could run on IBM machines, while Apple computers could run only their own programs. Apple was trying to sell computers like a consumer oriented company even though the market clearly demanded a different approach. "Ironically, it was John Sculley, with his background in consumer products, who realized that," McKenna said. "Steve, the one with the technical background, didn't recognize that soon enough."

Sculley brought a distinctive MBA approach to Apple. "That in itself is not always good," said Tim Bajarin, an Apple analyst. "But he was able to maintain the personality of Apple and to link it to very significant management skills that put Apple on a winning track. Before Sculley, Apple was a loose, undisciplined corporation. He came in to tighten it up but met a lot of resistance because of the mavericks in the company. He tried to bring Apple to a higher level of responsibility, to get better internal and external realtionships. Things gradually started to change."

Sculley sat in on meetings and made copious notes while saying little. He never raised his voice. "It was a new thing at Apple to have somebody listen to you politely," said a senior manager. "Before Sculley, going to a meeting was like walking into a storm." Sculley told Apple managers: "We're dependent on each other's strengths." That statement was welcomed by most people at Apple, who had been accustomed to fighting one another, but it had little effect on Steve Jobs.

Under Sculley's 1983 reorganization, Jobs managed to maintain control of the Macintosh division and, as chairman of the corporation and the largest stockholder, he was disproportionately powerful. He continued to view the Apple II products as dinosaurs and told marketing managers for Apple II that they were working in a clumsy, out-dated division. Sculley's reorganization had the effect of making Jobs even more powerful than he had been, although some people believe that Sculley was giving Jobs enough rope to hang himself. Sculley was lenient with Jobs, much to the dismay of people in the Apple II division, who were being bullied by Jobs while they were bringing in most of the company's profits.

"We were all absolutely astounded that Sculley seemed to be buying Jobs," said a senior programmer. "He sat with Jobs and listened to his ideas politely and often went along with him. Scotty used to shout him down, but now Jobs seemed to have the ear of the company's president and chief executive officer."

Sculley spent so much time with Jobs that people in the Apple II division disdainfully referred to their relationship as "a love affair." This was probably an inaccurate assessment in view of what was to follow. Apple's board was tired of Jobs's erratic behavior and had given Sculley directions to rein him in. Sculley replied: "That's a little hard to do when the division manager is also chairman of the board." The conflict between Jobs's Macintosh division and Apple II was already ripping the company apart, but it got worse. Sculley was aware of it, but he was too busy with other things to make a drastic move.

Sculley had seen 1983 get off to a good start, only to end with a series of Apple failures. The promise of Apple III did not materialize, nor did that of the Lisa, and Scully was worried that Apple's sheen, already tarnished, would lose all luster. As McKenna noted, "A failure with one product leads to the probability of failure with the next product."

Sculley's moves at Apple were seen as positive steps by other companies who manufactured personal computers. They followed Apple's lead and started to bring in professional managers, a term that Sculley despises. There was a rush to hire professional marketers in Silicon Valley. Atari hired James Morgan, pirating him from Phillip Morris, and Osborne Computer hired Robert Jaunich away from Consolidated Foods. For Osborne it was too late, and the company folded in 1984. That was a source of satisfaction for Jobs, who was fond of relating a conversation with Osborne.

"Just how good is the Macintosh?" Jobs said Osborne asked.

Jobs replied, "It's so good that you'll want to buy one for your kids long after we've driven you out of business."

Apple struggled mightily just to survive 1983. It was a year of terrible turmoil. Prices dropped and competition grew, squeezing industry profits. Quarterly profits fell for the first time in Apple's history. There was fear that, at worst, Apple might not survive or, at best, that it would lose its credibility and the market would start viewing the company as a loser.

There was one bright spot during 1983. The much maligned Apple II division introduced the Apple IIe and sold more than 700,000 units, about 400,000 more than during the previous year. The presence of IBM thundered all around Apple in 1983. Apple's share of the market dropped from 21 percent to 19 percent. IBM's announcement that it would spend millions on its personal computer line in 1984 sent shivers through Apple. With the failure of Lisa, the introduction of the Macintosh in 1984 gained even more importance at Apple.

At the end of 1983, Sculley and Jobs had their first major disagreement. Sculley wanted to merge the Lisa and Macintosh divisions, but Jobs resisted. Jobs wanted to postpone the merger until after the Macintosh was introduced the following January.

But Sculley insisted and Jobs gave in, probably because his keen sense of survival told him that the board of directors was with Sculley. Just a short time after the merger, he said of Sculley's decision, "He was right."

The merger of the two divisions should have given the Macintosh a big push because they essentially used the same technology. But, while Sculley was preaching the new Apple gospel of cooperation with third party dealers, Jobs wasn't having any part of it. He drove away anyone who wanted to cooperate and, in his obsession with the Macintosh, even had it configured so that it could not use software programs that had been created for the Lisa. The Macintosh turned out to be a stand-alone machine.

Nevertheless, spirits were high at Apple when the Macintosh was introduced at the annual stockholder's meeting in January of 1984. The normal evangelical zeal that marked the introduction of Apple products was even greater for the Macintosh—for those in the division. They were given front row seats and singled out as the elite, "the future of Apple," while members of the venerable Apple II division sat dismally discouraged in another room watching it all on closed circuit television.

But both Sculley, who was still relatively new on the job, and Jobs were looking to Macintosh to get Apple back in the fast lane. Sculley had seen many of Apple's weaknesses and had helped correct them by consolidating divisions and putting the company on an austerity program. He had not been on the job long enough to be a specialist in products, and he was just as hopeful as Jobs about the Macintosh. With Jobs, he had formulated a massive, one hundred million dollar advertising program to launch the Mac, aiming at the corporate marketplace.

The Macintosh called for a huge media blitz that would total fifteen million dollars during the first three months after the computer was introduced. Apple printed ten million copies of a twenty page Macintosh advertisement that was included in several magazines. The company cooperated with more than a dozen trade magazines to help produce covers that featured the Macintosh. Apple continued its blitz by mailing hundreds of press kits that were in the form of a lunch box that contained information about the Macintosh, as well as a Macintosh T-shirt. Jobs and Sculley conducted more than sixty interviews around the country, garnering a great deal of press coverage. All three television networks included the introduction of the Macintosh in their news shows. In New York, where Jobs had bought a two million dollar apartment overlooking Central Park, the chairman of Apple Computer presented a Macintosh to rock singer Mick Jagger of The Rolling Stones.

Apple's hype was in full gear, and most of the people in the Mac division were euphoric. Reporters had been courted and they flocked to Cupertino where they rhapsodized about the "smart, brash, foresighted" engineers who had created this marvel of new technology. One notable advertisement ran for sixty seconds during the January 1984 Super Bowl, where the Washington Redskins were taking a thrashing at the hands of the Oakland Raiders, 38 to 9. The Macintosh advertisement, which ran only one time, showed drone-like human beings sitting in front of a huge computer, meant to represent IBM. A fresh-faced young woman ran into the scene, threw an object at the computer and vaporized it in a flash of light. The young woman, of course, was meant to represent Apple. The voice-over said, "The thugs and wreckers have been cast out. Let each and every cell rejoice! You'll see why 1984 won't be like *1984*." The creators of the commercial from Chiat-Day Advertising received an ovation from Apple's board of directors at a meeting following Super Bowl Sunday. The commercial was never run again.

Apple's advertising program for the Macintosh was widely viewed as a stroke of genius. "Apple has positioned itself directly against IBM, a marketing stroke that was beautiful," said an analyst with market researchers International Data Corporation. "Apple created the perception that it was as big and omnipresent as IBM." Sculley defended the huge advertising budget by saying, "Since Apple was taking a divergent direction in technology, no one was ever going to know it unless we became as bold and innovative with our marketing as we were with our product. The one other company that's learned how to do it is IBM."

Apple, still underestimating IBM's strength, was taking the giant from Armonk on in a toe-to-toe slugging contest. "We want to be a clear alternative to IBM," Sculley said at the time. "We are not content to exist on the edge of a corporate giant." Sculley's thrust at IBM's heart was underscored when he hired William V. Campbell, a marketer and former football coach, away from Eastman Kodak. Campbell performed the back-breaking task of hiring 360 people and training them within two months to beef up Apple's sales to dealers.

Jobs and Sculley together created a promotional program called a "test drive" for the Macintosh computer. Under this scheme, potential buyers could take a Mac home for twenty-four hours and try it out to see if they wanted to buy it. By supporting this move, Sculley proved to be less than infallible in his marketing expertise. Macintosh was aimed at the corporate market, but the "test drive" program clearly targeted home users. It made many people consider Apple unfocused in its promotion of Macintosh. Unfortunately, the "test drive" was only one of a series of ghastly mistakes.

Analysts predicted that businesses were expected to purchase at least two-thirds of the $14.5 billion personal computer market in 1984. Apple, which had had no success in cracking that market, was counting on the Mac. But the going was rough. At the beginning of 1984, an analyst wrote that the fight for the corporate market was a two-horse race between IBM and Macintosh, but that Apple had not even made the betting interesting. "It has not yet been proven that you can go with Apple computers in the office and know, as the industry standards change, that you won't pay a penalty for using Apple," said Doug Cayne, a securities analyst for the Gartner Group of Stamford, Connecticut.

Jobs, more than anyone, seemed to be caught up in the euphoria of the big Macintosh promotion and advertising campaign. He excitedly proclaimed that, "Apple has the chance to become the second largest computer company in the industry by the 1990s." He also added that he wanted to "Mac-intize" the rest of Apple. The people in the "rest of Apple" would have preferred nothing more than to see Steve Jobs's hide nailed to a barn door. Steve Wozniak was so disgusted with all of the attention being given to Macintosh, and the ignoring of Apple II, that he stopped coming to work. He flew airplanes and promoted two multi-million dollar rock concerts that resulted in multi-million dollar losses. In the hullabaloo surrounding Macintosh, hardly anyone outside of Apple took notice of Wozniak's departure.

The Macintosh was already in serious trouble when Apple held a sales meeting under the tropical Hawaiian sun in October of 1984. Apple put just as much effort into this sales meeting as it did into advertising and public relations to whip its one thousand-strong sales force into a frenzy of excitement. During the presentation, the sales force whooped, yelled, and laughed as they watched a giant video screen showing a man trying to use a huge computer that had green slime oozing out of it. Apple had created its own version of the theme song from the movie *Ghostbusters*. As the slime oozed out of the machine, the speakers blared, "Who ya gonna call?" And the audience screamed, "Blue Busters!," "Blue" referring, of course, to IBM.

In spite of the hype at that October meeting, Apple already knew it had serious problems with the Macintosh and that it was making absolutely no headway into the corporate market. Its massive effort to win major corporate customers resulted in only one major sale. Peat, Marwick, Mitchell Co., one of the Big Eight accounting firms, bought and installed 4,500 Macintoshes. And that was about it so far as Apple's attack on the corporate marketplace was concerned.

Jobs had initially told Trip Hawkins that Apple would sell five million Macintoshes in its first two years. He boasted about it and said the computer could be sold cheaply because Apple would be buying parts in huge quantities. Jobs's sales projection was outrageously inaccurate. In fact, Apple sold only 200,000 Macintoshes from the time it was introduced through November of 1984. The machine had severe problems, largely because Jobs had not listened to the marketplace to see what it wanted, and he steadfastly refused to let third party manufacturers get involved. Worst of all, it was not IBM compatible.

Other manufacturers of personal computers for both home and office use realized that, to survive, they had to learn to live with IBM. They started designing personal computers that would run IBM programs. Sculley was just as much at fault as

Jobs for this costly oversight. He had vowed that, "We must remain a leader or slip quietly into the darkness of mediocrity." The Macintosh, while it incorporated dazzling new technology, did not impress corporate users, and its success was at best mediocre.

Jobs had insisted on going it alone in creating the Macintosh. There was no aspect of the computer in which he did not have the final say. He had never been a technological star yet he insisted on approving everything about the Macintosh, as well as dictating the features that he wanted incorporated into the machine.

The result was a computer that was doomed to failure from the beginning. Jobs had insisted that the Macintosh be "user friendly," that is, easy to use. By guaranteeing user friendliness, the Macintosh internal programming was complicated and expensive to produce. Because he was obsessed with elegance in appearance, Jobs refused to have a fan installed in the computer. That made it impossible for the Mac to handle a hard disk drive, which is necessary for heavy business use. The computer was slow and had a limited memory, and there were no add-on products to make it faster or to increase its memory. An oversight that is almost impossible to understand is that Jobs did not create a letter-quality printer to go with the Macintosh, another necessity for business users. For every program being written by other companies for Apple, at least five were being prepared for IBM.

"There was no in-house cynic to stand up to Steve Jobs and say, 'It's incredibly stupid to sell a business machine that doesn't support a letter-quality printer,'" said Tom Warrick, a lawyer in Washington who is president of a large Apple user's club. Regis McKenna said that Jobs suffered from having too many "Yes men" around him. "I told him that there was no one in the company who would stand up to him and say, 'No, Steve. That's not how the real world works,'" McKenna said. The problem with both of these assessments is that Steve Jobs did not allow _anyone_ to say "No" to him.

The Macintosh sold fairly well to individuals, but scored a direct miss when it came to its target—corporations. Journalists, who a few years ago had been awed by the new technology of personal computers, had become more sophisticated. Many newspapers and magazines had personal computer editors who specialized in the field and they were no longer entranced by the new technology. They asked hard questions and knew when they were being bamboozled by "techie talk." They picked up on the Macintosh problems quickly and wrote articles about Apple's problems, much to the corporation's chagrin. The newspaper and magazine articles prompted a memo to all Apple hands from Fred Hoar, who was Apple's vice president for communications. The memo read:

Adverse Publicity
Recently Apple has been the subject of some stories in the press which cannot be considered "puff" pieces . . . i.e., they do a fairly negative job of reportage . . . it is in the scheme of things that bad news makes better copy than good news, and also that many, if not most, reporters have trouble conveying subtlety and complexity, much less their editors.

Apple's managers became aware, however, that despite the disdain of the media, the company's problems did not stem from the press, but from the Macintosh itself. William Campbell noted, "A lot of corporate accounts have not accepted that we have a serious office product yet." Esther Dyson, publisher of a respected industry newsletter wrote, "Apple will never get in the front door. It will have to infiltrate." A disgruntled Macintosh user grumbled, "It's like having a Maserati with a one-gallon gas tank." An Apple manager complained, "Mac was being perceived as a cutesy, avocado machine for Yuppies and their kids, not as an office machine or as the technological leader that it is."

Wall Street, taking note of the situation, cut its estimates of Apple's earnings for 1985. Where analysts had previously predicted earnings of $2.50 a share, they dropped it to $2.25—and that was optimistic. Apple's stock slid downward by four dollars a share.

Sculley reacted to the situation by promising a Macintosh that would not be a closed system, which could accept add-ons, and retreated from his position of taking IBM head-on. He promised a new Macintosh that would run IBM programs. In effect, he admitted that Apple could no longer slug it out with IBM, but had to learn to co-exist with an adversary that was not only more powerful, but also faster on its feet.

Jobs was ordered to create enhancements for the Macintosh during 1984, but failed to meet his deadline. The new timetable for the enhancements were pushed back to sometime in 1985 and Jobs received his first scolding from Sculley, who had little patience with those who couldn't meet schedules. Sculley was also annoyed that while he had been promising cooperation with third parties, Jobs had turned a deaf ear and created a Macintosh that did not lend itself to enhancements that could be manufactured by other companies in the personal computer field.

Jobs, who felt that he had been given a reprieve instead of a warning, scaled down his overly optimistic sales projections for the Macintosh. Where he had been talking about two million unit sales in two years, he now hoped to sell 200,000 Macs during the Christmas season, usually the healthiest time for home computer sales. Clearly he was aiming at the consumer market instead of the corporate scene, which had originally been the target for Macintosh. Even so, his projections came up 50,000 units short and continued to decline on the average of 19,000 units per month. What's more, the heavy cost of manufacturing and introducing the Macintosh seriously eroded profits. The first serious crack had developed in the Sculley-Jobs relationship.

The Macintosh was the first attempt Jobs had made at creating a computer—and it was a failure. Nevertheless, he remained committed to the Mac technology and philosophy, even while sales continued to slide. He succeeded in compounding his difficulties with Apple by becoming even more protective of Macintosh, and taking his frustration out on the Apple II division. Sculley had attempted to improve morale within the company by consolidating divisions, but Jobs would have no part of that. He was intensely jealous of the continuing success of Apple II and chagrined over his own failure with the Macintosh. Jealousy, coupled with failure, in a man with a monumental ego can create enormous negative reactions. Jobs struck out viciously at the Apple II group, reiterating his often heard litany that employees in the group were creating clumsy, outdated, and inelegant machines.

"We all tried to stay away from him," said Bruce Tognazinni. "In Apple II, we used to say that the Macintosh division had God on their side. Morale in the Apple group was very low."

One member of the Apple II division, who no longer cared much about his future at Apple, presented Jobs with a copy of *Miss Manners.* Jobs dismissed the irony with a shrug. "I'm not a discreet person," he said. "He [Jobs] was so protective of us that whenever we complained about somebody outside the division, it was like unleashing a Doberman," said one member of the Macintosh team. "Steve would get on the telephone and chew the guy out so fast your head would spin."

Even though Jobs was splitting the company in two and failing with his own division, he stalked around like a dictator. "Steve Jobs is into power," said Trip Hawkins. "The bigger Apple got, the more he thrived on it. When he got control of the combined Lisa and Macintosh division, he was just impossible. He had far too much unilateral power. Sculley should have reined him in a lot sooner than he did."

Sculley, however, was faced with a paradoxical problem. On the one hand, Jobs, as a divisional manager, worked for him and, on the other, as chairman of the board, Jobs was Sculley's boss. "John was in a terribly difficult position," said an Apple manager. "His hands were really tied."

Jobs insisted on complete loyalty in the Macintosh division, but he even managed to create a slew of enemies in his own domain. "You were either with Jobs or against him," said Bruce Tognazinni. "We were all against him." Oddly enough, Jobs seemed oblivious to all of the trouble he was causing and the growing number of people, including the board of directors, who were turning against him. "As Steve continued to get more arrogant and demand more and more, there were just that many more people who were out to get him," said a former Apple executive.

Contributing to the frustration of the board, Sculley and, most of all, to the Apple II division, the venerable Apple II turned in a record performance in 1984. With Jobs hounding the

189

division's managers, and even refusing to allow the Apple II to be advertised as a business computer so it wouldn't compete with his Macintosh, the division sold 800,000 Apple IIe's and portable Apple IIc's. It generated revenues of nearly one billion dollars, which accounted for at least two-thirds of the company's profits. The high cost of introducing the Macintosh, plus shortcomings in the computer and manufacturing problems, bit deeply into company profits. Jobs was missing crucial deadlines while he continued to harangue the Apple II division. Jobs ruffled feathers even more with the Apple II group, whose members were required to have passes before they could enter the Macintosh area, when he escorted folk singer Joan Baez, for whom he held a brief torch, on a tour of the Mac manufacturing area. Miss Baez was an unlikely corporate spy, but her visit stung the sensitivities of the Apple II group.

Sculley, at long last, acknowledged the problem and tried to do something about it. To help boost morale, he held a beer bust and designated an Apple II Forever Day. He even convinced Wozniak to return to the Apple II division. Wozniak's arrival boosted the sagging spirits of the group, but not enough. Delbert W. Yocum, a manager who had worked his way up through the ranks to become head of the Apple II products group, blamed himself for not getting his division enough "mind share," which is computerese for "attention." He pledged to work harder to get more press coverage for Apple II and an increased share of Sculley's attention. Sculley did not need any prodding from Yocum. The company was split and the gap was growing wider with each passing day. Jobs not only created a furor, he was failing miserably in his first attempt to ship a product. It was not much of a performance for Jobs who, by then, was being promoted as the man who invented the first Apple computer, but was making such outrageous demands on others.

Throughout 1984, Sculley was beating the bushes to assure people that Apple wanted closer links with the computer infrastructure and more third party participation. He promised computers that would be IBM compatible, and open to enhancements from other companies. Jobs, meanwhile, stubbornly resisted getting the infrastructure involved with the Macintosh.

"Steve just became obsessive around the Macintosh concept of product line, even though Apple II accounted for the company's cash flow," noted analyst Tim Bajarin. "He split the company in half. Rather than one company that had different products, it was as if the Apple II group was one company and the Macintosh division was another."

People were wondering who was running the show at Apple, Jobs or Sculley? Sculley compared his tenure at Apple with his previous job as president of Pepsi Cola: "He [Kendall] and I put our personal friendship aside. He was running the company and I was running a division. Here, Steve and I are running the company together."

Sculley's effort to mend fences with vendors, dealers, and third parties was being thwarted by Jobs. Apple had a golden opportunity to gain strength because dealers and other companies were shocked when IBM began to manufacture much of its own software and to sell more computers through a company sales force. The computer infrastructure, which had become dependent on IBM, now wanted an alternative to Big Blue. Sculley obliged by scrapping plans for Apple to create its own software division, a move that was met with sighs of relief.

"Apple's success is in the best interest of independent vendors because it presents us with a target of opportunity," said Fred M. Gibbons, president of Software Publishing. Dealers also welcomed Apple as an alternative to IBM when the Armonk giant decided to sell more personal computers directly. Apple's relationship with dealers had been a rocky affair, but Sculley promised that the company would mend its ways. "Apple is not out to compete with us," said Norman Dinneson, president of ComputerLand of San Diego. Another dealer noted, "I'm not making much money selling Apples, but I like to see a good alternative to IBM." Sculley also managed to convince retailers such as BusinessLand and Sears Business Systems to stock Apple computers.

In the meantime, Jobs's refusal to cooperate with any of the promises Sculley made was creating bitterness with the infrastructure. AST Research, the world's largest manufacturer of IBM PC enhancements, created an Apple Enhancement Product

Division in the middle of 1984, much to the surprise of most people in the computer industry, who saw Apple as a company torn in half. Ash Jain, head of AST's division that made enhancements for Apple, was shocked that Jobs was not making good on Sculley's promises, but he did not think the situation would continue.

"We wanted to be less dependent on IBM," he said. "The situation at Apple was pretty bad. Sales were down and they had had one failure after another. The Apple III was a failure, the Lisa had been a failure. Jobs introduced the Macintosh in January 1984 and it was very heavily criticized by the industry. It did not have enough performance and it was a closed box that didn't allow it to be enhanced. There was a series of failures for Apple all the way around."

Industry watchers wondered why AST would start a division to manufacture enhancements for Apple computers when the company wasn't cooperating, and because they believed Apple's survival was in doubt. "People were telling us that Apple had a very bleak future," Jain says. "The position we had was that Apple was a big company and, no matter who you are, you make mistakes once in a while. Sooner or later, we felt that Apple would turn around and our division would be ready and poised to take advantage of the market."

Jain's product division was created in the summer of 1984 when the Macintosh was failing and Jobs was becoming even more arrogant in dealing with outside companies, as well as slicing Apple in half.

The Macintosh was a glaring example of Jobs's failure to listen to others. "You couldn't do anything with it except plug it into your power outlet and use it," Jain said. "If you wanted more power, you couldn't get it. If you wanted more memory, you couldn't do it. If you wanted more speed, you couldn't get it. You couldn't do anything with it except what was given to you by Apple." Jain contrasted the Macintosh with the IBM PC, which could be enhanced to perform a number of functions faster, was able to acquire added memory and could communicate with other IBM compatible computers. "The Macintosh was very restricted and that is why people were totally turned off by it," Jain said.

Jain was one of the most vocal critics of Steve Jobs during 1984, but he wasn't the only one. Yet Jain's criticisms were typical of the salvos being fired at Jobs. By late 1984, Jain was making three predictions about Apple and Steve Jobs that he believed would occur by the end of 1985: First, that Jobs would probably not be with the company; second, Apple would be acquired and cease to be independent if it kept Jobs; and, third, the company would have to create a Macintosh that would accept enhancements and be IBM compatible.

Analysts such as Tim Bajarin were publicly saying, "If it hadn't been for John Sculley, Apple wouldn't have made it through 1983, much less 1984."

The noose was tightening around Jobs's neck. Yet his actions defied Sculley, and their much-publicized friendship evaporated during 1984. Few people at Apple other than Jobs, Sculley, and the board of directors realized that a bitter power play had developed between Jobs and Sculley. They were much more concerned by rumors of mass layoffs in 1985. But Apple's board of directors had had enough. They goaded Sculley several times during 1984 to do something about Jobs, but Sculley was unwilling to act. According to those who watched Apple closely, Sculley hoped that he could manage Jobs because he believed the company needed a "folk hero" on the premises and Wozniak, disenchanted once again, was on his way out the door. The decisive moment occurred late in 1984 when Apple was predicting its first quarterly loss. Several members of Apple's board of directors, including the unsentimental Arthur Rock, approached Sculley.

"John," they said. "It's time to start thinking about getting rid of Steve."

CHAPTER 17

Power Play

Steve Jobs seemed unaware that a noose was tightening around his neck. He remained committed to Macintosh's new technology and disdainful of the contribution by the Apple II division. He held an enormous Christmas bash for the Macintosh personnel in 1984 while the people in the Apple II group found corporate coal in their holiday stockings.

The annual stockholders' meeting added insult to injury for the Apple II group. Jobs gave his Macintosh favorites front row seats as he preached the Macintosh gospel while Apple II employees again found themselves in a separate room watching on closed circuit television. Even John Sculley, who was aware of the morale problems within the company, joined in the general ballyhoo for the Macintosh, which had failed during the previous year. At the same time, Sculley was already making plans to do away with the Macintosh division. The Apple II staff were unaware of this, as was Steve Wozniak, who had returned to Apple a few months previously to work in the Apple II group.

Shortly after the stockholders' meeting, Wozniak found dozens of Apple II people ready to resign. Many of them had already submitted letters to Sculley. Wozniak decided to confront Sculley as a spokesman for the protesters.

"I went to see Sculley and told him that the Apple II people were being discriminated against," Wozniak said. "Sculley said, 'No, you're not.' But I pressed him because I was the second largest stockholder in the company."

Sculley was in a difficult position. He had already formulated a plan to reorganize the company and eliminate the-Macintosh division, but he was unable to let it be known because it would have destroyed morale. His plan would eliminate 1,200 jobs and strip Jobs of operating power. Wozniak, not knowing any of this, left the company in exasperation because he was weary of the bickering. He even sold all of his stock in Apple, although he did not resign from the company. Wozniak continued to be on the Apple payroll even though he formed another company called Cloud 9, which had as its goal the creation of an unspecified product. Other Apple II employees, who did not have the financial cushion that Wozniak had, remained with Apple, but Wozniak sympathized with them.

"Every time you went to a major presentation by the company, it was always Macintosh this, Macintosh that," Wozniak said. "The people in Apple II thought 'What are we working here for?' They couldn't believe it."

Trip Hawkins followed Wozniak's example, sold all of his Apple stock and resigned from the company. "There were a lot of morale problems because Apple II people felt like they had contributed all the revenue and yet were getting none of the recognition or credit," Hawkins said.

Sculley was determined to end the conflict and create "one Apple," by eventually replacing Jobs as head of the Macintosh division and replacing of him with a more experienced manager. As sales of the Macintosh continued to drop, the board urged Sculley to seize the reins and run the company. Sculley was reluctant to move too quickly, fearing the consequences of such a radical change.

Nevertheless Sculley confronted Jobs like a drill sergeant scolding a recruit and told him to get Macintosh in order. When Jobs realized that Sculley was serious, he retorted that Sculley didn't know anything about Apple and was inept when it came to running a high-tech company.

"The two of them started to have a real rift," said Trip Hawkins. "For a long time, Steve had the support of the board and felt confident. The board said that the company was screwed up and needed a different perspective. When the company started to slide they thought, 'You know, something has to be done.' Sculley tried to work with Steve on the changes, but he resisted. Sculley finally decided, 'Screw it. I'm the guy who's president. I'm the one who's going to get blamed if we don't make money. I've got the responsibility.'"

With the board behind him, Sculley hired Jean-Louis Gassee, the forty-one year old head of Apple France, who would eventually replace Jobs as head of the reorganized Macintosh division. Gassee was a hard-headed but scholarly mathematician who had built his own calculator when he was fourteen. As head of Apple France, he had turned it into the company's fastest growing and most profitable foreign division. Unlike Jobs, he had traveled a conventional career path, with management experience at Hewlett-Packard and Data General. It was Sculley's intent to make him marketing director of Macintosh and eventually to move Jobs into an unspecified position, then promote Gassee to run Macintosh.

Jobs resisted the idea of *anyone* taking away his control of Macintosh, and he was particularly concerned about a conventional businessman like Gassee running the division. "Steve is such a dominant person," said David J. Larson, the marketing manager who launched Apple IIe and IIc. "He really wanted Mac to be successful. He was genuinely concerned about an MBA coming in and not understanding the new technology. He didn't want someone around that he couldn't control."

There were shock waves running through Apple's board of directors concerning the Jobs and Sculley battle, but surprisingly few people—even high echelon executives—were aware of it. They were more concerned with rumors of the planned reorganization and fear that they might lose their jobs. There was an incredible strain between Jobs and Sculley, and they agreed to put their friendship aside. "This was not two guys fighting over personalities," Sculley said. "This was two guys fighting over the best way to run the company."

The battle for power between Jobs and Sculley came to a head at a board meeting on April 11, 1985 that lasted three hours. The topic of discussion was the planned reorganization of Apple and what role would be left for Jobs in the company. In the board's view, Apple needed a more seasoned manager for Macintosh. Jobs, who was unusually restrained, waffled. One time he would agree, another time he would oppose it. His thoughts seemed to be disorganized. He mentioned that he might be interested in running a new research/development department at Apple, then hinted that he might remain as chairman and run for Congress. The latter option was blue sky thinking because, although people had urged Jobs to get into politics, he had never registered to vote, which would have been a major liability in a political campaign. The board finally agreed to hire Gassee, but set no timetable for him to take control of Macintosh. Jobs was also told in no uncertain terms that Sculley, not Jobs, was running the company. "They made it very clear that Steve had to be taken out of day-to-day operations," Hawkins said. "He's the chairman," Sculley said later, "but it's clear that he works for me."

While the board set no timetable for Jobs to be removed as manager of the Macintosh division, Gassee had other ideas. He asked for a written guarantee of the date when he would become general manager. Jobs was furious at the demand and also felt that Sculley and the board had betrayed him. "He thought Sculley had pulled a surprise attack and stabbed him in the back," said a source close to Jobs.

Jobs immediately began to worry about relinquishing power under the new organizational structure. He began telling his friends in the Macintosh division that Apple was not big enough for himself and Sculley and that the board would have to choose between them. Then he called his chief lieutenants together and asked them if they would back him in a showdown with Sculley.

All of them agreed, but there was considerable lack of enthusiasm in their responses.

Jobs should have known at this point that he had no chance of success, but he immediately began an intense campaign to have Sculley fired. He telephoned individual directors and members of the executive committee, looking for support and telling them that Sculley didn't understand the intricate workings of a high-technology company such as Apple. Jobs's entreaties fell on unsympathetic ears, and one of the board members even told him to stop being childish and to grow up. But Jobs was determined and convinced himself that he still had an opportunity to win the struggle for power.

Sculley learned almost instantly of Jobs's plot to depose him and called an emergency meeting of the executive committee the next day. He pulled no punches. He told the executives what Jobs had been doing and told them bluntly, "I'm the one who's running Apple." Jobs was struck dumb when he realized that Sculley, indeed, had the power. Still, Sculley and the executive committee were reluctant to leave Jobs out in the cold under the forthcoming reorganization. They talked for three hours, trying to find a way for him to remain in an operating capacity, but failed. Jobs seemingly gave up and said he would take a long vacation while the restructuring occurred.

Jobs left the meeting and gathered his Macintosh executives together and told them with tears in his eyes that he was resigning from Apple. Then he turned and headed for the door, but two of his aides stopped him. His staff begged him not to leave, telling him that their lives, his life, and the history of Apple would be irrevocably changed if he left. After a long session, they managed to convince Jobs that he might still have a future at Apple. Jobs spoke with Sculley again about an operating position with the company, but Sculley told him bluntly that it was out of the question.

The next evening, Jobs had a pizza party at his home in an atmosphere of gloom. Attending were his chief lieutenants from Macintosh and Mike Markkula, his old mentor and friend. The talk centered around Apple's future. Jobs hoped to convince Markkula that he should have an operational role in Apple's future and wanted Markkula's help in getting support from the board. Markkula, who had once considered Steve Jobs a bright young man with a future as an executive, listened noncommittally while he munched from a bowl of cherries. Markkula's only comment to Jobs was that the board would carry out Sculley's plans for reorganizing the company. Clearly, Jobs had even lost Markkula's support. The very next night Sculley telephoned Jobs and told him again that he would have no operating position in the "new Apple."

Sculley had hoped to reorganize Apple slowly and to ease Jobs out as painlessly as possible. His friends said that Sculley was torn between doing what was best for the company and his feelings for Jobs. "It was a wrenching decision for him," said an associate. "He wasn't sleeping well, but he was still thinking with a clear head. He didn't want to hurt Steve, but he had to do what was in Apple's interest."

Sculley's hand was forced much sooner than he had hoped, partly because of Jobs's effort to overthrow him and his continual politicking for an operations position, and also because of a small business weekly newspaper called the *San Jose Business Journal.* Nick Arnett, who was a high-tech reporter and personal computer columnist for *American City Business Journals,* heard rumors about the power play at Apple. Arnett, an intense, intelligent reporter, learned about the power play from his informants at Apple.

"There's something going on at Apple," he told his editor. "It looks like Steve Jobs is on his way out." Arnett, while excited, was very cautious. He did not want to report an erroneous story, especially when it concerned a folk hero like Steve Jobs. The editor was also cautious. "You've got to get something more solid than rumors," he said. A few hours later, Laurie Kretchmeyer, another high-tech reporter for the *Journal,* appeared in the newsroom, her cheeks flushed with excitement. "Jobs is on his way out and the company is planning to reorganize," she told the editor. There was a hurried conference among the editor, Arnett, and Kretchmeyer and, several hours later, the three of them were satisfied that something monumental was happening at Apple.

"Let's go with it," the editor said.

The *Journal* was on deadline and the staff worked late into the night to get the breaking story into print. The next morning the *Journal* ran a banner story about the power play between Jobs and Sculley and the forthcoming reorganization at Apple. The story forced Sculley to act much more quickly than he had planned. Two days later, Sculley called an emergency board meeting at Apple, and his plans for reorganization were approved. Jobs was left out in the cold; he was still chairman, but a chairman with no power. The day after, the *San Jose Mercury News* featured a banner headline on the front page that read: APPLE DEMOTES JOBS.

At Apple there was pandemonium, especially in the Macintosh division, which saw its general manager fired. There was pandemonium within the rank and file, and even top executives were stunned. One Macintosh manager said, "They've cut the heart out of Apple and substituted an artificial one. We'll just have to see how it pumps."

Jobs was almost totally deflated, but he did not give up all hope, even after he was removed from the headquarters building and placed in a remote office that his secretary named Siberia. He told the few friends he had at Apple that he had lost the battle, not the war. The *San Francisco Examiner* speculated that Jobs, whom it called "a skilled corporate in-fighter," might still have a few tricks up his sleeve. Analysts believed that Jobs might yet make a comeback. Mike Murphy, who is editor of the *California Technology Stocks Newsletter,* noted the resilience Jobs had shown in the past. "Originally he opposed the Macintosh and fought it a couple of months. And then, when it wouldn't die, he became its biggest advocate. That's the crux of his role: to spend a lot of time on new ideas, oppose some and, when the good ones won't die, get behind them all the way." Sculley, knowing how stubborn Jobs was, drove a stake into his heart a few days later when he told a group of analysts, "There will be no operational role for Steve Jobs at Apple now or in the future." He added that Jobs would remain as the "soul of Apple." The stock market, long tired of Jobs, reacted by spurting up two points.

From "Siberia," Jobs telephoned every key Apple executive and offered to help them any way he could and made certain that all of them had his home telephone number. No one returned his calls and he discovered that important company memos were not coming to his desk. He knew he had been denuded, and it was a terrible blow to his pride.

"You've probably had somebody punch you in the stomach and it knocks the wind out of you and you can't breathe," Jobs said. "The harder you try, the more you can't. You've just got to try to relax so you'll start breathing again. If I tried to figure out what to do or sort out my life or all that stuff, it was just like trying to breathe harder."

Sculley maintained that he tried to interest Jobs in research and development, but that Jobs wasn't interested. He wanted an operational position with authority. "They were isolating him and putting him out to pasture," said one Apple manager. "He just didn't realize it right away." Jobs, banished and stripped of power, said, "It was very clear there was nothing for me to do. I need a purpose to make me go on." Unfortunately for Jobs, when he found that purpose, his vindictive nature came to the fore and he ultimately caused himself more grief and pain.

The power play between Jobs and Sculley was not nearly as important to Apple employees as the forthcoming reorganization, which created a great deal of fear, particularly in the Macintosh division. A major bloodbath was coming and everyone knew it. "They're getting the knives out and sharpening them," said one source close to the company. "I think you are going to see a lot of Apple resumés floating around the valley."

The prophecy was accurate. Within a month after Jobs was fired as general manager of Macintosh, Sculley implemented sweeping changes. He announced that Apple would permanently close three of its six factories before the end of 1985. He also fired 1,200 employees, most of whom were in marketing, including many who had been hired and trained in the past year. It stunned Apple. One person who visited the company said, "I saw a lot of long faces."

Even though 1,200 employees lost their jobs, it was different from the blood-letting of Black Wednesday. Bruce Tognaz-

zini, who survived both purges, noted, "There was a big difference between Black Wednesday and Sculley's move. Black
Wednesday was a day when people were fired based on whether
or not their supervisors liked them. Sculley put a lot of thought
into his reorganization. As early as 1984, he had been telling us
that Apple was top-heavy in marketing personnel. The company
couldn't afford those overlapping responsibilities. When Sculley
fired people, he did it with as much sensitivity and humanity as
he could."

During the Black Wednesday massacre, Apple did everything it could to avoid severance pay. When Sculley let 1,200
people go, mostly marketing people, they were given at least one
month's salary after their termination date. Scully had knifed
Apple to bare bones, and the stock market reacted once again by
spurting upward.

Jobs's downfall as head of Macintosh was greeted with
enthusiasm by the members of the Apple II group. They rejoiced
that their nemesis had been skinned alive. They were even happier when Sculley moved them from the Triangle Building,
some distance away, into headquarters. "The Apple II group had
been physically remote," Sculley said, "and that only contributed
to its being treated as a second class citizen."

Sculley's reorganization made Apple a more functional
company and eliminated the competition Jobs had fostered that
almost tore it apart. Delbert W. Yocum was put in charge of all
of Apple's engineering, manufacturing, and distribution. Gassee,
in charge of product development, reported directly to Yocum,
and William Campbell was made head of all U.S. marketing and
sales. Finally, Apple was solidified and not a house divided
against itself.

Jobs, in the meantime, agreed to become a sort of ambassa-
dor without any authority. He was dispatched to various coun-
tries to investigate marketing possibilities. In reality, he was
nothing more than a figurehead and, after a summer of licking
his wounds and remaining relatively quiet, he sought revenge.

During the summer of 1985, which was a long and lonely
one for Steve Jobs, he began to search his soul. He spent hours
with a pad and pen and wrote down the things that were impor-

tant to him. Gradually it dawned on him that he could start another company and still remain chairman of the board at Apple. One warm August day, he met with Paul Bird, a Nobel laureate in genetics from Stanford University. Over lunch, the two men discussed Bird's research material and Jobs was suddenly struck with a thought: Why couldn't Bird's material be distributed by computer to other institutions so it could be part of the curriculum? Bird replied that most universities in the country didn't have the software or hardware to make such an undertaking possible. Jobs had been interested in education when he was at Apple and the meeting with Bird caused a flash of his old confidence and a resurgence of spirit.

"That's when I really started to think about stuff and get my wheels turning again," he said.

Jobs began to discuss a new company with several of his close associates in the Macintosh division. The company he envisioned, while still nebulous, would deal in some way with personal computers and education. The people he talked with were enthusiastic about the project, but warned Jobs that he needed to let the Apple board of directors know what he intended to do. The bitterness that had existed between Jobs and Sculley had almost vanished with the passage of time. Jobs outlined his plan to Sculley in vague terms, maintaining that it would not compete with Apple.

Sculley took Jobs at his word and told the board that Jobs wanted to start a new company. The board, assured that the new venture by Jobs would not compete with Apple, agreed. Sculley was happy to tell Jobs after the meeting that the board agreed to the proposal. What's more, he was invited to remain on Apple's board of directors and told that Apple would be willing to finance ten percent of the new venture. Since Jobs's plans for the new company were vague, at the most, Sculley suggested that Jobs meet with him and Markkula in the coming week to discuss it in more detail.

Jobs was too impatient to wait for the meeting. That same night he met with his group and explained the situation. They all agreed that they wanted to go it alone, without any ties to

Apple. "We decided to cut the umbilical cord and go on," said one of Jobs's associates.

The next day Jobs met with Sculley and told him that he wanted to remain on Apple's board of directors, but that his new company, which he had decided to call Next, had no interest in Apple's financial participation. He gave Sculley a sheet of paper that listed the names of Apple's employees he wanted to take with him. According to Jobs's account, Sculley agreed, shook his hand and wished him good luck. Jobs said he felt a flicker of the old friendship when they parted.

Sculley has an entirely different recollection of the meeting with Jobs. "I was absolutely taken aback when Steve walked in and handed me the list," Sculley said. "I told him that he was taking key people, a lot of whom were crucial." Sculley immediately called an emergency meeting of the board and told it what Jobs intended to do. "The board felt they had been deceived," Sculley said. "He [Jobs] had said that he would take a few low level people not involved in anything that Apple considered important."

One of the people Jobs intended to take was Rich Page, the engineer who had spearheaded the development of the Macintosh. It was clear to the board that Jobs intended to go into direct competition with Apple. The board voted to fire Jobs as chairman and immediately filed suit against him. That night Jobs drove to Markkula's house and, in what must have been a painful meeting for both of them, submitted his resignation from Apple. Jobs was bitter about the episode. "We tried to assure them that we had absolutely no plans to use any trade secrets or technology," he said. "We can't tell them what we want to do because we honestly don't know. What we want to do is come up with some kind of successful parting with Apple so we can start our own company."

Jobs's dismissal as chairman of Apple thundered throughout the company and Silicon Valley. The suit filed against him by Apple captured the attention of the international media and reporters descended on both Apple and Jobs, who had retreated into his monastic home. Sculley complained that the situation was receiving more attention than an episode of *Dynasty*. Sculley said, "We all understand that start-ups are part of the culture, but this was Steve Jobs getting even, not just Steve Jobs going out to start something new."

The suit Apple filed claimed that Jobs was using trade secrets, taking key people from the company, and going into direct competition with Apple, using technology that had been developed at the company. "Things really got hot," said one Apple manager. As the suit dragged out, Jobs sold twenty-one million dollars worth of his stock in Apple, but was still the company's largest shareholder. The license plate on his car, proudly reading APPLE 1, came off and was replaced by another.

Though few Apple employees had any fondness for Jobs, they were in a state of shock. "I had no idea Steve was forming a company," said William V. Campbell. "Losing those people (in the reorganization) was a shock, but losing the chairman of the board was even more shocking." To others it seemed that Jobs had timed his departure to cause as much trouble for Apple as possible. Several critical projects came to a stand-still and the furor created by his firing and the suit made it difficult for Apple to hire new people, who were urgently needed for major projects. "The people who are really upset are the vice presidents," said an insider. "Their plans have really been upset."

For the most part, Apple's employees seemed to be relieved that Jobs was finally out of the picture altogether. The press had speculated that there would be a mass exodus at Apple when Jobs was fired. The press, however, did not realize just how few friends Jobs had at Apple. Hardly anyone quit and Wall Street responded to his firing by spurting up another point or two. "Most professional investors are happy to see Jobs out of Apple," said Don Sinsabaugh, a partner in Squaregold, Chefits and Sinsabaugh. "He ruffled a lot of feathers on Wall Street with his brash self-confidence. The most important thing is that Sculley will be able to run the company with a free hand."

With Jobs completely out of the picture, Steve Wozniak once again returned to the bosom of the company he co-founded. His disdain for taking part in corporate politics prevented him from linking his return with Jobs's departure. "It was a coming about in my life," he said. "I had been sort of bored, then I got interested again. I've even written some computer programs for some of the trade magazines." While Jobs was selling stock, Wozniak, who had sold all of his, bought 100,000 shares. "Well," he said, "I just felt like I ought to have some." Wozniak adamantly refused to get involved in the dispute between Jobs and Sculley, but he announced that Apple II was in the best condition ever. Furthermore, he said, "You could never really know where Steve Jobs stood. He could make a statement saying he was against people getting killed and it would sound like he wanted a person sent to the gas chamber. Sculley doesn't do that. What he's saying and what you hear are precisely the same things."

Some people believed that the board had brought Sculley to Apple with the intention of eventually getting rid of Jobs. "I hope that's true," said Trip Hawkins. "Unfortunately, I don't think it is." Bruce Tognazzini believes that the friendship between Sculley and Jobs was real, not just public relations hype. "At an executive meeting right after Jobs left, Sculley spent five minutes talking about Jobs leaving, then he spent twenty minutes saying how he prayed it wouldn't destroy their friendship," Tognazzini said. "It was pretty obvious that he was very sincere about it."

The suit against Jobs was finally settled out of court, in Apple's favor. Jobs was enjoined from hiring any Apple employees for three years and from producing products that would compete with Apple. Furthermore, any product that Next developed would have to be approved by Apple before it could be marketed. Jobs, in a final gesture of defiance, sold all of his shares in Apple except one.

Sculley was named chairman of Apple Computer in January 1986 and, at a shareholders meeting, he waved an olive branch in Steve Jobs's direction. "It's my hope that all of our founders, including Steve Jobs, feel welcome on the campus, as are Steve Wozniak and Mike Markkula." Jobs retorted through a spokesman: "Joni Mitchell said it best: 'Don't it always seem to go that you don't know what you've got 'till it's gone?'" Jobs's old friend, Dan Kottke stated what might have been an epitaph: "Sometimes he's a jerk personally, but he has interesting ideas."

After all the smoke had cleared, Sculley declared, "I didn't come to Apple to take it away from Steve Jobs. I tried to give him as much latitude as possible."

At age 30, Jobs had been deposed in a bitter power struggle and he was starting over. Apple, on the other hand, was looking forward to a much brighter future without him.

CHAPTER 18

After The Fall

Apple started 1987 as a two billion dollar company that had John Sculley's personal mark on it in every nook and cranny. Steve Jobs, while still a memory, is never mentioned officially at Apple. "It's absolutely forbidden," said one personal computer analyst. No one seems to mind, because Jobs brings back memories of helter-skelter, shooting-from-the-hip management. People on the inside and outside see Apple as a stable organization that is finally acting like the big company it is.

"I think what we tried to do is now starting to pay off," Sculley said. "We tried to hold on to the best features of Apple in terms of culture, but also recognized that even youth has to grow up and become more mature in other aspects."

Once a company that fought bitterly within its own ranks, Apple is now unified. The new motto is "One Apple" and employees can say it without blushing or thinking it's corny. Teamwork is the name of the game now. Jobs had singled people out as being either bozos or superstars, but that has changed, too. "Implementers are as much appreciated as designers," Sculley said. "Teams get as much appreciation as superstars." An engineer at Apple noted, "The company now reflects the will of the majority, while, under Jobs, it reflected the will of a chosen few."

By unifying Apple, Sculley was able to stop the bitter infighting among divisions and to give the company a clearer direction. "Sometimes before, we got mixed messages from the people who ran the company," said Douglas Solomon, Apple's manager for market intelligence. "Now we don't get as many mixed messages. We're trying to be more organized, planning more and thinking more long-range. Sculley is a rock. We know what we're doing." Erich Ringewald, a software engineer, said, "More people are happier at Apple than they were before."

The divisiveness that created so much turmoil, backbiting and secrecy is no longer in evidence at Apple since Sculley's reorganization. "No one has to hide anything anymore from other Apple engineers," said an Apple engineer. "When Jobs was around, if the Apple II group had done a project he hadn't okayed, he'd just cancel it. There was a genuine fear [that drove employees] to hide things from people in the company."

Sculley spent a lot of time on the road in 1985 and 1986 trying to repair the damage that Jobs caused to Apple's relations with the personal computer infrastructure. He has stated numerous times that Apple no longer wants to go it alone the way Jobs did, and has encouraged third party companies to develop software and enhancements for Apple. Ash Jain, head of the Apple Enhancement Products Division for AST Research, said, "Apple is much easier to work with than it was when Jobs was there. Sculley has committed the company to work with third parties, and Apple is one of the best companies I can think of to work with."

Sculley was also painfully aware of the performance flaws in Apple computers under Jobs. Jobs had insisted on building computers with capabilities that the market would have to accept rather than listening to what customers wanted. Sculley did away with that attitude in a hurry. "I'm trying to open channels that have been closed or neglected," he said. "A company the size of Apple needs not just great concepts but to be aware of marketplace wants. The different parts of the organization have to be well-tuned to each other."

Not everything has been coming up roses at Apple since Steve Jobs was fired and the company reorganized. Morale was an enormous problem in 1985 with one engineer noting that, "We were on the verge of hysteria." Sculley admitted, "Stress was our biggest problem in 1985. Every job in the company changed in some way." There was considerable fear within the Apple ranks during 1985, then Sculley's cost-cutting actions began to show a postive effect. He was able to reinstate profit-sharing, which had been cut under his austerity program. "The grumbling stopped when the first profit-sharing checks came around," said Brian McGhie, a software engineer.

Apple showed a small profit in 1985, but this was due to Sculley's drastic cost-cutting measures, rather than sales performance. Nevertheless, the company was on such a sound track that Sculley told a group of Wall Street analysts that Apple's quarterly earnings would triple over what they had been for the same quarter during the previous year. His prediction was more than 50 percent above what most analysts were predicting and the announcement caused Apple's stock to jump three dollars a share.

The quarterly earnings resulted from three factors: increased sales of the Macintosh Plus, the computer that replaced the original Macintosh, which was a failure; stronger international sales; and Sculley's austerity program. The international sales were more attributable to a weaker dollar, however, than to any kind of ingenious marketing program. Tim Bajarin was moved to say, "They are looking steady. Sculley obviously has the bull by the horns. Apple is getting much smarter in their marketing, and they don't contradict themselves anymore in their advertising."

The success of the Macintosh Plus must have been a blow to Steve Jobs's ego. The original Macintosh that he introduced failed and he was unable to meet timetables for enhancements that were needed. With Jobs out of the picture, Apple was able to make the improvements that were needed on the personal computer. Sales of the computer headed steadily upward whereas they had slid consistently with Jobs at the helm. Apple sold

174,000 Macintoshes in 1984, 245,000 in 1985, and 480,000 in 1986. The Mac is no longer viewed as a computer that is unsuitable for the corporate market, where it had received such a cool reception.

"The Macintosh Plus added tremendous power," said Bajarin. "It was very limited before. It's also been successful with the new phenomenon of desk-top publishing and with its laser printers." Sculley broke out of the mold of pitting Apple against IBM by announcing enhancements created by third parties that would make the Apple II and Macintosh compatible with IBM by late 1987. "Two years ago, I would have said that Apple would never make it in the corporate market," Bajarin said. "Looking at it today, with new applications and power, there's no question that it's going to get into major corporations. Apple is poised to deliver products to every segment of the market, from education, to the home, to small businesses and to large corporations."

Sculley withdrew Apple from direct competition with IBM in 1985, but renewed its assault on the corporate marketplace, where IBM is dominant. Instead of challenging IBM directly, he targeted the corporate market with products that did not compete directly with Big Blue. Sculley "stopped thumbing his nose at IBM," said one analyst, and convinced Apple managers that they had to find a way to co-exist with it. "We're not so much afraid of IBM anymore, " said Bruce Tognazzini. "We've finally gotten over this terrible arrogance that shot through Apple." Sculley spoke at a symposium hosted by Hembrech and Quist in San Francisco in May 1986 and underlined his determination to exist side by side with IBM. "People are realizing that it's not IBM versus Apple in this philosophical battle where one party has to be dragged out by its feet."

There are no longer the frenzied highs and lows that plagued Apple in its first years of existence. The company is steadier and the employees happier. Apple has a focus and direction that it lacked under Steve Jobs, even though people still wear jeans and T-shirts to work. The casual dress belies the discipline that Sculley demands, but that discipline does not seem to have dampened creativity. "Sculley has retained Apple's spirit, but has brought a sense of business pragmatism to the company," said

Bill Krause, the chief executive officer of 3Com Corporation in Mountain View. Sculley recognized the fear that Apple's innovative spirit would be stifled by a less indulgent atmosphere. "Apple is a more disciplined, grown-up company today," he said. "People have learned to recognize that discipline is not a threat to innovation."

Sculley's work at Apple seems to have put it on more solid ground than it has ever been on before. The company reported net sales of $1.9 billion in 1986 and net income of $154 million.

Sculley was still making peace overtures to Steve Jobs in the middle of 1986. "Just because Jobs and I aren't friends anymore doesn't mean I don't care about the things we did," he said. "A lot of ideas he had—the Mac and the Laser Writer—are starting to work. A lot of things Steve and I used to talk about together are very valid. The problem was implementation, a chance to turn the dream into reality. I know what it takes to be a success."

With Apple on a high road, and the power struggle with Jobs won, Sculley is happy. "Now that things are going well, I'm having a ball," he grinned. "I can't think of anything I'd rather be doing in the world."

Steve Jobs was devastated by his fall from grace at Apple Computer. Shortly after being stripped of power as head of the Macintosh division, he was seen wandering through his old offices late at night. Sometimes he would stop and lovingly run his hands over a Macintosh computer. When he was fired as chairman of the board, he retreated into his lonely two million dollar mansion. He was bitter, angry and, most of all hurt. The vitriol of the lawsuit against him by Apple overshadowed his personal anguish, which he suffered mostly in silence.

Reporters camped outside his house, hoping for a chance to talk to him, but Jobs remained isolated. A reporter for Mac-World, a hobbyist magazine for users of the Macintosh computer, waited for days to speak with Jobs but, when he saw him emerge from his home, he appeared so gloomy that the reporter fled. Jobs did tell reporters, "I'm not bitter. I'm not bitter." Another time, he blurted out, "I'm okay."

Some thought that he was protesting too much. "He became a tragic figure," said Bruce Tognazzini. "The other two

co-founders, Markkula and Wozniak, are happy, but he's tragic."
Jobs had time to reflect on his life, and on Apple, and comforted
himself with the thought, gained from his study of Eastern philosophy, that the journey was more important than the
destination.

"He considered himself washed up," said one old Apple
hand. "He thought he was finished. He said he would be a fool
to try and top what he did at Apple."

Jobs eventually came out of his shell and it was obvious that
he felt a close kinship with Apple in spite of his fall. "Apple
exists in the spirit of the people who work there, and the sort of
philosophies and purpose by which they go about their business," Jobs said in a rambling statement. "If I'm a million miles
away and all those people still feel there are things, and they're
still working to make the next big personal computer, then I will
feel that my genes are still there. If Apple becomes a place where
computers are a commodity item, and where the romance is
gone, then I'll feel that I've lost Apple."

Silicon Valley overflows with people who would like to
work for him in Next, the new company he founded. A steady
stream of hopeful people come to his door and he is flooded by
mail. One of those who form the cadre of Next says, "Everybody
wants to be involved in a start-up. It's part of the dream." All of
this interest comes with full knowledge that Jobs is a difficult
person to deal with. One analyst said: "Steve's management style
is tough to handle on a day-to-day basis. But on the whole, he's
worth a lot of money and he's a significant driving force. If you
get involved with him on a project, there's a chance that *you*
could make a lot of money."

Jobs's company, Next, is supposed to be delivering a product
in the fall of 1987, still unspecified at the time of this writing.
Instead of starting a company with a fist full of dollars from the
sale of a Volkswagen van, he has millions of dollars behind him,
and he is convinced that he can do something spectacular. "I did
it once in a garage," he said. "I did it again in the metaphorical
garage at Apple, with the Macintosh. I'm confident that I can do
it again."

He remains a driven soul and, at age thirty-one, believes that he has a responsibility to keep working. "If I just went and laid on the beaches for the rest of my life, which I couldn't do anyway, it's a pretty ridiculous message to people who are thinking about starting their own company, thinking about risking everything you have on an idea," he told a reporter.

Jobs remains a figure of intense interest in Silicon Valley and people are waiting to see what he comes up with Next. "Knowing Steve Jobs," said Tim Bajarin, "I wouldn't bet against him."

Bajarin could be right. Just as his detractors began to seal his tomb, Jobs sprang to life like Lazarus. H. Ross Perot, a Texas billionaire who is even more of a legendary figure than Jobs, invested twenty million dollars in Next, buying 16 percent of the company. Perot, who started Electronic Data Systems Corporation when he was thirty-two, saw Jobs on television talking about his new company. Perot was impressed by the thirty-one year old Jobs and what he said. The two came together and joined forces. "He told me that we're going to hit one out of the ball park," Jobs reported.

With Perot on board, Jobs's chances of another major success are greatly increased. Perot carries with him years of successful business experience. Just before he invested in Next, he had sold seven hundred million dollars worth of shares in General Motors. Perot has the respectability to encourage other venture capitalists to buy into Next, even though many of them feel that Jobs has inflated the price of his company, which has no product, at $121 million.

Perot is also a genuine American hero. He was popularized a few short years ago in a book called *On Wings of Eagles,* written by the popular novelist, Ken Follet. The non-fiction book told of Perot's efforts to form a commando team, composed of businessmen who worked for him, to rescue members of his company who were trapped in Iran following the Ayatolla Khomeini's rise to power. Even though Perot was in danger of being captured himself, he risked his life by slipping into Iran under a false name to encourage his trapped employees.

Although Perot is loyal to those who work for him, he is not an easy taskmaster. He expects results and usually gets them. Jobs will not find Perot, now on the board of directors of Next, a man who will succumb to his flighty style of management. But he has found a formidable ally and, if he succeeds with Next, the stigma of his "accidental" success at Apple may at last vanish.

Epilogue

Steve Jobs was both a victim and beneficiary of circumstances. He was a young rebel who experimented with drugs, with a mediocre grasp of high technology, who became chairman of one of the most dynamic companies in the history of American business.

He is enigmatic in that he sought a humanistic relationship between employee and company, yet his actions at Apple Computer showed no compunction about insulting and degrading people within and outside of Apple. Although he sought enlightenment and spiritual fulfillment and harmony, he created the most devastating kind of cacophony. He never outgrew adolescence, regardless of how self-assured he made himself appear in public. In that regard, he exemplifies Silicon Valley, which abounds with colorful characters who never really reached maturity. The Valley itself is just now starting to grow up, as Steve Jobs must do if he is to come close to matching the earlier success of Apple Computer.

He was brash, dictatorial, and overly confident, but those very same characteristics allowed him to approach multi-million-aires for financing when Apple was operating out of a garage. Ironically, those traits, also led to his demise at Apple Computer.

Jobs was the catalyst that brought Stephen Wozniak and Mike Markkula together to create Apple Computer. It was an accident of friendship, but even Wozniak, the inventor of the first Apple computer, admits that there would not have been an Apple Computer without Steve Jobs, the scrambler of the days in the garage. Jobs's most significant contribution to Apple Computer was that he brought Wozniak and Markkula together. Markkula was the key to the success of Apple Computer because he recognized the commercial possibilities of the computer Wozniak had created.

As Apple grew more successful and its public relations efforts promoted Jobs as the technological genius behind Apple, he appeared to believe his own publicity. Yet he was never a technical star, never more than average in his technological expertise. He could have remained as chairman of Apple indefinitely because the company's publicity had made him into a worldwide folk hero. Instead, he chose to fight for a position that he was never qualified to fill and ended up plunging into despair, faced with the gut-wrenching task of trying to start over and regain his previous status.

Jobs's personality is still deeply ingrained at Apple in spite of efforts to erase him from corporate memory. His influence lives on in the casual dress and the sense of the absurd which make Apple a unique company. The zaniness he brought to the company abides in the spirit that had rubber ducks swimming in the fountain outside the headquarters building in Cupertino one day, followed by an inflated shark chasing them the next.

Most importantly, no matter what his faults might have been, he will be remembered as one of the fathers of the personal computer age and of an industry that is estimated to generate more than fifty billion dollars a year. Jobs, through Apple publicity, is still inextricably attached to the company he co-founded in spite of the company's effort to erase him. Nick Arnett, former high-tech writer for the *San Jose Business Journal* may have summed it up best when he wrote, "Without Jobs, Apple is just another Silicon Valley Company and, without Apple, Jobs is just another Silicon Valley millionaire."

The first part of Arnett's statement may be true, but after pulling H. Ross Perot out of his magic hat, Jobs has served notice that he has no intentions of being one of the many nameless millionaires in Silicon Valley.

Index

219

miniaturization, 38
minicomputers, 36, 84, 91
MITS, 99
Moore, Fred, 55
Moore, Gordon, 8
morale within Apple Co., 100, 194
Morgan, James, 181
Morgan Stanley, 129, 130
MOS Technology 6502, 61, 62
Motorola, 61, 76
"mouse," 136
Mucusless Diet Healing System, 44, 49
Murray, Mike, 145

National Computer Conference (1980), 142
National Semiconductor, 9, 82, 84, 88
Nelson, Frances, 124, 125
New York Times, The, 3
Newton, Bob, 69
Next Co., 204, 213, 214
Nova minicomputer, 38
Noyce, Robert, 7–10, 56, 63, 75

One Bit Adder-Subtractor, 18, 19
Oregon Feeling Center, 51, 52
Osborne Computer, 152, 181
oscillator, 26

Packard, David, 6, 58
packaging, Apple, 93–95, 98, 102, 103, 186
Page, Rich, 204
paternity suit, Jobs, 123, 131, 132, 151, 153
Peanut. See IBM PCjr.
Peat, Marwick, Mitchell Co., 185
People's Computer Company, 55
Pepsi Cola Co., 165, 167, 168, 191
peripherals, 142, 143, 150
Perot, H. Ross, 214, 215, 218
philosophy, Eastern, 22, 43, 44, 49, 50, 53, 75, 213
philosophy, corporate, 159, 161
phone phreaking, 25–27, 30, 57, 59, 103 See also "blue boxes:" "Cap'n Crunch"

Pong, 47, 57
switching, 95
primal scream therapy, 51, 52, 54
Processor Technology, 76
profit sharing, 178, 210
public relations, 80–83, 111–113, 130, 142, 170, 171, 187, 199
profit sharing, 178
printer, letter–quality, 186

Radio Shack, 91
Rainbow Farm, The, 41
RAM, 9
Raskin, Jef, 118, 119, 121, 122, 134, 136–139, 157, 159–161
Rational Fasting, 44
Reed College, 40, 41
Regis McKenna Agency, 48, 82, 94, 97, 112–114
Remington Rand, 3
Reutimann, Bob, 102
Rock, Arthur, 109, 110, 112, 193
Raskin, Jef, 157, 159–161
Rosen, Ben, 111, 112
Roshi, Suzuki, 75

San Jose Business Journal, 199, 200
Sarofim, Fayez, 129
Schwartz, Mel, 69
Scott, Michael, 154–157, 160–165
Sculley, John C., 165–212
Jobs compared to, 166
Jackson, Michael, compared to, 169
Sears Business Systems, 191
Securities Exchange Commission, 129
semiconductors, 5, 36
Sequoia Ventures, 84
shareholder meetings, 143, 144
Shockley Semiconductor labs, 6, 7
Shockley, William, 4–7, 12
silicon, 4, 7
Silicon Valley, 4, 6, 7, 13, 36, 61, 63, 79, 85, 112, 127, 133, 181, 204, 213–218
single-board computers, 84